FOR DEVON,

EVERY WORD, ALWAYS

## OTHER BOOKS BY JAY PARINI

*Singing in Time* (poetry)

*Theodore Roethke: An American Romantic* (criticism)

*The Love Run* (novel)

*Anthracite Country* (poetry)

*The Patch Boys* (novel)

*An Invitation to Poetry* (textbook)

*Town Life* (poetry)

*Bay of Arrows* (novel)

*John Steinbeck* (biography)

*Benjamin's Crossing* (novel)

*House of Days* (poetry)

# THE LAST STATION

## A NOVEL OF

## TOLSTOY'S LAST YEAR

# JAY PARINI

# THE
# LAST
# STATION

AN OWL BOOK
HENRY HOLT AND COMPANY
NEW YORK

Henry Holt and Company, Inc.
*Publishers since 1866*
115 West 18th Street
New York, New York 10011

Henry Holt® is a registered trademark
of Henry Holt and Company, Inc.

Copyright © 1990 by Jay Parini
All rights reserved.
Published in Canada by Fitzhenry & Whiteside Ltd.,
195 Allstate Parkway, Markham, Ontario L3R 4T8.

Library of Congress Cataloging-in-Publication Data
Parini, Jay.
The last station: a novel of Tolstoy's last year /
Jay Parini.
p.    cm.
ISBN 0-8050-5823-0
1. Tolstoy, Leo, Graf, 1828–1910, in fiction, drama, poetry, etc.
2. Soviet Union—History—1904–1914—Fiction.  I. Title.
PS3566.A65L3    1990                          89-71659
813'.54—dc20                                     CIP

Henry Holt books are available for special promotions and
premiums. For details contact: Director, Special Markets.

First published in hardcover in 1990 by
Henry Holt and Company, Inc.

First Owl Books Edition 1998

*Designed by Kate Nichols*

Printed in the United States of America
All first editions are printed on acid-free paper.∞

1   3   5   7   9   10   8   6   4   2

*There was a muddy center before we breathed.*
*There was a myth before the myth began,*
*Venerable and articulate and complete.*

*From this the poem springs: that we live in a place*
*That is not our own and, much more, not ourselves*
*And hard it is in spite of blazoned days.*

Wallace Stevens,
"Notes Toward a Supreme Fiction"

# THE LAST STATION

# 1

# SOFYA
# ANDREYEVNA

The year has turned again, bringing us to the end of the first decade of the new century. I write the strange numbers in my diary. 1910. Is it possible?

Lyovochka is asleep now, and he will not waken till dawn. A while ago, I was drawn by his rattling snore down the hall to his bedroom. His snore sounds through the house like a creaking door, and the servants giggle about it. "The old man is sawing wood," they say, right in front of me. They no longer respect me, but I smile back at them.

Lyovochka's snoring doesn't bother me, since we sleep in separate rooms now. When we slept in the same bed, he had teeth: they lessened the snore.

I sat on his narrow little bed and pulled the gray blanket with the key design up to his chin. He started, forcing a monstrous grimace. But he didn't waken. Almost nothing wakes Leo Tolstoy. Whatever he does, he does completely: sleep, work, dance, ride, eat. They write about him constantly in the press. Even in Paris, the morning papers adore tidbits of gossip about him, about us—true or untrue, they don't care. "What does Count Tolstoy like for breakfast, Countess?" they ask, lining up on the front porch for interviews throughout the summer months, when the weather in Tula makes this a pleasant destination. "Does he cut his own hair? What is he reading now? Have you bought him a present for his name day?"

I don't mind the questions. I give them just enough to send them happily on their way. Lyovochka seems not to care. He doesn't read the stories anyway, even when I leave them on the table beside his breakfast. "They are of no interest," he says. "I don't know why anyone would care to print such rubbish."

He does, however, glance at the photographs. There is always a photographer here, snapping away, begging for portraits. Chertkov is the most troublesome. He thinks himself an artist with the camera, but he is just as foolish with that as with everything.

Lyovochka slept on, snoring, as I smoothed his hair. The white hair that tumbles on his starchy pillow. The white beard like spindrift, a soft spray of hair, not coarse like my father's. I spoke to him as he slept, called him "my little darling." He is like a child in his old age, all mine to coddle, to care for, to protect from the insane people who descend upon us daily, his so-called disciples—all led on, inspired, by Chertkov, who is positively satanic. They think he is Christ. *Lyovochka* thinks he is Christ.

I kissed him on the lips while he slept, inhaling his babylike breath, as sweet as milk. And I remembered a bright day many years ago, when I was twenty-two. Lyovochka's beard was dark then. His hands were soft, even though he spent a fair amount of time with the muzhiks, working in the fields beside them, especially at harvest. He did this for recreation, really. For exercise. It was not so much a point of honor then, as it would be later, when he liked to imagine himself, at heart, one of the noble muzhiks he adores.

He was writing *War and Peace*, and every day he would bring me pages to recopy. I do not think I have ever been happier, letting my hand darken those pages, letting the black India ink summon a vision as pure and holy as any that has ever been seen or dreamt. Nor was

Lyovochka ever happier. He has always been happiest within his work, dreaming his grand, sweet dreams.

Only I could read Lyovochka's handwriting. His crablike hieroglyphs filled the margins of his proof sheets, driving the printers wild. Corrections blotted out corrections. Even he could not make out what he had written much of the time. But I could. I read his intentions, and the words came clear. In the afternoons, drinking linden tea, we would sit for hours by a peat fire, discussing changes. "Natasha would never say such a thing to Prince Andrey," I would tell him. Or "Pierre is too simple-minded here. He is not as stupid as he pretends." I would not let him write badly. Nor would I let him drowse in his study or spend too much time on horseback or in the fields. Lyovochka had more important work to do. I drove him to his desk. I was important to him.

But I do not matter now.

Not like in those early years, as on my name day, September 17, when I was twenty-two, as slender and beautiful as a daffodil.

We had three children then. Taking care of them, looking after the entire estate (Lyovochka has never been good with details or management—not then, not now), and copying his manuscripts, my days were exhaustingly full. But I did not complain, even when he spent endless hours chatting in his study with that silly bluestocking Marya Ivanovna, who had attached herself to him like a limpet.

I knew she would not last. Of all the women in his life, only I have lasted. They could not wear me down, and they will not.

That was in 1866. I remember because it was the year our blessed tsar, Alexander, was saved by the hand of God. A miracle. He had been taking his daily walk in the Winter Garden when a deranged youth (from a well-known family, alas) fired at him with a pistol. The quick hand of a muzhik saved the tsar, dashing the gun to one side.

That same night, in Moscow, Lyovochka and I attended the theater, as we often did in those days. The performance began with everyone in the audience standing to sing "God Preserve the Tsar!"

I have never seen such weeping! For weeks after, I gave thanks at special masses held in the Chapel of St. Nicholas, near the Kremlin. Russians needed their tsar then. They need him now, though one would never know it listening to my husband and his friends. It is a wonder the police haven't silenced them. If Lyovochka weren't as powerful as the tsar himself, I dare say they would.

Of course, Lyovochka won't hear me on this subject. He despises the tsar, on principle. But in our early days together he was a monarchist, too. He worshiped Alexander, who had freed his cousin, Major-General Prince Volknosky, who had been one of the Decembrists sent to Siberia by Nicholas I. His wife, the princess, had gone into exile with them, leaving behind a small child.

On that name day, long ago, the late-summer light fell slantwise through the yellow birches. I spent the morning by myself, wandering in Zasyeka Wood, smelling the rich earth, the late-blooming flowers. One maple, to my surprise and horror, was already scarlet, lit like a bell in a strange light. I stood beneath it, unable to control my tears.

Lyovochka appeared from behind the tree. In a white blouse, looking more like a muzhik than a nobleman, he dazzled me with his stare. Such intensity! Had he followed me here?

"Why these tears, my little Sonya? What's wrong?"

I bit my lip. "Nothing," I said.

"Nothing?" he said. "Something."

"This tree," I said. "Look! Already the leaves have turned. Soon the whole wood will be bare."

I could hardly tolerate the winters in Tula, then or now. There is no escaping the cold, the blue wind and snow. The trees, with their black branches, crowd my mind. I find it impossible to think.

"You aren't crying because of this red tree," he said. "You are crying for Sonya."

I protested. Wasn't it my name day? Wasn't I the luckiest woman in all of Russia, to have married the most promising writer of his generation, to have three small, beautiful children and a large house in the country?

But he was right, of course. I wept for Sonya.

That night the servants prepared an elegant early dinner on the terrace, setting a table in the late-afternoon sun. My sister Tanya had brought a lovely pheasant pâté from Moscow, which she served on a cool cipolin platter—a gift from Mama. There was black bread fresh from the oven. There were large wet grapes in white bowls, with oranges from the south in red bowls. And borscht and, later, duck in a Parisian glacé. There was lamb, too, and a bit of goose. Sweet cakes of bran and honey tumbled from a basket. Lyovochka poured the wine, much more of it than anyone should have drunk!

A number of young officers from the Tula regiment appeared, in smart dress uniforms with silver buttons. Lyovochka did not hate the military then. His years in the army were not so far behind him then, or his memory of the Caucasus. He would lie beside me in bed, telling me about Prince Gorchakov and the siege of Silistra. I treasured those nights, those stories. And I miss them, as I miss the young officers who ate, so often, at our table.

We gathered about the long table with its crisp linen tablecloths and English china. The crystal caught the sunlight and sparkled with a brightness that was almost painful. "Today is the Feast of the Martyrs," Lyovochka told the assembled company, proposing the toast. "The *Blessed* Martyrs," he said, correcting himself, as one or two of the officers chuckled. "There is Vera, whose name is Faith. And Nadezhda, who is Hope, and Lyubov, which means Charity. Their mother is Sofya, meaning Wisdom. To thee, my Sofya, source of all wisdom, love of my life. . . ." Glasses clinked. I bowed my head, determined not to weep.

From the garden, well hidden by trees and bushes, came the gay strains of my favorite opera, *La Muette de Portici*. Lyovochka rushed to my side, drawing me into his arms for a brief public display of strong affection. I could feel the pressure of their eyes upon us as we kissed. But I did not mind. "Just one dance—before dinner?" Lyovochka asked me. I dipped my eyes, shyly, to the floor, but I danced beautifully in those days, before my knees were stiffened by too many damp mornings in the country.

Over his shoulder, I saw that Marya Ivanovna was looking into her empty plate. This occasion, I think, ended her little obsession with my husband. It was a lance thrown into her chest by Lyovochka himself!

After dinner, the real dancing began. Only the aged aunts and their wizened friends refused to join us whirling on the stone terrace, spinning in celebration of the Martyrs.

Lyovochka insisted, as always, on the *kamarinskaya*, a dance with intricate, quick steps. A few tried to sit it out, but he would have none of it. Lyovochka was the ringmaster, driving us—especially the younger officers—into ever more wild and lavish gestures.

Long before the others left, I was led by Lyovochka to the bedroom. Our abrupt departure was almost embarrassing, but I didn't mind. One of the young officers caught my eye as we left; I knew what he was thinking, and it terrified me slightly.

Before I could even undress, Lyovochka was kissing me frantically on the neck and shoulders. I lay back on the broad bed and let him do what he had to do. It was not unenjoyable then, as it would become. Soon his trousers were down about his knees. I closed my eyes when his large red hands reached under my dress, the flat palms pressing hard on my nipples. And I let him take me, as he would, quickly. I wished he understood about these things, but I could not tell him. I let him fall asleep, half dressed, nuzzling into my shoulder.

When the dawn broke over Zasyeka Wood, he was gone. He had taken himself, as usual, to his study. I found him there later, his lips pursed, the candle still burning in the daylight. His quill dug deep letters in the page; his eyes flickered with a wild energy that I loved. He did not notice me, even when I put my hands on his shoulders and breathed, softly, on the back of his broad, white neck.

# 2

# BULGAKOV

"But sex?" asked Chertkov, rubbing his forehead with the palm of a hand disfigured by eczema. "You are only twenty-four." He leaned forward across the desk. "Not an easy age for abstinence."

I withdrew the smile that had formed on my lips against my will. Vladimir Grigorevich Chertkov has no sense of humor. Apart from his plumpness and bad skin, this humorlessness is the most noticeable thing about him.

"I know that Count Tolstoy does not approve of sexual relations."

"He despises them," Chertkov replied. "And, if I may advise you, he does not use his title. He renounced it years ago."

Chertkov unnerved me. I felt uncomfortable not using Tolstoy's title. I had been brought up in polite company, taught to defer to those with power. It annoyed me that Chertkov imagined I wouldn't know about the renunciation of that title. I know practically everything about Tolstoy that can be learned from his writings, and much else besides. There is a thick smoke of gossip surrounding the name of Leo Tolstoy, and I had inhaled that smoke on every possible occasion.

"You must call him Leo Nikolayevich, like the rest of us," Chertkov added. "He prefers that."

Chertkov's chameleonlike skin puffed loosely about his bald, pear-
shaped head. I could almost see through his forehead to the frontal
lobes of his brain. He spoke stiffly, tapping his puffy fingers on the
bare table. "I take it you have read *The Kreutzer Sonata?*"

I nodded, though I hoped we would not discuss this particular
work. *The Kreutzer Sonata* is Tolstoy's one failure, as I see it. Is there
anything in common between Pozdnyshev, the hero of that tale, and
Leo Tolstoy? I cannot believe it. It's the story of a man who murders
his wife. Many readers—I don't go this far myself—consider it a tract
against marriage, a missile of hate, a vile book. It is so unlike *Anna
Karenina*, where Tolstoy celebrates the marriage of Kitty and Levin,
raises it like a banner across the cold Russian sky. But Pozdnyshev!

"I don't want to belabor the point of chastity, but I arranged for
a servant last year who proceeded to ruin two young housemaids
who had been with the Tolstoy family for many years. It upset Leo
Nikolayevich terribly. I want to make it clear that this won't be a
problem."

I shook my head in outward assurance but inwardly was horrified
that I should be classified with a servant. I think my anger showed
in my cheeks. I tried to cover them with my hands.

"I'm sorry to bring up a delicate subject," Chertkov said. "One
can never be too specific, I always say."

"It's all right," I said. "I understand."

The job seemed to slip away from me, and I panicked. More than
anything, I wanted to be Tolstoy's private secretary.

Chertkov circled the desk and stood beside me. He put a cold
hand on my wrist. "I have heard only good things about you from
Makovitsky and the others. And I have read carefully what you have
written about Leo Nikolayevich. So has he. It is somewhat . . . youthful. But quite sound."

"Tolstoy has read my essays?"

Chertkov shook his head in confirmation. I beamed. It appeared
that everything would fall, amazingly, into place.

"I don't want to prejudice you against Sofya Andreyevna, but it would be impolitic of me not to mention her disagreements with Leo Nikolayevich," Chertkov went on. "It has been an unfortunate marriage—for him." He began to pull his silky black beard, drawing it to a point beneath his chin. The beard gives him the look of a Tartar. "Frankly," he continued, "she is not one of us. I would go so far as to say that she despises us and would do anything in her power to see that her husband's work does not go forward."

"But they've been married for nearly fifty years! Surely, this . . ." I was not sure what I meant.

Chertkov leaned back against the desk and smiled. "You are an honest fellow, Valentin Fedorovich. I see why you came so highly recommended. Dushan Makovitsky is not overly intelligent, but he's a good judge of character."

"I have heard about these problems between—"

"Don't let any of this trouble you," Chertkov said. "But remember that she will say dreadful things about me." He seemed uncomfortable saying this and shifted. "Sofya Andreyevna and I have not always been on bad terms. When I was first exiled, she protested to the tsar. And she often wrote to me in England, passing along news of Leo Nikolayevich. Now she does not want me near her husband. It made her furious that I bought the house at Telyatinki, even though I am not allowed to live there."

"Disgraceful," I said, surprised at my own vehemence.

"I'm what you might call living contraband," he said, smiling. It was the first time he had smiled since I'd called on him. He reached out again, taking my hands in his.

"My dear Valentin Fedorovich, you have been offered a great gift. You will see Leo Nikolayevich every day. You will take meals with him. You will walk in the forest by his side. And you will find your soul warmed daily by his fire. I hope that you will love him as I do. And that you will learn from him." He let go of my hands and walked to the window, parting the curtain to look at the falling snow. "What he says will ring in your head forever."

I don't know why, but I began to think of my father as he spoke.

My father has been dead for a year. He often spoke to me in his soft, guttural voice, delivering fatherly advice. I took none of it seriously, but I appreciated his efforts. He knew that, since my conversion to Tolstoyism, I was hungry for God, hungry to learn, to discuss ideas, to perfect my soul. My father admired all of this, but he said I had to be careful. A civil servant for thirty years, he had managed to avoid thinking about anything. But I refuse to accept his intellectual bankruptcy as my legacy. I want to become, like Chertkov, a disciple.

A servant in a rough wool jacket entered. This deficiency of proper attire is Chertkov's compromise with Tolstoyan values. He is not a willing member of the class into which he was born, though he has not relinquished all the trappings. Krekshino is a fine house, with spacious grounds and several outbuildings for horses. I had seen perhaps half a dozen servants—and assumed that a dozen more hid themselves in the bowels of the kitchen, or elsewhere on the grounds. The furniture in the house is unpretentious but solid—mostly English and French. I did not like the heavy velvet curtains that darkened the rooms.

"Tea, sir?" the young man asked.

I accepted a steaming glass of China tea with a nod of appreciation.

"Come here," Chertkov said, motioning me to the large leather chairs beside the fire. I watched as he dropped to his knees and worked a large, old-fashioned bellows, fanning the logs in the iron grate to a flame. The chimney seemed to roar, inhaling the sparks. "We must become friends," he said. "We have so much to accomplish, and there are many enemies."

His cheekbones flared when he spoke, and he seemed always to be repressing a burp. Dressed in a fresh muslin blouse with a shiny leather belt, he looked like other Tolstoyans I have met. His boots were unstylish but well made—a gift from Leo Nikolayevich, he told me. "He made them with his own hands—a craft he has learned in recent years. He makes boots for everyone."

Chertkov sipped his tea in an almost prissy manner. Although I very much admired him, liking him would require an act of will.

"Here is a letter from Leo Nikolayevich," he said, handing me a sheet covered with Tolstoy's messy scrawl. "He has not been well. You can tell from the unsteady hand. It is partly Sofya Andreyevna's fault, I must tell you. She has destroyed his ability to sleep with her constant nagging." Anger bloomed in his chest. "She is a desperate woman. There is no telling what he might have accomplished were he married to a more suitable person, someone who shared his idealism and convictions."

"I have heard that she's dreadful."

He nodded gravely, soaking this in. "You will take many meals at Yasnaya Polyana, but Sofya Andreyevna makes few concessions to her husband and his friends."

"She isn't a vegetarian?"

He shook his head with disgust. "Neither are her sons. Only Sasha can be trusted—among the children, that is. Confide only in her or in Dushan Makovitsky, your mother's friend. He is a good man."

"Dr. Makovitsky says that Sasha does much of her father's secretarial work."

"She types everything for him. There's a little room down the hallway from his study called 'the Remington room.' You'll doubtless spend a good deal of time there. Sasha needs help. The volume of letters seems to increase monthly with people frantic to get a word of advice from Leo Nikolayevich. He replies personally to most of them." Chertkov smiled again, revealing chiseled teeth with dark spaces between them. "Leo Nikolayevich adores his daughter, by the way. This drives Sofya Andreyevna mad."

"Does the countess type?"

"No, but she used to copy all of his work by hand. She was so possessive about it—and meddlesome."

I felt uneasy now. One does not like to come between married people, whatever the circumstances.

"You will help with the secretarial work, of course—mostly filing and answering letters. The point is that Leo Nikolayevich needs a man with your intellectual gifts around him. Somebody, like yourself, who has read and understood his work. Gusev was invaluable that way."

I had heard a good deal of Nicholai Gusev, who was Tolstoy's secretary for some years. The government of Tula exiled him from the province, as they did Chertkov, for "subversive activities," a sentence that might well fall on my head one day. I do not mind. Exile is a great Russian institution. The Russian soul has been tempered, like blue steel, in Siberia.

"Take these letters to Leo Nikolayevich, if you will," Chertkov said, handing me a small, tightly sealed packet. "One can't be sure what gets through to him, I'm afraid." He bit his lip. "Sofya Andreyevna does not respect his privacy."

"She would actually intercept his letters!"

He nodded, suppressing a grin. "I have another little task for you. A secret task, I should say." He leaned forward in his chair. "I have instructed Sergeyenko, my secretary at Telyatinki, to give you several English notebooks constructed for a special purpose."

I wanted to look aside but didn't dare.

"Sergeyenko will show you how to use them. In brief, you will keep a private diary for me. Write with an indelible pencil and use transfer paper. The interleaves can be torn out of the notebooks quite easily. Bring these weekly to Sergeyenko, who will send them to me here. I want to know exactly what happens at Yasnaya Polyana." A queer yellow light filled his eyes. "Let me know who is visiting Leo Nikolayevich. Tell me what he is reading, and make a note of what letters go out or come in. And let me know what Sofya Andreyevna has been saying."

A long pause followed, during which I restrained myself from comment. "Naturally," he continued, "I'd like to know what Leo Nikolayevich is writing. Too much of his time, I fear, has been wasted on this anthology of his. You might help by taking on some of these editorial duties. Do more than he asks of you. Urge him to get back to his philosophical work."

"Is he writing another novel?"

Chertkov belched into a silk handkerchief. "Novels are for women, for pampered, bourgeois women who have nothing better to do with their time."

"But *Anna Karenina*—"

"It's a decent example, but still quite foolish."

"Vladimir Grigorevich, I . . ."

He stared at me with tiny eyes that did not seem human. They were the eyes of a weasel.

"I liked *Anna Karenina*."

"You're a young man, Valentin Fedorovich! Young men like novels. I did, many years ago. My mother, in fact, was a friend of Turgenev. Fiction is for people who have not yet properly begun their search for God. What subjects intrigue these novelists? I will tell you. Lust and adultery." His upper lip curled, exposing his teeth like alder roots in a swamp.

I dipped my head forward and mumbled.

Chertkov drew his lips into a sidelong sharklike smile. "I like you very much, dear boy. I'm sure that Leo Nikolayevich will be grateful to you for whatever help you can give him." As he spoke, he pulled thin black leather gloves over his hands to hide a particularly raw patch of eczema. I felt sure, at last, the job was mine.

"I hope I will be able to help him," I said.

"You will. I see that."

I grinned stupidly, and Chertkov, as if annoyed with me, stood up. "Good-bye now," he said. "I look forward to receiving your diaries. And remember: Don't let anyone find out about them. Not even Leo Nikolayevich. It would distress him."

We shook hands, exchanging a few words about my preparations for the trip to Tula, by train, the following week. He escorted me into the dark front hall. Our footsteps echoed off the high ceiling and slate floor. A servant held out my coat and hat for me.

"I would not entrust you with this position if I didn't believe you were one of us," Chertkov said, his black-gloved hands resting on my shoulders. "I'm terribly worried, you know. Leo Nikolayevich is frail and nervous, though you will never hear a word of complaint from him. It is painful that I should have to live apart from him in his last days."

I nodded, but his comment did not seem to require affirmation.

"I'm grateful to you, Vladimir Grigorevich," I said.

He deflected my comment with a wave of one hand.

"Godspeed," he said, pushing the door open against a swirl of snow. "And remember what I said: *write everything down!*" He kissed me on either cheek and pushed me into the fierce January wind. A black sleigh waited for me in the drive, with a driver bundled in so much fur that he did not look human.

We drove off at a trot along a winding road through a line of bare elms. Huddled in my kaftan, with the light snow ticking on my forehead, I felt exalted and terrified—like Elijah being whisked to heaven in a whirlwind fire.

# 3

# L. N.

**LETTER TO PYOTR MELNIKOV,
A WORKER FROM BAKU**

YASNAYA POLYANA, 22 JANUARY 1910

It seems to me that two issues concern you: God—what is God?—
and the nature of the human soul. You also inquire about God's
relation to humankind, and wonder about life after death.

Let me take the first question. What is God and how does he
relate to humankind? The Bible says a lot about how God created
the universe and how he relates to his people, meting out rewards
and punishments. This is nonsense. Forget it altogether. Put it out of
your mind. God is the beginning of all things, the essential condition
of our being, and a little bit of what we take to be life within us and
revealed to us by Love (hence we say, "God is Love"). But, again,
please forget those arguments about God creating the world and the
human race and how he punishes everyone who disobeys. You must
erase that from your mind in order to consider your own life freshly.

What I have said is all we know of God, or can know.

About the soul, we can only say that what we refer to as life is
merely the divine principle. Without it nothing would exist. There is

nothing physical about it, nothing temporal. So it cannot die when the body ceases to exist.

You also—like all of us—want to know about life after death.

In order to understand me, pay close attention to what I say next.

For mortal man (that is, for the body alone) time exists: that is, hours, days, months, and years pass. For the body alone, there also exists the physical world—what can be seen, touched by the hands. What is big or little, hard or soft, durable or fragile. But the soul is timeless; it merely resides in the human body. The *I* that I spoke of seventy years ago is the same *I* I refer to now. Nor does the soul have anything physical about it. Wherever I am, no matter what happens, my soul, the *I* that I refer to, stays the same and is always nonphysical. Thus, time exists only for the body. For the soul, time and place and the physical world have no reality. Therefore, we can't really ask what will happen to the soul or where, after death, it will go, because the phrase *will be* suggests time, and the word *where* suggests place. Neither time nor place has meaning for the soul once the physical body has ceased to be.

That speculations about life after death or heaven and hell are shallow and mistaken should by now be clear. If the soul were going somewhere to live after death, it would have been somewhere before birth. But nobody seems to notice that.

My feeling is that the soul within us does not die when our body dies, but that we cannot know what will happen to it and where it will go—even though we *do* know that it cannot die. About punishments and rewards: I think our life here has meaning only when we live in accordance with the commandment to love one another. Life becomes distressing, troubled—bad—when we ignore this commandment. It would seem that whatever rewards and punishments our deeds warrant, we shall receive in this life, since none other can be known.

# 4

# SOFYA ANDREYEVNA

I know it for sure now. They'll do anything to come between me and my husband. It would be hard enough, God knows, without them pursuing us like Furies. What's worse is they think I don't know about their plan to write me and my children—Leo Tolstoy's children and grandchildren!—out of his will. I always know what's going on behind my back. I can tell it by their looks, their whispers and winks, even their deference. They somehow imagine I don't notice the secret messages delivered when my back is turned. Only yesterday a servant carried a letter from Sergeyenko to Lyovochka right under my nose, but, of course, I recognized his big, loopy handwriting on the envelope! Do they think I was born yesterday?

They spread rumors about me to the press. Last week an article appeared in Moscow claiming, "Countess Tolstoy has become estranged from her husband. They barely talk. They do not share a similar view of politics or religion." What nonsense! And it has all been spread by Chertkov and his friends, who have succeeded in coming between me and Lyovochka, in spite of our forty-eight years of marriage. In the end, however, I will triumph. Our love will triumph.

I'm treated as a stranger here. But am I not the very person who bore Leo Tolstoy his thirteen children (not bad for a preacher of chastity!), the woman who sees that his clothes are washed and mended, his vegetarian meals prepared to his liking? Am I not the one who takes his pulse before he falls asleep each night, who gives him enemas when his bowels are blocked, who brings him tea with a large slice of lemon when he cannot sleep?

I am a slave. An outcast in my own household. To think that I was the daughter of a famous Moscow physician! My father admired Leo Nikolayevich for his position in the aristocracy, yes, but also for his literary accomplishments. Who wouldn't? Even then, it was obvious that he would become an important writer. He was the talk of Moscow and St. Petersburg. I can remember my mother saying to me, "One day you will read about Count Tolstoy in the Encyclopedia."

When my sisters and I were teenagers, Papa would put tapers in the window once a week, as was the custom then—to signal our "at home." We waited, Lisa, Tanya, and me. We all loved Count Tolstoy desperately, though Papa and Mama assumed that Lisa, as the eldest, was the obvious mate for him. I was the middle girl, slender and dark-eyed, with a soft, reedy voice and teeth like ivory. I was the envy of Lisa, who was a cat—clawing and mewing, slinking about the house. Lisa had brains, yes. She was an "intellectual." But she was pompous and, if I do say so myself, a fraud.

Tanya could have been more dangerous. She was all mischief and commotion, eyes black as coal, with hair cut straight across her forehead like an Oriental whore. When she walked across the room, every muscle in her body signaled to the world. I hated her then. Who could tolerate the fetching way she would dance and sing, her grandiose schemes for "making it" in the theater? As if Papa would let one of his daughters spread her tail feathers on the Moscow stage! Poor Papa.

I don't think I was as difficult as the others. Nor should it have surprised anyone that Count Tolstoy chose me over my sisters. Though not brazen about it, I had accomplishments. I could play the piano—not like I do today, though not so badly either. My watercolors were passable. I could dance as well as most girls of my rank and position. And I could write like the wind—stories and poems, diaries, letters. Then, as now, Lyovochka had an instinct for self-preservation. He has always known how to get what he needs.

I first met the count when I was ten. He had come to visit Papa in the Kremlin, where we had an apartment, his dark mustache drooping, his uniform perfectly pressed, the boots so shiny you could see his knees reflecting on his toes. A ceremonial sword hung from his belt. He was about to join his regiment in the Danube, he said, affecting a quiet, slightly melancholic swagger. I stood meekly in one corner while he and Papa talked.

They sat in the front parlor, directly across from each other. Papa couldn't see me, but I could see the count, his knees pressed together, his hands large and red, folded awkwardly on his lap like sea crabs. As Papa spoke, the count's eyes seemed to flash with attentiveness. His stare, then as now, was compelling, irresistible. He hunched forward on the low cerise chair. The yellow epaulets and the double row of brass buttons on his uniform were almost too much for me to bear!

He and Papa talked for two hours in muffled tones, as if plotting the overthrow of the monarchy. What was all the hush about? Were they deciding which of us girls would be the future Countess Tolstoy? I don't think I could have wondered such a thing. After all, I was only ten years old. But my heart went out to Leo Tolstoy. I decided then and there that, one day, I would be his wife. When he left, I stole back into the parlor and tied a pink ribbon around the back leg of the chair he'd sat on.

After that, Papa spoke often of the young count, for whom he had a special affection. Once he let me borrow his novel *Childhood*. I read it in one long night, by candlelight, while my sisters slept. Every sentence blazed like a match tip. The images whirled in my head for weeks. No wonder all of Moscow was agog.

But that was years before any of us was really old enough for marriage. Suddenly, we were ready. Lisa was, anyway. And Mama was fed up. This courting business—the gentlemen callers, the endless teas and tension—had gone far enough. She wanted Lisa off her hands as quickly as possible.

In July a brainstorm overtook her; she would visit her father at Ivitsi, in the province of Tula, not far from the Tolstoy family estate at Yasnaya Polyana. It just so happened that we three girls (and little Volodya, of course) trotted along as well.

Mama said Lisa was the ideal mate for this eccentric, overly intellectual count, and she always made sure that Lisa sat next to him on the sofa in Moscow. Lisa would natter on about the latest philosophical works hot off the German presses. "It often occurs to me," intoned our Lisa, her small voice trilling like a bird's, "that the German Higher Criticism has made ill use of Hegel's dialectic. Don't you think so, Count?" Lyovochka's face would glaze over.

What was actually on the count's young mind was hunting in the Caucasus, though he would occasionally dazzle (and alarm) us with a speech about the wonders of Immanuel Kant. Sometimes, catching my eye, he would wink, and once, in the hallway, he squeezed my hand when nobody was looking.

Much as self-advertisement disgusts me, I will admit I was lovely in those days, with a tiny waist a man could happily surround with his powerful hands! That hot July morning, when the maid came to say the coach was ready to take us to Count Tolstoy's estate, I knew that he would soon be my husband.

Papa waved his handkerchief from the steps of Grandfather's small manor house as the ancient coach creaked and wobbled down the dirt road. Miles down the road we came to the soft, undulating cornfields typical of the Tula region. The corn, wheat, and rye, the long, symmetrical bands of muzhiks bending over their work in happy unison rolled past, then the forest of Zasyeka, with its thick, green woodland smelling of pine and mud. We came upon the village of Yasnaya Polyana, which did not impress me. A miserable clutch of thatched huts, shaky isbas, and stone barns. The village pump, with a tin pail slung beneath the spout, was spurting muddy water. The big wooden door of the church swung wide, and a middle-aged widow in a black veil stood beside it, chattering away to a toothless old nun the size and shape of a tree stump. The widow bowed gravely at our coach as we passed, feigning deference—the typical hypocrisy of the Russian lower classes.

Leo Tolstoy lived in his large ancestral home, which bore the same name as the village, Mama told us. Like all good teachers, she had a way of seeming enthusiastic about the obvious. She went on to explain how the count, like most young men of his rank, had been addicted to gambling. ("Your father, of course, was the exception," she said.) Playing cards with an unscrupulous neighbor, he had bet the central part of his house to stay in a game. He lost, and the unforgiving neighbor actually hauled off the main body of Yasnaya Polyana, leaving the wings behind, freestanding and ridiculous.

"He no longer gambles, I believe," Lisa said. "Nor does he drink overmuch. He is practically a teetotaler. And he is *very* devout." She sucked her lips into a pert rosebud that made me want to slap her. But I restrained myself, knowing what I knew about the count's real intentions.

"I'll bet he's worse than ever," Tanya said. "All young men drink and gamble, and Lord knows what they do with women."

"That tongue of yours is going to wag you all the way to a nunnery," Mama said, fussing with her hair.

We passed between two whitewashed towers at the entrance to the grounds of Yasnaya Polyana. The big stone house that had been refashioned from the abandoned wings stood at the end of the long serpentine drive, with parallel rows of silver birches rising along it like an honor guard. The meadows beyond them looked rich and silky, spotted with buttercups. And butterflies, too! The house competed admirably with nature for our attention. It was a long house on two floors, white as alabaster, with a Greek pediment topping a veranda over the entrance. A beautiful house, I whispered to myself. I was determined to be its mistress.

Lyovochka's Aunt Toinette, a shriveled thing in a country dress, welcomed us. *"Bienvenu! Comme c'est bon!"* she kept chirping. It seemed incongruous, this distinctly peasantlike woman—a real *krestyonka*—speaking Parisian French with almost no accent.

Mama accepted her welcome in garbled French, which, to my ear, sounded more like Chinese. *"Merci beaucoup! C'est une belle maison! Une belle maison! Mais oui!"* she cried.

Lyovochka, looking red-faced and out of breath, came hurling through the door apologetic, saying that he hadn't quite expected us. But he didn't make us feel guilty. Like a French courtier, he kissed everyone's hand in turn, lingering that extra moment over mine. I lit up inside, ablaze with love. I did not know where to look or what to say.

"Let me show you the orchard," he said. It seemed odd, especially to Mama, that he wanted us to see the orchard before we toured the house itself, but Mama was not going to object.

"We just adore orchards," she said. "Don't we adore orchards, girls?"

"I haven't thought much about it," Lisa said. She could be so tedious.

We paused by a thicket of bushes strung with ripe, red fruit. "Raspberries!" Tanya screamed, as if she'd never seen them before.

Lyovochka handed around pails, and we were all told to begin picking, right then and there—even Mama, who made the best of what she considered an unfortunate situation. "What charming raspberries," she said. "Don't we just adore raspberries?"

I stepped off with a pail behind one of the big bushes and had been happily, mindlessly, picking berries for a few minutes when Lyovochka sprang, like a bear, from behind a swatch of leaves.

"You frighten me!" I said.

He took my pail away and held my hands. "I'm sorry," he said. "I am."

"You should be."

He did not let go of my hands. "These are city hands," he said.

He held them and looked at me for such a long time. I said, "Would you like a berry?"

Like a defiant child, he plucked a berry from my pail and popped it between his coarse lips. I spotted his fat red tongue and looked away.

"I must go," he said. And disappeared.

Now I knew that my instincts were correct. It's strange how one can know everything at once about the future—not the details, but the overall picture. I knew that my life would be spent here, on these grounds, with Leo Tolstoy. I also knew that I would be his harshest critic and his best friend. And that heartache lay ahead of me, unspecified but cruel.

I carried this secret, miraculous knowledge with me, hoarded it like an amulet. It would ruin everything if they found out before the time was ripe.

Tanya, Lisa, and I lodged together in the vaulted room on the ground floor that nowadays is crammed with stinking, uncouth disciples: insane noblemen, beggars who are proud of their fallen state, toothless nuns, idealistic students, revolutionaries, criminals, vegetarians, foreigners. The mad economist Nikolayev is here, preaching Henry George's theory of the single tax. He slurps his soup on the linen tablecloth, splashing those to his right and left. Drankov, the cinematographer, is here, too. I don't mind him, although he is constantly taking our picture.

I thought Lyovochka would propose to me after dinner, but he didn't. By the time we left, two days later, nothing had happened. Worse, he acted as though we had never exchanged a moment of intimacy. I began to doubt my perspicacity. Perhaps I had been mistaken all along? Perhaps he had behaved the same with Lisa? Even with Tanya? As we departed, I could barely fend off despair, though I maintained a cheerful countenance. I comforted myself with the fact that Lisa was more miserable than I. She wept openly as we clattered off behind a troika, and Mama scolded her. "He will ask you in his own good time," she said, disappointment curdling her voice.

Two days later, at Grandfather's house, Tanya wakened me. "It's the count!"

"You're teasing me."

"No, it's true! He's come on a white horse."

Leave it to my Lyovochka. Grandstanding, as usual. "A horse," he once said, "is the symbol of the rider's soul."

Grandfather welcomed him eagerly, grinning and bowing. He was so queer, with his close-shaven skull and black skullcap, a razorlike nose. His hairy fingers, like the legs of a tarantula, seemed always to be moving. His eyes were independent of each other, like fish eyes, poking out from opposite sides of his narrow head.

Lyovochka was covered with white dust and sweat. He affected a shy, boyish grin, apologizing for his condition.

Grandfather told him not to think twice about it. It was an honor, he said. "And how long did it take you, Leo Nikolayevich? It's such a long way to come on horseback."

"Three hours. Perhaps a bit more. I was in no hurry. It's a lovely day, isn't it?"

"Let me get you a drink?"

"That would be very kind of you, sir."

We huddled in the shade of the hall, listening to their exchange. I wore a muslin dress that day, a white one for summer, with a lilac-tinted rosette on the right shoulder. I trailed a long ribbon down one arm, the kind we used to call *Suivez-moi, jeune homme*.

"He has come for you, Lisa," my mother said. She could barely restrain her giddiness and pride. "Today is your day."

"I wouldn't sleep with a dusty man like that," said Tanya to Lisa.

Lisa turned her nose up. To give in to her sister's taunts would be unbecoming of a future countess.

The day followed a summery course of gay (though hardly extraordinary) meals, with lots of party games and silly jokes. The strain of waiting for the count to strike seemed unbearable to poor Grandfather. Mama was hardly any better. Her conversation lapsed into inanities that, fortunately, the count never noticed.

It happened after dinner. Everyone had left the dining room but myself and the rather obviously hyperventilating count. He turned to me and said, "Could you wait a moment, Sofya Andreyevna? It's so pleasant in here."

"It's a charming room, isn't it?" I said, lying through my teeth.

"The food is excellent here."

"Grandfather likes his food."

We shifted from foot to foot. Get on with it, I thought.

"Come sit beside me on the sofa," he said. "You wouldn't mind that, would you?"

I smiled and followed him to the little sofa along the side wall. He sat down first, impolitely, but his doing so allowed me to choose my position. For the sake of modesty, I left a few inches between us.

He pulled a green, baize-covered table up to our knees and took a piece of chalk from his coat pocket. I watched him closely as he leaned over the table and began to scribble on its soft cover.

He wrote: "Y.y.a.y.d.f.h.r.m.c.o.m.a.a.t.i.o.h.f.m."

I stared at the peculiar inscription.

"Can you decipher this?"

"It's a string of letters, Leo Nikolayevich."

Was this some sort of after-dinner game played by the aristocracy? My stomach tightened.

"I can help you," he said. "The first two *y*'s represent the words *Your youth*."

"Your youth and your desire for happiness remind me cruelly of my age and the impossibility of happiness for me," I cried, having reconstructed the entire sentence. It was a miracle!

When the meaning wakened in my head, I shuddered. Everything fell clear.

Lyovochka, meanwhile, was rubbing out what he had written and starting the little game all over again.

This time, he wrote: "Y.f.i.w.a.m.f.t.L.H.m.t.c.t."

I knew exactly what he meant once I understood that *L* was for

Lisa. "Your family is wrong about my feelings toward Lisa. Help me to clarify this."

An actual proposal did not follow for several weeks, but I knew now that poor Lisa was finished. He loved me alone.

When Lyovochka visited us in Moscow in September, I gave him a story I had written. It was about a tender young girl who had a suitor called Dublitsky—an old, rather ugly nobleman. He wished, more than anything in the world, to marry her, but she wasn't sure if she really wanted him. I don't know why I wrote such a story. I didn't actually think of Lyovochka as old and ugly, though he was a little of both. I gave it to him without realizing it might cause pain. His response came, by post, a few days later:

*Naturally when I read your story, my dear one, I saw that I was Dublitsky. How could I think otherwise? I realized that I am what I am: Uncle Leo, an old, uncommonly plain—even ugly— character who should concern himself with God's work and nothing more. I should do God's work and do it well, and that should be enough for me. But I become miserable when I think of you, when I recall that I am Dublitsky. I am reminded of my age and the impossibility of happiness. For me, anyway. Yes, I am Dublitsky. But to marry simply because I need a wife is something beyond my ken. I can't do it. I would ask of my future wife something terrible, impossible: I insist on being loved as I love. Forget about me. I shall not bother you anymore.*

I'd have stabbed myself in the breast a thousand times if that could have made a difference. I cursed myself for giving him my story. What had I been thinking? For days I was inconsolable.

A week later, I sat at the piano, comforting myself with a light Italian score, a waltz called "Il Bacio," the kiss. There was a knock at the door. It was Lyovochka, his eyes sunken like potholes beneath his bushy brows. I may misremember this, but he smelled of lavender.

He sat beside me at the piano and said, "I've been carrying a letter in my pocket for several days now. Will you read it, Sonya? It's for you."

I quietly took the letter down the hall to my room, locking myself in to read it. My hands trembling, the characters difficult to see through my tears, I read: "Would you possibly consent to be my wife?"

"Open this door!" Lisa shrieked. She knew exactly what was going on. "Sonya! Open this door."

I peeked out.

"What has he written to you? Tell me frankly."

"He has offered me his hand in marriage."

Her face tightened. She seemed fit to burst, like an overripe tomato. "Refuse him, Sonya! Say no!" She began to pull at her own hair, "I will die if you don't. It's intolerable!"

Such a scene! I adored every minute of it, of course, but I kept my composure. At least somebody in this house was worthy of the title Countess Tolstoy.

Mama came scuffling down the hall when she heard the commotion. She dragged Lisa, kicking and squealing like a pig, back to her room. "What the count must think!" Mama cried.

"You must go into the parlor and deliver your response," she said to me flatly. All possible pleasure had drained from the scene she had so long anticipated.

I found Lyovochka standing against the wall, his face white as a sail. He wrung his hands.

"So?" he asked. I heard a note of resignation in that question, and my heart went out to him. The poor, dear man!

"Yes," I said. "Yes, I will marry you, Leo Nikolayevich."

Soon an avalanche broke over our heads, what with servants rushing about, Lisa weeping beside me, Tanya shouting in her vulgar way, Mama offering drinks. Everyone was there but Papa, who pretended he was ill. In truth, he was upset that the count had revealed such bad manners. He should first have asked Papa. Indeed, he should have asked for Lisa's hand. It took several days and much coaxing by Mama to bring him round, but he acquiesced. He always did.

Life became miserable again too quickly. Lyovochka, in a fit of honesty, gave me his diaries. I was honored, at first, and thrilled. It seemed wonderfully romantic to read the most private thoughts of one's future husband!

One sentence hangs in my memory like a black crow: "I consider the company of women a necessary evil and avoid it when possible. Women are the source of all frivolity, all sensuality and indolence, all the vices to which men are prone." He went on to recount the whole disgusting story of endless nights on the town in Moscow, St. Petersburg, even Tula and Sevastopol! Whores and peasant women of all stripes had shared his bed!

I read on with disbelief, learning that he had lost his innocence as a boy of fourteen in Kazan, led to a brothel by his elder brother Sergey, who'd specialized in debauchery from the beginning. After he had performed the disgusting act, he stood by the harlot's bedside, weeping. It was as if he foresaw all.

And there was more. I heard for the first time about Axinya, the peasant woman who had served his vile needs for three years before our marriage. I could have borne this were it not for their son, Timothy, who haunts us still. The hideous, dim-witted Timothy, who snorts and guffaws, who prowls our house like a demon spirit from hell. Worse, he looks just like Lyovochka: the same height, the same slightly rounded shoulders, the unmistakable eyebrows and wispy spume of a beard! He has Lyovochka's profile, too, with the fleshy nose and jutting chin. A loathsome parody of my husband, he lurches about Yasnaya Polyana, carrying wood, doing errands, creeping in the shadows.

I have begged my husband to get rid of Timothy, to send him to Moscow, at least. We are never there anyway. But the Master wants his sins to cluster about him. He wants to suffer, to see that grotesque reflection of himself at every turn.

I married Leo Tolstoy, the great author, on 23 September 1862, at eight o'clock, in the Church of the Nativity of the Virgin, right under the Kremlin's long, imperial shadow.

"How can I live without your company?" my sister Tanya said, as I was leaving the church.

"Try, my dear. Try."

I was pleased to slough off the old life. I was tired of being beholden to Papa, plagued by doubts about my future life. My life was settled, once and for all.

Oh, was it settled.

# 5

# DR. MAKOVITSKY

They laugh at me. They giggle and sneer behind my back. Even the servants have caught on to their little game. Just the other day I heard the maids saying, "The doctor is such a little runt—and a dunce." They get this kind of talk from Sofya Andreyevna, I suspect. She dislikes me. But what can one expect from a woman like her, who wastes her days snuffling around behind Leo Nikolayevich's back like a dog, trying to unearth some new bone of discord. She suspects that Chertkov has convinced her husband to draft a new will that bequeaths his writing to the world after his death. He has always said he wants to do this, and it's the obvious thing for him to do. But Sofya Andreyevna wants the royalties. How else could she support all the servants, the big house, the torrent of guests and outings and .trips to Moscow, dresses from St. Petersburg? Her avarice is as legendary as her inability to understand her husband's principles. As Leo Nikolayevich often says to her, one should not expect to make a profit from books written for the sake of humanity. It offends him that anyone, let alone the poor, should have to pay to read what he has written.

But I feel sorry for Sofya Andreyevna. It's not that she is a bad woman. She simply does not understand what her husband has accomplished. Her soul is not copious enough to absorb his dreams for the improvement of humanity. On the other hand, they don't require immense effort to comprehend. The poor shall inherit the earth. The first shall be last, and the last shall be first. And so forth. Everything Leo Nikolayevich says has all been said before. In the realm of religion and ethics, one does not invent the truth; one discovers and proclaims it.

Leo Nikolayevich is the great proclaimer.

I am not, however, so foolish as to think that *he* is Christ. Christ is Christ. But Leo Nikolayevich is certainly one of his prophets. I am lucky to know him as well as I do. I am more than his personal physician. I am his friend.

I began reading Tolstoy as a medical student in Prague. Strolling amid that city's amber stones or sitting in the cathedral while the organist practiced for Sunday morning services, I would meditate on his message. Later, in Hungary, I dedicated myself to his writings. Soon I wrote to him asking for advice, informing him that I had been sought out by local Tolstoyans to lead their group.

He wrote back: "It is a great and gross mistake to speak about Tolstoyism or to seek my guidance on this matter or to ask my decisions on problems. There is no Tolstoyism or any teaching of mine, and there never has been. There is only one general and universal teaching of the truth, which for me, for us, is most clearly expressed in the Gospels."

I understood this, yes. But I also knew that God spoke especially clearly through Leo Tolstoy. Divine light shone through his prose. And I tried to live by that light as I made my daily rounds in the village. The medical profession is well suited to a life of service, and I returned to my narrow room each night in the boardinghouse exhausted but fulfilled, happy inside. I would read his books by a blazing wick till midnight. His *Confession* moved me greatly, as did "What I Believe," where—with astonishing simplicity—he says what he thinks.

Who is Christ? This question has preoccupied Tolstoy for many decades. He answers, "He is who he says he is: the Son of God, the Son of Man, the truth and the life." But he is *not* God. That is the essential mistake made by our church theologians. What Christ gave us was a way of understanding our lives in a perspective that cannot be destroyed by death. It is the fear of death that hangs like a buzzard over mankind's head, a perpetual torment. As Leo Nikolayevich has said, one should whisk that fear away. Say, "Be gone, buzzard!" And then comes freedom.

As a token of my faith, I have forsaken women. True, I am not a handsome man. I am small. But my hands are a doctor's hands: delicate and fine. I stitch and cut. I bandage and assuage. I am a doctor. Though I am hardly an old man, not having yet passed fifty, I am quite bald, and this seems to offend many women. My beard, which I trim each morning, seems to grow whiter by the month. But I have fire. There is a fire in my head, in my heart. I am in love with God. I can feel the fire of God in my soul. I am part of him. I *am* God, as everyone is God who recognizes the God within himself.

I can even recognize a bit of God in Goldenweiser, that fraud and mountebank, that pianist and Jew. Why Leo Nikolayevich allows that man to hang about this house, to play his piano, to eat at his table and walk beside him in the orchard, defeats my understanding. The superiority of the Slavic race to the Israelites has always been known. As a man of science, I cannot fail to observe the colossal sequence of defeats that the Jews have sustained. Wherever they go, they are suspect. They fester and grow in almost any soil. Leo Nikolayevich does not understand about Jews.

But every man has his blind spots. Leo Nikolayevich is not God. Nevertheless, I love him. I love him completely. I cannot believe my luck, that each day of my life since I came here six years ago, in 1904, has been spent here beside him. I have thus been privileged to listen to his words. I write them all down. I have mastered a kind of shorthand, so I rarely miss anything important.

It can be quite annoying at lunch or dinner, however. Sofya Andreyevna teases me for writing under the table whenever Leo Nikolayevich speaks. She shouts, "Dushan Petrovich, you're scribbling again! Naughty, naughty!"

I have an excellent memory, however—a gift from God. Each night, before sleeping, I settle down at my little deal table and recall his words, working from notes gathered during the day. I take great care not to embellish what he says. The words of Leo Nikolayevich need no improvement! Each pause, each gesticulation and aside—all perfect. And it's all there, in my diary. Word for word—a permanent record. My gift to humanity.

Apart from the annoyance of Sofya Andreyevna, my life here has been pleasantly routine. I spend each morning, while Leo Nikolaye-vich is writing, in the village. An isba has been converted into a surgery for my use, and I see a dozen or so patients there every day. Whooping cough, bad throats, intestinal obstructions, fevers, measles, consumption, venereal diseases. Cases of hysteria. Lice. I see every-thing. But I love our Russian peasants. They are the soul of endur-ance. They are simple and God loving. God fearing. This is why Leo Nikolayevich loves them, and why I do, although most of them are pathetically superstitious. They do not understand that I represent the science of medicine. What I practice is not magic. For magic, I direct them to the monastery outside Tula. Let the monks heal you, I say, if you don't believe in my methods. Not one of them has yet taken me up on this offer.

Today was a special day. Against Sofya Andreyevna's wishes (which made it all the more attractive), I collected Leo Nikolayevich from his study at nine-thirty. He had already been at his desk for two hours, which is unusual for him. He normally begins at nine. But he had planned on our trip into Tula this morning, so he got up and started to work before the rest of the household was awake, doubtless treasuring the early morning clarity that overtakes the soul.

We went into Tula in the troika—a relatively short and effortless journey, except in winter, when heavy drifts can block the road. Today it was unusually warm, and the roads were clear, even though it snowed lightly all night. The fields spread about us in their whiteness. It was so beautiful! Leo Nikolayevich commented several times on the freshness and stillness of the day. His health had not been good recently—some chills, some coughing—so I made sure he bundled up in several coats and wore a thick hat. I put a blanket over his legs to block the wind. He drooled slightly, and a glaze of ice soon formed in his beard, but he did not appear to notice.

Leo Nikolayevich was moved by our little excursion, which we had been planning for some weeks. Tula's newspaper, the *Molva*, had been filled with nothing else. Some muzhiks from the Denisov estate had been charged with stealing mail from the postal service. They were to go on trial first, followed by something more important, something dearer to Leo Nikolayevich's heart than mail thievery. I. I. Afanasev, whom Leo Nikolayevich met several times at Telyatinki, had been accused of circulating pamphlets advocating socialism and revolution.

"It is always distressing when a man is accused of nothing more than expressing a view of life which is saner than that which already prevails," said Leo Nikolayevich, talking more to himself than to me as the troika clattered over the wooden bridge into Tula. He took on that ponderous look which sometimes overwhelms and distorts his features.

When we arrived at the courthouse, the street was thronged. Not unlike at the Kursk Station in Moscow, earlier in the month, when Leo Nikolayevich found himself drowning in a mob of well-wishers, thousands of them, all of whom screamed his name at the top of their lungs. Today, word had spread that Tolstoy would appear as a witness for the defense in both cases, and people came out hoping to catch a glimpse of him. All kinds of people, but especially beggars, who imagined that "the Count," as they persist in calling him, could work a miracle for them. Many reached out merely to touch his coat in passing.

"Clear a path for Leo Nikolayevich!" I shouted, and four young soldiers in dark green overcoats rushed to help us. We five formed a wedge, like geese going south, with Leo Nikolayevich in the wake of the V. He kept his head down, ignoring the shouts of "God bless you, Leo Nikolayevich!" I was terrified that he would stumble or collapse, as he sometimes does, but he walked with a determined step. If anything, the attention buoyed him.

The courts were too cold for a man of Leo Nikolayevich's eighty-two years. Though logs had been laid in all the fireplaces, the high ceilings and bare halls conspired against all possibility of comfort. And Leo Nikolayevich quickly succumbed to the frigid temperature. His lips soon began to quiver, turning blue as nails; I feared he might have another one of the minor strokes that have plagued him lately. They leave him temporarily speechless and without exact memory.

"Keep your coat on, Leo Nikolayevich," I said. "Even the sun is cold today."

He grinned that toothless grin of his, stretching his lips. "You are my doctor, aren't you?"

"I am indeed. So listen, for once." I am forever trying to get him to behave sensibly about his age.

An official of the courts led us to a small box, where we sat on a wooden bench with other witnesses and official observers. The gallery was crowded, and the judge—an aristocrat and member of the local militia called Bozorev—bowed slightly to Leo Nikolayevich as he entered and took his place behind a table.

The first session concerned the muzhiks who stole the mail. Leo Nikolayevich believed the peasants had been framed, and I communicated this information to the judge. Leo Nikolayevich patted his knees with his long fingers, as if keeping time with a private melody. He seemed lost through much of the proceedings. But he came to life during the testimony against Afanasev, who belonged to a fringe group of socialists and revolutionaries. An oxlike prosecutor in a regimental uniform accused Afanasev of circulating materials designed to create discontent among the muzhiks. Afanasev was not directly accused of plotting to overthrow the government of the tsar, but the implications were grave. Those wishing to speak in his behalf, such as Leo Nikolayevich, were slated for the afternoon session.

We had lunch in a bare little room next to the courts, a piece of rough brown bread and a slice of goat cheese drunk with hot tea brought by a vendor. As we talked about the proceedings, Leo Nikolayevich grew animated. He believed in the elementary principles of free speech, he said, principles quite alien to the Imperial government of Russia. He admired Afanasev, who is young and idealistic. Indeed, he sympathized with the young man's goals, though he doubted that violent revolutions would ever lead to the establishment of a just society.

"People seem to forget that we all must die," he said. His hand trembled as he tore off a small bit of bread to mouth slowly with his gums. "We ought to spend our energies not on useless conflicts but on doing what is clearly good. If a revolution is not something genuinely new—such as the abolition of *all* government—it will certainly be nothing more than an imitation of what we have already seen, and that will be worse than what it replaces."

I did not find this entirely sound. "But the tsar is wicked," I said, whispering, even though we seemed alone. "Any government would be better than this one. Surely none could be worse."

Leo Nikolayevich spoke calmly, unafraid of being overheard. He is among the few Russians who can be said to have immunity from prosecution by the tsar. "There can be no improvement in the condition of the Russian people," he said, "nor any people, through revolution that does not exist on a moral basis. A moral basis presupposes that force will not be used."

I quickly got all this down on my notepad. It was good. Very good. But I objected to the impracticality of his stance. I, too, believed that the will of God must be followed in all things and that immoral revolutions could only hurt the Russian people. But I saw no reason why it could not be God's will that a reasonable form of government forcibly replace a tyrannical one. I expressed these reservations, but Leo Nikolayevich seemed immovable. Perhaps he was putting himself in a mood appropriate to the afternoon session.

We got back to the chambers before the rest of them; it was even colder now. Leo Nikolayevich hunched forward, working his mouth as though lumps of bread were still lodged in his cheeks and needed mastication. He gasped once or twice, and I quickly took his pulse. It was racing madly. I urged him to return immediately to Yasnaya Polyana.

"I will not speak," he said. "But you must stand in my place. Say that I disagree with all that has been said against Afanasev. Tell them that I consider him a young man of high ideals and goodwill, and that he should not be punished."

When the judge returned, I stood to apologize for Leo Nikolayevich, saying that his health made it impossible for him to speak in public. But I communicated, briefly, his position with regard to Afanasev, and the judge thanked us warmly. At this point, Leo Nikolayevich stood, bowed to the judge and the assembly, and left the courtroom, leaning heavily on my arm for support.

Not a sound could be heard as we left, not until a voice lifted, lonely as a puff of smoke on the horizon: "God save Leo Nikolayevich!" I looked back. It was Afanasev.

We stopped for another glass of tea on the way out, since Leo Nikolayevich felt a chill. We had not been sitting there terribly long when a young man appeared. He had a message for the count, he said, smiling at me as though we shared some intimacy. He said, "I have been asked to report that the case against the muzhiks has been dismissed. They are free to go home." He paused, letting the richness of that news sink in. "And Afanasev has been given the minimum sentence. Three years confinement in a fortress."

"That's horrid!"

"Dushan Petrovich," Leo Nikolayevich said. "We should be glad he was not condemned to death, given the unrest throughout this country. The government is only too eager to see that examples are made of men like Afanasev. Three years in a fortress is not so bad for a young man. He will read and write. I will send him books."

Leo Nikolayevich was aglow in the evening, kindly to everyone, listening attentively to Sofya Andreyevna. He put a drop of white wine in his water goblet—a sign that he was feeling festive.

Boulanger was there, playing (insufferably) the good little disciple, as was Nazhivin, a young writer, who insisted on sitting next to "the Master," as he called him—to everyone's chagrin. He cooed like a pigeon when Leo Nikolayevich spoke, his throat clucking away. I disliked him intensely, especially when he grew philosophical and repeated, verbatim, Leo Nikolayevich's own remarks, as though he'd just thought of them himself. Leo Nikolayevich remained polite with him. I can't think why. Indeed, he nodded vigorously when Nazhivin parroted a particularly well-known Tolstoyan locution. It was most embarrassing.

Sofya Andreyevna ushered everyone into the drawing room at the front of the house, and we sat about while she played Beethoven's Pastoral Sonata on the piano. Large tears came to Leo Nikolayevich's eyes, and he wiped them on his sleeve. He often weeps when music is played, either on the piano (usually by Sofya Andreyevna, who fancies herself a world-class pianist whom circumstances have forced to hide her light under a bushel) or on the gramophone. On the other hand, music moves me not a whit.

It has been ruined for me by Goldenweiser, the idiot Jew. Night after night he performs at the keyboard for the Tolstoy family, who are too kindly to turn him out. Leo Nikolayevich is pushed about, submissive to all, eager to preserve the calm at any cost. But the cost is great.

One day he will understand why I oppose Goldenweiser. He will also understand that Sofya Andreyevna must be removed.

# 6

# BULGAKOV

Most days resemble other days. They fall in rows, mowed down by time. One does not much regret the loss. But a few glorious days stand out in memory, days where each moment shines separately, like cobbles on a strand. One yearns to repossess them, and mourns their distance. Such was my first day as Leo Nikolayevich's secretary.

It was mid-January, a foggy morning, exceedingly warm for this time of year in Russia. I woke early in the small room just above the kitchen. This was my second day at Telyatinki, and I was to meet with Tolstoy after breakfast. Masha, who had recently joined the devout band of Tolstoyans who live and work at Chertkov's house, brought me a glass of tea in bed. She is a tall girl, Finnish in appearance, with high cheekbones and short blond hair that falls straight on either side of her head. Her almond-shaped, green eyes dipped to the floor when she entered my room, having knocked so lightly that I was unaware of her presence till she opened the door.

"Come in," I said, clearing my throat and sitting up in bed.

She put the tray down on the table beside my bed.

"It's very kind of you to bring me tea. You needn't have done that."

"Tomorrow, you will make your own tea," she said. "But today you may consider yourself lucky."

Her shyness seemed to evaporate as she cut a fresh slice of lemon and dropped it into the tea.

"I like being waited on."

"We do not grant special privileges around here. Everyone is equal at Telyatinki."

"A real democracy!"

"You're teasing me."

"I'm sorry. Shall I not?"

"As you will," she said. She pushed the blanket back to my knees and sat down. No woman had ever sat beside me while I lay in bed, except my mother. Everything in Masha's manner proclaimed that she was, by God, a straightforward, progressive, practical girl. A real Tolstoyan.

"Have you met everyone already? Sergeyenko has no sense of humor. I should warn you," she said. "He's extremely kind, however."

The kindness had eluded me. Sergeyenko, Chertkov's secretary, is the son of a close friend of Tolstoy. He ran the establishment at Telyatinki in Chertkov's absence. Unfortunately, I had taken a dislike to him almost immediately upon my arrival the day before. He is a youngish man, plump, in his late thirties; like Chertkov, he has a narrow black beard. There is something a little dandyish about him, except that he takes almost no baths; he smells sour, like rotting wool. He had got straight to business immediately.

"Vladimir Grigorevich is anxious that you should begin your reports from Yasnaya Polyana," he said, having taken me into his bare little study off the front hall. He pulled the mysterious notebooks with the interleaving pages from a burled oak desk. "You should know that, for reasons of security, we must keep the existence of these diaries—your diaries—a secret."

I promised to obey his wishes, but I felt empty inside. Secrecy did not seem, to me, the essence of Tolstoyism. This was no way to begin a relationship with the man I most admire in the world.

"Did you not like Sergeyenko?" Masha asked now, interrupting my reverie.

"He seems sincere," I said.

Her small but lovely breasts puffed out her muslin blouse, just a little. Her long arms, slender wrists, and delicate fingers were alluring. I quietly breathed her in, filling my lungs with the soft air that clung to her.

As we talked, I learned that she had taught in St. Petersburg. It was unpleasant work—an elite school for the spoiled children of bureaucrats.

"As a young girl, I wanted to be a nun," she said.

I could not restrain a slight grin.

"You find me amusing?"

"I'm sorry," I said. "I can't imagine you as a nun."

"Why?" She did not seem angry, merely curious.

What could I say? That she was too beautiful to be wasted on a nunnery?

"You don't look like a nun," I said—a pathetic bridge across an awkward place in the stream of conversation. "I mean, nuns are old and . . . wrinkled."

She knew I was bluffing and leaped from the bed. "I'd better get back to the kitchen. I'm on duty this week. It will be your turn soon enough."

"Democracy in action."

She didn't like the current of cynicism and turned away.

I wanted to ask her about her interest in Tolstoy, but she seemed in no mood to dwell on herself. She stood, smoothing the folds in her skirt, still uneasy about me.

I thanked her again, a bit profusely, for bringing me the cup of tea.

"Perhaps one day you'll bring me a cup," she said, closing the door behind her.

It occurred to me that remaining chaste might not be easy at Telyatinki.

■ I was driven to Yasnaya Polyana by a young farm steward named Andrey. A thin, olive-skinned fellow with tight curls on his head, he has the high cheekbones and slightly upturned eyes of the Mongol. He played the balalaika beautifully on the evening of my arrival, somewhat to Sergeyenko's dismay. (Sergeyenko thinks that music is frivolous and that readings from Scripture or the philosophers are appropriate evening entertainments.)

"The count's a simple man," said Andrey, holding the reins. "He don't frighten you. Not like Chertkov."

"Does Chertkov scare people?"

Andrey withdrew. "He's all right."

"I know what you mean about him," I said, trying to reassure him.

We bumped along over the frozen mud. The fog was still thick, hanging in the trees like cotton on a comb. It swirled, pooling in the valley, curling around whitewashed isbas, licking its tail into the corners of Zasyeka Wood. The air had a slight coppery tang.

My stomach was a leather balloon, compressed, hard. I was vaguely nauseated. This was worse than going to school for the first time.

"Do you know Tolstoy personally?" I asked.

"I see him riding in the afternoons, always alone. But he don't come to Telyatinki much. The countess won't let him. She's jealous of his friends, you know. A real bitch."

"Countess Tolstoy is a bitch?"

"I shouldn't say it, not so blunt."

"You should always say what you think."

I felt like a hypocrite saying such a thing, but—as a person of superior rank—I felt it was my duty to state the obvious moral.

Andrey said, "I don't want to turn you away from the countess. You'll hear plenty bad enough said about her. Just wait."

From the first I hadn't heard a decent word about Countess Tolstoy in the company of Tolstoyans. She seemed like my grandmother, Alexandra Ilinisha, who rode roughshod over my poor grandfather, Sergey Fedorovich. A traditional gentleman of leisure in St. Petersburg, he died last year, of apoplexy, at the age of seventy-nine. He had spent the last half century of his life ignoring Grandmother. He walked in the public gardens or hid himself in his study, where he read the latest French and English novels. Wearing a panama hat in summer, with a piqué waistcoat studded with breloques, he was the sort of man Tolstoy would have despised. Yet I liked Grandfather. He was generous and sweet natured, and very learned. He had directed my early reading. In fact, he had led me to Tolstoy, of whom he personally disapproved. "He has betrayed his class," was Grandfather's principal criticism, which he couldn't really explain to me or elaborate. Nevertheless, he was delighted that I had taken to books; *any* books would do.

"He's kind of a simple man," said Andrey, again.

"Who?"

"Tolstoy! Never raises a voice against nobody."

A picture of Tolstoy was developing in my head, that of a henpecked, gentle, silent, austere father figure who fends off the world like my grandfather did, somewhat ineptly.

It was nine when we turned into the gates of Yasnaya Polyana. As in a novel, the fog began to lift, revealing the bone-white facade of the manor house in the near distance. The light grew harsh, delineating the wintry scene with a printmaker's exactness: the tall frozen elm outside the house, the birches to one side of the road, the thatched roofs of various cottages on the estate. Weeds poked through the snow's recent dusting over the fields, and the estate seemed deserted now, bare but stately and serene.

Andrey deposited me at the front door and departed, leaving me nervously on my own. I took off my hat and gloves and knocked on the heavy door. An elderly man in a dark formal jacket, with white gloves, opened it.

"You're the new secretary?"

"Valentin Fedorovich Bulgakov," I said.

He nodded, bowing slightly. He did not volunteer his name, and I didn't ask. He led me to a cloakroom where I could leave my coat and hat. I had put the letter of introduction from Chertkov in my jacket pocket, and I felt to make sure it was still there.

"The count has gone for a walk," the man informed me. "He would like you to wait for him in his study."

I was led into Tolstoy's private chambers through a light-drenched, empty house—a fairly typical country house of an aristocratic Russian family, though more sparsely furnished than one might expect. The wooden floors, the color of honey, glowed.

"You would like some tea?"

I declined, thanking him, and was directed toward the cracked leather couch against the far wall. I sat down and crossed my legs, feeling out of place here—like one who wanders into church on a weekday. When the man was gone, I stood up again, jittery but curious. The room was smaller than I had imagined it would be, with pale, dirty walls. It smelled faintly of hemp and tallow, an old man's smell. An ornately scrolled, thick-legged writing table stood in the center of the room, an altar of sorts. I touched it gingerly, running my hand along the smooth desktop, then sat in Tolstoy's chair. I felt as if I had mounted a powerful horse that was about to charge off all by itself, oblivious to my wishes.

Stacks of letters, all with envelopes torn open but probably unanswered, lay in clumps on the desk. A stone jar full of pencils and fountain pens stood to one side of the blotter; a pot of India ink was loosely covered beside a ledger. There was a notebook lying open. The handwriting was large but difficult, that much I could tell from a distance. I would have loved to peek into the notebook, but I didn't dare, backing away from the desk.

A double row of books hung in a rack on the wall. The bottom level contained a miscellany of texts: philosophers, religious thinkers, biblical studies, novels from England, France, and Germany. A few

Russian novelists and poets. I plucked an odd-looking volume with a buff cover from the shelf and leafed through it. It was a play called *Man and Superman* by George Bernard Shaw, of whom I had not heard. A copy of a letter slipped from the pages onto the floor, and I picked it up. It was from Tolstoy to the author of the play, written in English. My eye fell on a passage near the end of the lengthy screed:

> *Indeed, my dear Shaw, life is a great and serious business, and each of us must contrive, in the brief time we have been allotted, to discover what our job is and do that job as earnestly as we can. This applies to all men and women, but especially to one such as yourself, a man with the gift of original thought who can pierce to the heart of serious questions. Thus, trusting that I will not offend you, I will say what seems to me to be wrong with your book.*
>
> *The first defect is that you are not serious enough. One should never joke about the purpose of human life, the reasons for its perversion, or the evil that consumes humanity from day to day . . .*

I broke off, hearing footsteps, hastily tucked the letter back into the volume, and returned it to the shelf. I was quivering now. This was a great man indeed. One who could write so plainly to a man like this Mr. Shaw from England. It's easy to praise people. To point out faults is another matter.

The footsteps passed, and their sound dwindled at the end of the hall. Now I looked up to the top row of books—the lovely Brochhaus Efron Encyclopedia, with its blue spines and gold lettering, stretched halfway across the room. Next to it was a row of Tolstoy's novels, bound in buckram. I lifted a volume off the shelf: *Boyhood*—his first published book. I turned the pages, reading a few sentences, then plucked *Anna Karenina* from the set. I took a quick look at *The Four Gospels Harmonized and Translated*. In this massive work, Tolstoy manages to discern the true Gospel of Jesus—the story of a man who gave up the world for God, for man; in doing so, Jesus became God-like—His exemplary life, cleared of generations of mystical debris, is uncovered—"harmonized and restored"—in this book, though few readers have found Tolstoy's commentary easy to follow. It will take decades to clarify and elaborate on the work Tolstoy began.

I loved thinking that these volumes were Tolstoy's very own. I clasped my hands behind my back, determined to touch nothing else. Various portraits on the wall caught my eye. There was Dickens in the flush of youth, his quick eyes blazing, and the poets Fet and Pushkin. I sat down again on the leather sofa, focusing my eyes on the ornate little table beside it, an antique, with a bell on it (for summoning me, perhaps?), and a vase of blue glass, filled with ornamental straw.

The door opened before I had even heard footsteps. It was Tolstoy, who stepped into the room like a sweet, old grandfather, apple cheeked and beaming, his fur-lined Siberian boots trailing clumps of snow. He wore loose, baggy trousers and a blue linen blouse, tied at the waist. He rubbed his red hands together.

"I'm so glad you're here!" he said. "I'm so glad!"

His greeting was almost fulsome, but I did not question his sincerity. There was no room for that.

I handed him the letter from Chertkov, but he put the envelope on the desk without a glance. "Vladimir Grigorevich has already written about you at great length. I need your help quite badly. My new collection is hard work—it requires so much effort, and I am such an old man. Too old. But let's talk about you. How is your own work progressing?"

I thanked him for his interest, but he dismissed my gratitude, saying that my writing had caught his attention, as it had Chertkov's. I was grateful.

We talked about the work I might do on *For Every Day*, which Tolstoy had once thought of calling *Circle of Reading*, suggesting that one should keep reading and rereading the sayings it contained, continuously, as a circle is continuous. (Chertkov preferred the other title, so it was called *For Every Day*.) My work will be to compile an anthology of wise sayings for daily use in contemplation by the average Russian. An alternative to the Scriptures, or something to be read alongside them. I am to help in gathering and selecting quotations, and Tolstoy will read and approve (or disapprove) of what I do.

We sat together on the couch like children, our legs side by side, while Leo Nikolayevich (as he immediately told me to call him) spoke. Each day thirty or forty letters arrive from well-wishers, people in a state of spiritual crisis, angry readers, political revolutionaries, madmen. Leo Nikolayevich sifts through these himself, labeling the envelopes with a chalk marker: N.A. (no answer), A. (appeal for help), and S. (silly). Some of the silly letters and letters of appeal will be put in a tray each morning, and I will be asked to construct some response to them. Leo Nikolayevich reserves for himself those that most interest him. All letters will, after drafting, be taken to the Remington room for typing by his daughter Sasha. "You will like Sasha," he said. "She's a lively girl, very attentive."

The day will unfold from there, routinely. He explained that, unless he rings for me, he prefers to work undisturbed until two, when the entire household sits down to lunch in the dining room, with Leo Nikolayevich presiding over a discussion of some current topic. After eating, he likes to walk the grounds or, if he feels well enough, ride into the village or along a dirt trail in the forest on Delire. At five he returns to his study and takes a glass of tea, then works until the call comes for dinner, which is promptly at seven. I have an open invitation to remain whenever I choose. After dinner there is music or chess. He retires early most nights with the hope of reading, though now he reads less, or so he said.

"You do not look well, Valentin Fedorovich," he said to me. "Do you feel all right?"

"I slept rather badly last night. It may take a few days to adjust to a new bed."

He put his frail hand on my forehead and asked me to lie on the couch. I protested, of course, but he insisted.

"Lie here. Take a brief nap. I find that brief naps can help a great deal when one doesn't feel well." He put a blanket around my knees. "I will bring you a glass of tea."

As he left the room to get my tea, I savored the unreality, the touching absurdity, of my situation. Here was the greatest author of the West, Leo Tolstoy, fetching tea for me, his new secretary, nearly sixty years his junior. This was a man I could easily love. Indeed, as I lay there on my back, surveying the crumbling plaster on the ceiling, I loved him already.

# J. P.

## LATE WINTER RAMBLE IN ZASYEKA WOOD

*The woods in winter fill with birds:*
*a clash of sparrows, jackdaws,*
*jays that flip among the shaggy boughs.*

*I step through brush, unharmed,*
*its brittle gauze of leafless branches*
*that can twig your eyes and make you bleed.*

*In the wind above the red Norwegian pines*
*a ragged crow waits, lazily*
*aloft, a cold eye hung*

*and hard as diamond in the ice blue sky.*
*Last summer, in a field nearby,*
*I saw that crow, its sharp beak*

*working on a fresh-dead dog. I watched them*
*lift off, veer into these woods*
*for some dark feast, black crow and dog.*

*What's moldering beneath this crusty snow?*
*I put my ear down by a stream*
*to hear the gargling water underground,*

*lost syllables, lost tales, alive*
*beneath the ice. Whatever we can love*
*stays warm inside us, even when*

*we lose the name of life,*
*when sooty shadows lengthen on our spines,*
*when birds above us are the only song*

*we'll hear again. I walk across*
*the frozen lid of water, where it sags*
*but doesn't give. The world's my home still,*

*even though I've got less days to count*
*than once, when dreaming I could fly,*
*I climbed a tree and leaped into the wind*

*with sleeves air-filled. Ah, falling*
*into soft snow, falling from a height I knew*
*would matter only if I hit a rock or stump . . .*

*I put my lips against an icy root,*
*where sap is running though it's not yet spring.*
*It's warm in winter,*

*as my mouth fills with dry snow, sweet-*
*sticky bark. I bend to pray:*
*Lord, let me know you as I know these woods,*

*Zasyeka's warm and winter fluttering,*
*blue wings and black, the taste and tastelessness*
*of sappy snow, the flicker of these moods.*

# 8

# SASHA

Mama came into the Remington room this morning as I was typing, carrying a shawl. A blue shawl spun to a woolly froth, which she insisted I simply must have over my legs. "You've never been a healthy girl," she said, tucking the ends around my knees. I reminded her that it was Masha who had always been ill, not me. Mama just wanted to snoop.

"So what is this you're typing?" she asked, casually. "Letters? A new story?" The woman has no grace.

"A nosy woman soon loses her nose," I said.

"Alexandra Lvovna!"

Whenever she wants to feign disapproval, she calls me by my Christian names. Even the servants around here call me Sasha. I am not pretentious.

"He's working with Bulgakov on *For Every Day*," I said. "You needn't worry. He's been saying nothing *in print* about you." We both know that Papa writes the truth about her in his diary. That's why she wants to read it all the time, and why Papa tries to keep it hidden. It's become a silly game of hide-and-seek.

"You've become rude and unladylike," Mama said. "I don't know why Papa makes you do all his dirty work," she added, gesturing toward the typewriter.

"There's nothing dirty about the work I do for Papa." I turned my back and began typing again.

"Do you like Bulgakov?"

"Well enough," I said. "He's polite. A bit naive, perhaps. But he's young." In fact, I find him disingenuous, even shifty. But I would not tell Mama such a thing. She is always looking for potential allies, and Bulgakov strikes me as one of those people who quickly turn the color of any room they enter.

This past year Mama has become impossible, positively bleeding with jealousy and bourgeois rancor. Weeping, preening in the mirror, prowling about the house all night like a crazed animal! Papa does not deserve this. I cannot understand why God put this particular burden on Russia's greatest author.

Masha, my sister, was Papa's favorite before she died. She always appeared to understand his ideas, though I doubt she did; still, it's not worth criticizing the dead. Since she passed away, I have made myself indispensable to Papa, and he is grateful to me. He loves me now, much as I love him. Masha loved him, but she was weak. Her cheeks were pale as eggshells, her lips were always blue, quivering even when she was silent. She professed Tolstoyan values, including chastity, but how she tumbled into the arms of Obolensky, that fool, who was all fancy breeding with no cash to back it up. Papa cried at her wedding, but the tears were not joyful ones. I, on the other hand, have resolved to dedicate myself to Papa. I have read his books and, unlike most of those who surround him, I have *understood* them.

And I will never marry. Why would the daughter of Leo Tolstoy wish to serve another man?

Mama can hardly bear it that Papa lets me type his work. She used to recopy his manuscripts in that finicky hand of hers. She likes to recall how day after day, during the composition of *Anna*, she would wake up dreaming about Vronsky, Levin, Kitty, wondering what would next befall them.

Sometimes I envy her those early days when Papa was fresh, writing novels and stories. But his work now is more important. Novels are bourgeois entertainment unless the author adopts a clear moral tone. This is why Papa dislikes William Shakespeare. "You can never tell where Shakespeare stands," Papa says. "He's invisible. It is the duty of an author to present himself to the public. To say, *this will do, and this will not do.*"

Papa adores the clean copy that I bring him every morning, though he quickly spoils it, scratching out words, putting in new phrases, whole sentences, and paragraphs in the margins or between lines. He likes to make balloons at the side, full of corrections that I'm supposed to understand and incorporate into further drafts. I hate when I have to creep into his study to ask for clarification. Of course, he's infinitely patient. He thanks me every time, as if anyone wouldn't be glad to do as much for Leo Tolstoy.

I'm working late tonight, the lantern buzzing beside the typewriter, trying to finish today's projects. What a day it has been! Sergeyenko's father was here, one of Papa's oldest friends. Father is always like a little boy around Sergeyenko, joshing and teasing. I love to see that. He brought us a gramophone for a gift, including a voice recording of Papa made some months before in Moscow. Mama put the record on that ghastly machine, with its brass horn and terrifying knobs. It was set up in the dining room on the table opposite the door, where everyone could gape at it. Our servants—the footmen, the cook, even a few stable boys—gathered in the hallway to listen. Some peered through the balustrade into the dining room as Papa's voice boomed through the house in its queer distortion. It was Papa, yes. But it was *not* Papa. The glass vase on the mantel tingled to the point of shattering.

The machine pleased everyone but Papa. I understood exactly why he crouched like that in the Voltaire chair, drawing himself inward like a turtle hiding within its shell.

My brother Andrey came from Moscow, looking dapper, grating on Papa as usual with his chatter about countess this and colonel that. He cares nothing for his father's feelings and knows little of his ideas.

"It's wonderful, isn't it?" Andrey kept saying, fussing with the gramophone to make it talk louder and louder.

Papa said, "Like all foolish inventions of this so-called civilization, this machine will soon become a bore," and left the room.

The remark upset Sergeyenko, whose father had brought the gramophone and the record in the first place. But he knows Papa and his ways.

"Your father is something of a Luddite, I fear," he said, scratching his beard.

Mama, bless her, immediately took Papa's recording off the gramophone and put on a Glinka duet—also a gift from Sergeyenko. This brought Papa back into the room, smiling. He sat back in his chair, putting his hands on his knees and shutting his eyes. When the duet was finished, Mama put on another of the records we had been given: Ballinstin's version of the serenade from *Don Giovanni*. Papa produced a wide smile that showed his pink, wet gums. "This is very nice," he said, patting his legs with both hands. "Very nice." Sergeyenko glowed.

An hour later we gathered for tea. Mama had invited Bulgakov to stay. He seemed to gape at everyone and blew his nose repeatedly on a dirty handkerchief. I can hardly stand him and cannot imagine what Chertkov saw in him. Papa's last secretary, Gusev, was ever so much better, a sincere man who understood Papa's ideas better than Papa does himself. Even Chertkov said so.

Andrey, like Mama a lover of discord, rambled on about patriotism, soon turning to the superiority of western Europe over Russia and questioning the proper relation of landowners to the muzhiks. Tanya's husband, Sukhotin, grew excited and began to lecture about the price of land. When he finished his little address, Sergeyenko added that the Russian peasant has grown increasingly furious with landowners in the past decade, and rightly so. They deserve better treatment, he said, punctuating the air with a finger.

"I have seen with my own eyes a whole village full of muzhiks thrashed by a small band of soldiers," Andrey replied, scanning the room to register the impact of his statement. "There must have been five hundred families on hand, but not one person objected. They're sheep, the muzhiks. Nothing but sheep!"

Papa's eyes became dark pools. His brow wrinkled, and he seemed on the point of speaking when he restrained himself, knowing that whatever he said would be taken the wrong way. It grieved me to see this.

"The muzhiks drink too much," Mama said, salting the wound in Papa's heart. "The army is worth only what the government is willing to spend for them on alcohol. I've seen this proven by statistics." She sipped her glass of tea and lifted a plump little cake from the silver tray. "It's certainly not for lack of land that the Russian muzhik leads a life of poverty," she added. "Their poverty is spiritual. They have no willpower."

Papa fastened his yellow knit jacket around his shoulders, as if a bitter wind had just blown through the house from the northern steppes. I saw by a flicker of his brow that he could no longer maintain a lofty silence.

Smoothing his beard with one hand, he leaned forward. "If the peasants had money, they would not surround themselves, as we do, with footmen costing ten rubles a month. We behave like idiots."

"No, dear, they would spend it all on drink and whores," said Mama.

Papa looked at her glumly.

"You know, the Russian landowner finds himself in a filthy situation," Mama went on. "Do you think it's impoverished landowners who treat themselves to all these modern gadgets, things like gramophones? Of course not. They're bought by wealthy merchants living in the towns, by capitalists and plunderers!" Mark Antony would not have addressed his troops less boldly.

"What are you suggesting, dear?" Papa asked. "That we are somehow less villainous than they because somebody gave us this gramophone as a gift?"

He laughed, and everyone laughed with him, perhaps a little nervously.

Meanwhile, Dr. Makovitsky was scribbling everything Papa ut-

tered on the tiny pad he keeps hidden beneath the table. You can tell
when he is writing because his mouth twists and the lower lip pro-
trudes queerly. I noticed that Valentin Bulgakov appeared quite agitated by what he saw. I don't think he had ever heard my parents
argue in public before, and it can be terribly upsetting if you're not
accustomed to it.

"Dushan Petrovich!" Papa said, shaking the doctor from his
stenographic trance. "Bring me that letter from the revolutionary.
The one I showed you a few days ago. I believe it's still on my
desk."

Papa read aloud from it to everyone. It was a curious thing to do,
given the letter. One part of it stays in my head and haunts me.

> No, Leo Nikolayevich, I cannot agree with you that human rela-
> tions are improved by love alone. Only those with an education
> and a full belly can talk like that and get away with it. What
> shall we say to a hungry man with children, the man who has
> staggered through life beneath the yoke of tyrants? He must fight
> them. He must liberate himself from bondage. Now, before your
> own death, I tell you, Leo Nikolayevich, that the world is thirsty
> for blood, that men will continue to fight and kill, not only their
> masters, but everyone, even their children, so that they shall not
> have to look forward to their evil as well. I am sorry that you will
> not live to see this with your own eyes and be convinced of your
> mistake. Nonetheless, I wish you a happy death.

Andrey bowed his head over his glass, silenced. Mama said that
since the letter came from Siberia, the man was probably a criminal
in exile and his opinion should be dismissed.

"He is certainly in exile," Papa said. "But I see no reason why
he should be called a criminal."

"Why else would they send him to Siberia?"

Papa shook his head. He rose with some difficulty, bowed, and
took his leave of the company. It is his custom to retire to his study
after tea, usually to read or correct proofs.

I, too, left the room, though I felt no obligation to excuse myself. Politeness has its limits.

Not long after, as I was typing, a shy knock came at the door.

"Come in," I said.

"You're working late tonight, Sasha," said Bulgakov. His jacket was buttoned to the neck, and his beard was glossy. I realized in the yellow lamplight that he is not unattractive. His cheeks burned with the roseate hue of young manhood. I like the fact that his beard is wispy and guess that he does not have much hair on his chest. Indeed, there is something womanish about him, something tender and unformed.

"I have four letters to finish before dinner," I told him, without rising. I wondered why he had come to me like this.

"May I come in?"

"Certainly, Valentin Fedorovich. Sit down."

He pulled a cane chair up beside me, uncomfortably close, and looked over my shoulder. I could feel his breath on my shirt.

"Do your parents often speak to each other so . . . bluntly?" he asked.

"It is no secret that my parents have fundamental differences," I said, trying to be judicious. In this household, you can never tell what will be repeated, or to whom. "Mama does not understand my father's goals. He is a spiritual creature, while her chief concerns are material."

"But I like your mother."

"She means well, of course." I sounded insincere, but what was I to say? That Mama is irrational, false, and greedy, self-centered and generally impossible?

"Your father is the greatest author in Russia today," Bulgakov said.

"Quite."

"I feel privileged to be here, Sasha. It is an honor I never dreamed of."

I simply nodded. It pleased me to hear my father referred to in these terms, however jejunely. The family takes his genius too much for granted.

Bulgakov began talking of his family, his ambitions. He had been converted to Papa's ideas through an acquaintance with a small group of Tolstoyans in Moscow, and now he hopes to live for God. The injustice of Russian society upsets him, he said. He was thoughtful and sincere. I really liked him, to my surprise. Unlike so many people around here, he has read Papa's work carefully and found his own way to express many of the same ideas.

Suddenly Mama marched into the room, shouting, "Valentin Fedorovich! Come downstairs. I must show you a letter I received only this past week from a woman in Georgia." She led him awkwardly from the room. He was embarrassed, but he did not have the sense—or the wherewithal—to resist her.

That woman simply cannot bear it when anyone is alone with me. Let her read her ridiculous letter to young Bulgakov. He means nothing to me. I have my work before me, and this is enough.

# 9

# SOFYA
# ANDREYEVNA

If I'm in the right frame of mind, I actually like these wintry, overcast days when you live in a white cocoon. White cloud-scud sky, with snow hanging on the branches, meringue slices of clean, white snow. The ground is soft with the dust of snow, and your feet make a slight, muffled sound when you walk along the frozen paths. I like the blackbirds, too, and sparrows, so tenacious, enduring. Nothing scares them away. When I see blackbirds on the fence in the orchard, my heart fastens on them.

There is something going on behind my back, something to do with the will. Yesterday, I asked Lyovochka directly, "Has anyone approached you about your will? Has anything changed? You would tell me, wouldn't you, if anything happened?"

He thinks he can give away everything we own: the house, the land, the copyright to all his works. Has he no sense of responsibility?

"You mustn't worry, Sonya," he said. "Nothing has happened." But I'm worried.

Is it so much to ask for, that my husband's children should inherit his property, including the right to republish his work as they see fit when he is gone? They, too, must live. It is some years since we agreed that I should maintain control over everything he wrote before 1881. I am happy enough to let the world take the rest, leaving me with *Anna Karenina*, *War and Peace*, and all the early novels—the only ones that keep selling anyway. It's almost comical that my husband believes the later works matter beyond a small circle of religious fanatics. Who wants to read books of theological speculation? Books that tell you that you've been doing everything wrong through your whole life?

I've been lying in bed with a headache, watching the snow fall, drinking tea. I cannot read. My head is tight as a drum, pounding. And I do not have the gramophone in my bedroom.

Music has been my one escape, an island in this tilting sea around me. Had my life gone better, I would have been a professional pianist. Tanayev, my teacher, assured me that my talent would have been sufficient. But Lyovochka has denied me even this.

He was impossible about Tanayev, so mean and jealous, like a silly schoolboy. My interest in that dear, sweet little man was entirely professional—or almost entirely. He is not, after all, an appealing man—not in any conventional way. He is short and porky, with red hair thinning on top; he refuses to trim that scrubby auburn beard of his. But his style! What style!

Tanayev understands how a woman in society should be treated. Alas, it has been a long time since I have been around people who understand that, people such as the friends who would call on Papa—courtiers and generals, men of rank in society. No wonder I feel lonely here, in the wilds, surrounded by Goths.

I remember seeing Tanayev for the first time, on the stage in Kiev. Tanya and I went to that concert by chance, but we both knew at once that we were in the presence of genius. We wept madly when he played the *Appassionata*. After the concert, waiting for his carriage, the poor man was surrounded by screaming, foolish women. Pelagya Vasilievna, who had been his childhood nurse and now accompanied him everywhere like a doting grandmother, tried to push them away.

But it was useless, such was their passion. One foolish girl grabbed his red silk kerchief, ripping it to shreds. I could not bear to see such a travesty and instructed our footman to do something.

He walked bravely through the mob, shouting, "Make way for the Countess Tolstoy!" Though embarrassed by the attention, I followed him. The crowd grew very still, and a path opened for me, almost miraculously, to the feet of Sergey Ivanovich. I felt like the Queen of the Ball.

"It is a great honor," Tanayev said, kissing my hand.

"You played marvelously well tonight," I said. "Especially the *Appassionata*. It is my favorite sonata."

"I thank you, Countess. Beethoven is not for everyone."

I invited him to ride in my carriage, since his was nowhere to be seen, and he graciously accepted.

It was on the way to his hotel that I mentioned, in passing, that I, too, played the piano.

"By comparison with you, of course, I'm a dreadful amateur," I said.

"You do yourself an injustice, I'm sure," he said.

"I wish that were true."

"Perhaps I could give you some lessons. Would that interest you, Countess?"

"Me? You would instruct me?"

Imagine! He was an impossibly dear man, taking on such a beginner. That night, I lay awake in bed quivering. I would be taught by the man who had himself been discovered at the age of ten by Nikolai Rubinstein! The man who became Tchaikovsky's protégé and friend! The teacher of Scriabin! My luck, it seemed, was turning.

That was shortly after the death of my dear little Vanechka. He was my best, my sweetest and dearest little boy, so kind and loving. I cannot bear to say his name or think of him. On the night he died, I went to his bedside and felt his tiny, fevered head. "I'm sorry to have wakened you, Mama," he said. "Sweet child," I cried. "My sweetest child!"

Lyovochka never understood my grief. Nor did he see that Tanayev offered a balm. Dear Sergey Ivanovich led me from darkness into light. But how bitter my husband grew, full of jealousy and hatred, small-minded, petty. His so-called disciples come here day after day now, worshiping him like Jesus Christ himself, and Lyovochka allows this to happen. He is so greedy for publicity, so thirsty for praise. If only they knew what I know . . .

Sergey Ivanovich came to Yasnaya Polyana frequently, but always against my husband's will. The great Russian author, heir to Pushkin, peer of Dickens and Hugo, would lock himself in his study, avoiding the dinner table, sulking like a child whose mother has refused to give him a sweet. Sergey Ivanovich, of course, behaved superbly.

Our best times together were in Moscow. Sergey Ivanovich would play for hours at the grand piano in the front parlor. How he could play the polonaise! After, we would drink tea together, talk, or take little shopping tours of Hunters Row. Sergey Ivanovich loves his food, perhaps a little too passionately, but I was willing to cater to his whims. We would steal away to Trembles, the bakery, and buy dozens of tiny mince cakes, bonbons, and chocolate truffles. All the way home we'd stuff ourselves, giggling in the back of the sleigh, while old Emelyanych, our driver, scowled. What blissful days!

I thought that finally happiness had found me. Then Lyovochka wrote me one of his famous, stupid letters:

> *I find it infinitely sad and humiliating that a worthless and un-appealing stranger should now be ruling our lives and poisoning our final years together; sad and humiliating to be forced to ask when he is leaving, where he's going, when he will rehearse his stupid music, and what music he will play. It's terrible, terrible, base and humiliating! And that it should happen at the end of our lives, which until now have been honest and clean—also at a time when we appear to have been drawing closer and closer, in spite of the many things that divide us . . .*

How he went on! My Lyovochka likes nothing better than to thrash himself, to don the hair shirt and mortify his flesh. But why does he always have to thrash me, too? The subject of Tanayev drove him crazy. Of course, it flattered me that he should, at his age, have become jealous of my attentions. Before Sergey Ivanovich came along, he paid no mind to who sat with me on the sofa or wrote me little notes or invited me to tea. I would never have expected this turn in Lyovochka, since jealousy is the province of those with nothing else to do. But Sergey Ivanovich annoys him in the most irrational way!

Thinking it over, I believe it has something to do with Tanayev's womanliness. Sergey Ivanovich is not the brute, masculine type that Lyovochka, in spite of himself, admires. He would never be caught dead riding in the woods on horseback or, in his youth, shooting animals. He likes to take bubble baths, to perfume himself, to wear bright colors—the sort of behavior that irritates Lyovochka beyond description.

Ah, the letters that passed between us. Lyovochka hated my trips to Moscow and was sure that I went to our house on Dolgo-Khamovnicheski Street for the sole purpose of meeting Tanayev. For once, he was right. I *was* meeting him, and I loved those meetings! But nothing shameful passed between us. It was innocent, pure and simple!

One doesn't have to become a man's lover to love him. I know that. But Sergey Ivanovich is simply not the sort of man who takes lovers anyway, not in the usual sense. He does not require the baser satisfactions—something the old goat could never comprehend.

Once, only once, he kissed me.

But that is history. We do not see each other now. We do not communicate. Lyovochka put an end to it, with a letter sent from his brother's farm in Pirogovo: "It disgusts me to see you once again taking up with Tanayev in this manner. Frankly, I cannot continue to live with you under these circumstances. . . . If you cannot put an end to this, let us part company."

Let us part company! After a rueful laugh, I wept. But the letter continued, sketching out four "solutions" to our "problem":

1. *The best thing is for you to break off all relations with Tanayev at once, never minding what he might think. This will release us instantaneously from the nightmare that has been tormenting us both for over a year. No meetings, no correspondence, no exchange of portraits, no little mushroom gatherings in the woods.*

2. *I could go abroad, having separated from you entirely. Each of us could then lead his or her own life.*

3. *We could both go abroad, thus facilitating your break with Tanayev. We would remain abroad for as long as it took for you to break this infatuation.*

4. *The most terrible solution is the fourth, and it causes me to shudder. We could attempt to convince ourselves that the problem will right itself and do nothing.*

Why did he torment himself with such hairsplitting madness? I did not know what to answer him, finding the entire subject baseless and foolish.

For much of autumn I had been living in Moscow, studying the piano with Tanayev, attending concerts almost every night at the Conservatory. Toward winter, Lyovochka appeared on Dolgo-Khamovnicheski Street, his eyes red like open wounds, his hair and white beard flying apart. It struck me forcibly that he was deranged.

He said not a thing about Tanayev all day, but I knew exactly what lay behind his stalking about the house like a wild boar. Lyovochka is nothing if not obvious. As we lay in bed that night, surrounded by what he so charmingly refers to as our "disgraceful luxury," I spoke openly about the problem. I had considered it carefully, deciding it was not worth continuing my relations with Tanayev as presently constituted.

"Lyovochka," I said, sitting up in bed. "I will end my lessons with Sergey Ivanovich. No more lessons. No more long stays in Moscow on my own, either, if that upsets you so much. But I do ask one favor: that he may visit me once a month—or every other month, perhaps. I want him to feel free to come, occasionally, to sit beside me at the piano for an afternoon, much as any friend would do."

Lyovochka lifted himself to a sitting position, staring ahead like an embalmed corpse. He was shuddering, as if chilled to the marrow. I grew afraid.

"Is that too much to ask?" I said. "A simple *friendship* with Sergey Ivanovich?"

"What you just said proves that your relationship with Tanayev has already exceeded the limits of friendship," he responded, his voice high and quavering. "What other person's monthly visit would bring you so much joy? If this is the case, why not see him weekly, even daily! You could rejoice every moment of your life!"

The conversation went from worse to impossible. He called me a "concert hag" and flew into such a rage I thought he would asphyxiate himself with anguish! But I got back at him. Perhaps "got even" is a better way to put it. I would not be conscripted, co-opted, hemmed, and bordered. I would wage a war of the people, a war on behalf of my deepest needs. In the end, I would win.

"Go ahead!" I said, "Murder me! Slice my throat from ear to ear!" I thrust myself backward across the quilt, exposing the tender region beneath my chin.

He fulminated, silently, for several minutes, then resorted to his chief weapon: his sex. Like a young lion, he fell on top of me, kissing my throat, then my forehead, rubbing my breasts with his course red hands. I realized there was no point, not any longer. I could not fight Leo Tolstoy—not now. But I quietly resolved to continue my resistance.

For the sake of politeness, I invited Sergey Ivanovich to Yasnaya Polyana for a brief visit, some months later. He came. And Lvovochka remained civil. But everyone knew it was over.

My one hope now, a faint but unmistakable beam of light tunneling down through the clouds of my life here, is Bulgakov. I realized shortly after he stepped through our door that this was a young man with sense; he is not, like the dread Gusev, another of Chertkov's mindless minions. Why do they kowtow to him like an Oriental prince? That tub-faced, sallow, spiteful man! If I could pluck his heart out with my bare fingers, I would do it. I would hang by my neck till dead for the pleasure of killing him. At least he is banished from Tula. The governor has good sense: Chertkov *is* a dangerous revolutionary. But he is also a fool. Bulgakov, whom he surely does not know except superficially, will never enforce his nasty little schemes. Chertkov has made a lovely little mistake here.

Yesterday, I waited outside the room where Bulgakov works.

"Excuse me, Valentin Fedorovich," I said, when he stepped through the door. "Would you come to my sewing room? We could take a glass of tea and talk."

"Thank you, Countess," he said. "I would be honored."

"Please, my friend!" I put a hand on his arm. "Call me Sofya Andreyevna. We do not stand on formality around here, as you may have observed."

His arm was like iron, straight and strong. Though he is terribly thin, he did not seem weak. His eyes have a brightness and permanence about them, and when he speaks, he looks directly at you. None of the other Tolstoyans do this. They feel guilty around me— the weasels! But not Bulgakov. He is sweet and kindly by nature. He is intelligent, yes, but thoughtful and gentle. He does not feel superior because he has read Plato or some obscure German. Nor does he believe, like Chertkov and Sergeyenko, that eating no meat absolves him of all other sins!

"You are a fine young man," I said, rocking in my chair. "Very clear eyes. Nice features." A fire had been laid for me, and tea was brought in crystal glasses.

"Thank you, Sofya Andreyevna," he said. "It pleases me when my looks give someone pleasure, though I doubt that one should take credit for one's features. I had very little to do with their invention."

"You might have ruined them by now. I have seen many young men ruin their looks by drinking and eating and running with loose women. You have kept yourself pure—a real Tolstoyan, I can tell!" I fought to keep a lid on myself. If he sensed a note of ridicule in my voice, it might destroy everything between us. Like most young men, Bulgakov is oversensitive. He has not yet been around many adults, especially of the female sex.

"I admire Leo Nikolayevich immensely."

"Good. He will like that. No amount of admiration surfeits him."

Bulgakov was uncomfortable, so I changed my tack. "He is deeply grateful for the help you've been giving him. You've come up with a great many useful passages. He told me so himself. I think it surprises him that such a young man could be learned. When he was your age, he was whoring in the Caucasus."

The dear boy cleverly ignored my derisory remarks about Lyovochka—a good sign. Tact is among the more socially useful forms of insincerity. It is noticeably lacking among my husband's associates. Lyovochka, of course, has never had to worry about not offending people. If you are Leo Tolstoy, you merely reveal the Truth.

"*For Every Day* is a noble project," he said. "It will help people to live more contemplative lives."

"Contemplative lives!" I said. "You say lovely things, Valentin Fedorovich. A gift for the apt phrase!"

He was staring past me, out the window, where the snow was falling.

"The winter has been good to us," I said. "Even with the snow. Not more than we can bear. I used to dread winters in the country. But Leo Nikolayevich adores it here. I can hardly ever get him to go to Moscow, except for the briefest visits. The crowds upset him. They mob him now—like an emperor. It's hardly safe for him to travel."

"I heard about what happened at the Kursk Station."

"There were thousands of them, screaming and cheering, pushing around us! Thousands! The tsar himself does not attract such attention."

He liked to hear me praise Lyovochka, especially his books. Unlike Gusev, who was a crass illiterate, Bulgakov has read everything by my husband. *War and Peace* he called "a monument" and asked about

its origins. So I told him about the five years it took to complete—
back in the mid-sixties. Can it be so long ago? We saw almost no
one during that time. Lyovochka wrote furiously, with no regard for
the things of this world, no fretting over disciples, no Chertkov or
Sergeyenko hovering beside him and tearing every sheet off the desk
before the ink was even dry! I, his young wife, worked beside him
through every stage.

"I hunched over his manuscripts with a magnifying glass, trying
to make out the infinite corrections, till my head almost burst with
pain," I told him. "But it was bearable pain. I would awaken each
day dreaming of Pierre and Natasha, of Prince Andrey and his father,
even old Kutuzov!"

Bulgakov listened keenly. He is in love with Lyovochka. I could
see that in his eyes.

"My life is difficult now," I said. "You know that Leo Nikolayevich and I have had disagreements."

"I'm sorry."

"What is obvious cannot be ignored."

"I'm aware that there is a good deal of trouble between you."

"He thinks of me as his enemy, not his friend. But Leo Nikolayevich, my Lyovochka, is old and sick. We nearly lost him a few
months ago, you know. He went unconscious for a day. His pulse
nearly stopped."

Bulgakov nodded. Furrows of sympathy deepened in his brow. His
gaze was innocent as a pond.

"You must help me, Valentin Fedorovich. I want only what is best
for Leo Nikolayevich and his family. They want to separate us. You
have seen as much, I'm sure. I could tolerate the situation if it only
concerned me—I would dislike it, but I could stand it. What is unreasonable is for me to sit back while they steal his children's inheritance."

"They would never do such a thing."

I tried not to laugh. "They will do whatever is necessary to
accomplish their ends."

My young visitor grew ill at ease. I decided not to ask for his help. Not yet. I had first to be sure of his friendship, though I could see that a bond existed between us.

"I will give you a present," I said, pulling from my dresser a small notebook I had bought in Moscow several months before. It had a neatly embossed cover, and the paper was handmade in Amalfi.

"You're much too generous, Sofya Andreyevna, I'm afraid I—"

"Please! It's yours, Valentin Fedorovich. For keeping a diary. You must always keep a diary."

"It is a popular activity in the province of Tula."

"You're teasing me. Never mind. I will expect you to search your conscience daily, then to record the truth."

"The truth may not be so easy to find."

"You've been listening to your friends at Telyatinki. There's enough truth about for all of us. Write what you see. That's always the place to begin. Trust your eyes!"

He kissed me on both cheeks and bowed. His politeness was refreshing, and it made me long for Moscow. The crudeness of life around here is intolerable. I was not brought up to live like an animal.

I sat quietly by myself for a long time after Bulgakov left, thinking about him. And all morning I have thought about him still more, while the snow continues to fall, a dry, dusty snow that swirls on the window ledge, freshens the white fields, the whiter distance. I hear sleigh bells coming and going. Something is going on, but I am afraid to inquire. I feel certain that if the wheel does not turn my way soon, I shall be finished. I shall die, after which my children and grandchildren will be left with nothing. I pray that Valentin Fedorovich will help me.

# 10

# L. N.

5 JANUARY 1910

I am sad. The people who live around me seem terribly alien to me. I have been trying to think how to react to the irreligious people of this world. Perhaps the best approach is to treat them like animals: love them, pity them, but make no attempt to enter into spiritual relations. Such attempts at connection would only produce unkindly feelings. These people do not comprehend my reality, and by their lack of comprehension and self-assurance, employing rational argument to darken the truth, refuting truth and goodness, they provoke me to unkindness. I express myself very badly, but I feel one must cultivate in oneself a special attitude toward such people so as not to impair one's ability to love them.

# 11

# DR. MAKOVITSKY

"I had a dream, Dushan," Leo Nikolayevich said this morning. "Shall I tell you my dream?"

He did not seem well. His beard was straggly and yellow. I took his pulse and temperature. They were normal, but his eyes appeared more glittery than usual. I asked him how his vision was, and he said, "You're always worried about my health, Dushan."

"I'm your doctor, Leo Nikolayevich!"

"I don't care what you are. I'm an old man. Old men are unlike young men in one important respect: they are not healthy. I am going to die soon. So let's worry about something more important."

I am quite happy, often, to dwell on trivial subjects. But I put away my medical things, not wishing to irritate him. Irritation increases his pulse rate.

"Do you know what Pascal said about dreams?"

I shook my head. I am not well read.

"He said that it's a good thing that our dreams are disconnected, otherwise we could never tell them from reality."

"I rarely dream," I said.

"Nonsense! We all dream. It's just that we bury the memory. They are too painful. They tell us too much about ourselves."

It occurred to me that nothing is quite so boring as listening to other people's dreams. On the other hand, Leo Nikolayevich's dreams interest me profoundly as indications of the way his mind works, as evidence of his genius. God speaks through him. I recognize the heavenly cadence in his voice.

I took out my notebook. It doesn't appear to bother him when I transcribe his thoughts, though he occasionally teases me about it.

"Last night I dreamt I was at a formal ball in Moscow, one much like the balls I attended as a young officer. When the orchestra struck up a certain dance, I realized that I knew the music perfectly well but that the steps had changed. I could not understand what everyone was doing, and they began to laugh at me, to point their fingers and laugh."

"You have always been out of step with your time," I said, but Leo Nikolayevich did not respond. I put my head down and continued to write.

"How can you write when I'm not speaking?" he asked. "Are you making things up, Dushan Petrovich?"

"I would never make up anything. You know how much I value what you say."

"I know, I know." He stood up now and began to pace his study floor. "I have had too many troubled dreams this winter," he said. "Some of them sexual in nature. I have often been tortured by fantasies."

"This is natural," I said.

"Is that so, Dushan? Have you had sexual dreams lately?"

"I do not dream."

He ignored my remark. "Here is one of the dreams I keep having. It concerns a young, black-eyed Tartar girl I met in Sevastopol during the war. She lived in Eski-Simferopol, in fact—a little village not far from the front. I was stationed there. It was quite unreal, that village—a haven of exiles from Petersburg society—parasites, all of them.

You would never know that thousands of young Russian soldiers were dying—or heaped in stinking piles—just a few versts away. They played cards and dressed for dinner and held balls."

"You loved this Tartar girl?"

"I never loved her, Dushan. You romanticize everything. I made foul use of her body for my own purposes." He grinned slightly.

"You committed sexual intercourse with her," I said.

"Indeed. Sometimes twice a day."

I could not help but shudder. I could not imagine Leo Nikolayevich in this act.

"I upset you, Dushan Petrovich. You are a man of delicate conscience. I should be more careful what I say in front of you."

"I'm sorry. I—"

"You're a virgin, I know."

"Leo Nikolayevich, I—"

He waved his hand to silence me. I was relieved.

"Her name was Katya. I have never forgotten her. If she were here, I would beg her forgiveness. But—may I speak so bluntly?—I continue to dream of her body. I recall too perfectly our times together, the exact positions of our bodies, the taste of her, everything. Even a few of the jokes. . . ."

His eyes grew watery now. It seemed, to me, that we understood each other.

"Leo Nikolayevich," I said, at last. "You torture yourself with memories. This all occurred many years ago."

"More than half a century. Katya will be an old woman now, shriveled, with white hair and dry, wrinkled breasts. She will hardly remember my name, I suspect. She may well be dead."

"You are the most celebrated writer in Europe," I said. "She would have heard your name, even if she hasn't read your books."

"She couldn't read, Dushan. How would she know?"

It occurred to me, with mild horror, that most of Russia could not read. Yet it also seemed true that everyone—even an illiterate *krestyonka* in the Crimea—must have heard the name of Leo Tolstoy somewhere, somehow. The papers have always been full of stories about him.

"I had another dream last night. Did you hear me scream? I dreamt I was a big black bull. I entered a field of a thousand cows, beautiful white cows, and I made my way through the lot of them, mounting them from behind, one by one. Suddenly, clouds filled what had been a brilliant blue sky. Lightning shot from cloud to cloud, and thunder shook the ground. A pit opened up, and the wind pushed against my side, toppling me over. I was dropped into that deep pit by the wind, whereupon I was struck by a bolt of lightning. My skin exploded into flames."

"I heard you scream," I said. "I almost came to your room. But you apparently fell back to sleep quickly."

"Sleep and waking are much the same to me now. I suspect the same may be true of death. It will hardly differ from the life I lead these days."

"That is very pessimistic," I said.

"What a dear man you are," he said, putting a hand on my shoulder. "I don't think I could live here another day without you."

"I intend to stay," I said.

"Thank you, Dushan. Thank you."

He kissed me on both cheeks now, and I kissed him. His cheeks were wet, which moved me greatly. This past year has been difficult for him, and the toll is severe. His nerves jangle and buzz. His eyes are red, his skin milky, his hands tremble, and his lips quiver. I fear that he may die soon and that the quarrels with Sofya Andreyevna will hasten the end.

I watch her connive, pretend to have fits, dissembling daily. The woman is rapacious. She wants luxury of a kind that offends her husband, who wishes only to live simply. Her talk at the dinner table is frivolous and self-serving, like that of a Petersburg matron. It disgusts me, though I have held my tongue. There is no point in making a fuss. I'm a guest here, after all.

I sit alone in my room most evenings after dinner, reading. I fall asleep easily. The routine here is pleasant, but the emotional pressure exhausts me.

Leo Nikolayevich assumes that I am a virgin. Technically, I suppose I am. I wish, in fact, I were. Sexual relations have always upset me when I think about them. I was never a good-looking man. In my youth, this troubled me. How many nights did I lie awake, taunted by fantasies and horrified by my own ugliness?

Once, when I was a medical student in Hungary, desire overwhelmed me. I had been drinking, and I paid a woman to come back to my flat. She was not expensive, nor was she worth what I did spend. Her teeth had lost their enamel and were distressingly clear; she had rude marks on her legs, the result of problems with her circulatory system, I decided. Her breasts sagged.

She undressed upon entering my flat. I watched her with my heart fluttering in my throat like a winter wasp. She danced around me, teasing me, making little jokes about sexual intercourse. I had to close my eyes.

She sat beside me on the bed and rubbed my temples, slowly. I asked her to rub my shoulders, and she suggested I remove my clothes. I had never been naked before a woman, and I only partially complied, stripping down to my underwear. She snickered slightly, as one might expect a whore to do.

"What is your name?" she asked me, in a soft voice I can still hear.

"Anton," I said.

"You have something to hide, Anton?" she asked.

"Do what you are paid to do," I said.

She laughed piercingly, and I had to restrain myself. It is disagreeable to find oneself enraged, ready to strike a blow. But I controlled myself and rolled onto my stomach on the bed, letting her knead my shoulders. She worked slowly, beautifully, down my spine with her strong hands. I could feel the roughness of the skin of her fingers, like a pumice stone.

When she insisted that I roll onto my back, I hesitated. My erection could not be disguised. But I did so, and she put her hand upon it, gently, then her mouth.

I will never understand why I let her complete this grotesque, unnatural act. It would have been far less damning in the eyes of God had I actually committed sexual intercourse with her. But I felt utterly helpless, weak as a whippet, unable to speak or move. I let her proceed to the terrible finish.

When she was done, she said, "And how did you like that, my dear Anton? Pretty good, no? Shall I come back tomorrow night?"

"There is money for you in that envelope on the dressing table. Please take it and leave me alone. I never want to see you again."

"You *enjoyed* that, didn't you?"

"Please," I said. "Please let me alone now."

She looked unexpectedly downcast as she left. And I realized now how old she was, perhaps forty or fifty. To my surprise, I felt sorry for her. She was just another of God's creatures. What she did for a living was a burden, her burden. Had she, perhaps, been a princess in another life? Or an animal of some kind?

"Everything is holy," Leo Nikolayevich said to me recently. "Everything that lives is part of God."

I agreed with him and told him of my fascination with the Hindu religion and reincarnation. He dismissed the idea, saying it is "interesting but not plausible."

I am less convinced. Sometimes I worry that I accept whatever he tells me without questioning. At times, Leo Nikolayevich is so utterly unconventional, ready to defy any tenet of Orthodox Christianity. Other times, he seems oddly scriptural and dogmatic. But I rarely argue with him. It is not my nature.

What I know is that I love God, that my duty is to serve man, and that by serving man, I serve God. I also serve the mystery and spirit that inhabit the body of Leo Tolstoy. I have been privileged to dwell under his roof, to have access to him on a daily basis. I have been singled out by God for this assignment, however difficult at times the task may seem.

# 12

# BULGAKOV

I rode back to Telyatinki on a horse borrowed from Chertkov's stables, a white mare with a powerful, slightly concave back and black hairs on its rump. As I rode, a storm gathered in the west. Clouds thickened at the edges and turned opaque, with large purple underbellies. A thunderhead drove a school of mackerel-like wisps into the darkening east. It is rare to see such drama in winter. Now the pink rim of Zasyeka Wood turned violet. Sunlight glowered on the fields, with long shadows cast by every tree and hillock. A rich wind, damp and gusty, blew up from the south. I kept thinking about Masha.

She has become my closest friend at Telyatinki, though we have to be careful we don't spend too much time in each other's company. Sergeyenko is a dreadful puritan about such things, and though he doesn't actually ban sexual relations, he makes sure that everyone understands Leo Nikolayevich's ideas on the subject. "Better to marry than to burn" is Sergeyenko's rather too Pauline philosophy. He often reads aloud from the *Confessions* of St. Augustine of Hippo, with whom he shares an aversion to sex (though Augustine's later puritanism arose from a rakish past). He also favors those Buddhist scriptures that preach the insignificance of the physical world. The spirit, he says, is all that matters. "We are ephemera. Flotsam and jetsam thrown up by the universal spirit."

It's not that I utterly disagree with Sergeyenko—or Augustine, for that matter. It seems useless to let one's physical desires control one's life or interfere with the progress of the soul. The object of sexual relations is necessarily reproductive. One copulates to propagate the race. Taken so, copulation fits nicely into the broad scheme of human activity. But the needs of the spirit dwarf the requirements of the flesh—that is, they ought to. There is no point in living like an animal, ignoring the goal of existence, which is union with God. Man is man because God gave him the powers of reflection. These powers enable him to understand his place in the divine creation.

Mind is the great gift, the Promethean fire handed to human beings by the gods, which is why Leo Nikolayevich places so much importance on study, on contemplation. My grandmother always told me to pray without thinking. But thinking is the only way to make sense of life, to learn to live with the fact of death, the possibility of extinction.

In my teens, I found myself drawn to indecent images and thoughts. I realize now that the issue of decency is bogus. Is it decent for the tsar to force young Russian men to kill young men from other countries, in the most brutal ways? Is it decent for society to allow people to starve in the streets, to die alone in miserable little isbas, to live like rats in Moscow sewers? Slavery of any kind—economic, military, social—is indecent. But sexual activity, how men and women choose to combine their physical parts, is completely neutral. It is merely the energy devoted to it—the time it takes away from proper mental and spiritual work—that debases it.

I saw Masha in the distance, cutting wood with a double-bladed ax. Not what most Russians think of as women's work. I stopped my horse and watched as sunlight glistened off the sharp steel blade. Her thick fur hat nearly covered her eyes.

"How can you see what you're doing?" I asked, approaching on horseback.

She kept swinging. "You're done for the day?"

"Leo Nikolayevich was playing chess with Sukhotin. He didn't need me this afternoon. I was asked to stay for dinner, but I decided to come home."

"Why?" She paused, stretching her back. Wind lifted her long hair and made her dress flap. Her ankles were slender, protected by canvas spatterdashes.

"I felt like it." I let that sink in. "Anyway, there's going to be a storm."

"I made a pot of soup, Valya. We can eat together in the kitchen when I'm done with chopping."

I do not like the idea of women chopping wood. But the women among the Tolstoyans oppose separate work. Masha is adamant on this subject.

"You will be the next tsar, Masha," Sergeyenko teases her.

Leo Nikolayevich's attitudes toward women are mildly reactionary, even though he imagines himself liberal. He would never let Sasha chop wood.

"I'm hungry," I said.

"You're always hungry, Valya."

She had invented the name Valya from Valentin, which she claims is far too serious a name for me.

While she finished at the woodpile, I put the horse in his stall, unsaddled him, brushed him down. His rich black coat steamed in the cool barn. A couple of boys, local muzhiks, forked hay from the loft into the wooden stalls. I felt warm inside, happy. The mingling smell of straw and mud filled the little enclosed night of the barn. Shards of sunlight splintered through the roof.

As I walked toward the big house, it began to sleet, a diagonal slush that drilled the mud, that whitened the brown grass, that popped off the wooden steps and broad pine boards of the porch. Telyatinki is a rambling, ungainly structure, somewhat crudely made of scraped logs, with a simplicity inside that reminds one of a country school-house. The plank floors are waxed, then buffed to a mirrorlike sheen. We take turns doing this work on a biweekly rotation drawn up by Sergeyenko, who has a passion for schedules and lists.

Masha joined me in the kitchen. She poured a thick, salty broth with carrots and beets into clay bowls that we had fashioned ourselves the week before and hardened in the oven. We ate with big wooden spoons, alone. There was plenty of black bread, which the women bake every Sunday afternoon, and freshly churned white butter. Neither of us spoke for a while.

"How is Leo Nikolayevich feeling?" she asked, breaking the silence. "Everyone here is worried."

"He has a bad cough."

"He should be careful. A man of his age can go quickly. My grandfather was perfectly well one day and dead the next."

"He says he will last only a few months, perhaps a year. And he means it."

"I wonder if he's serious. If he were serious, he would take precautions."

"All I know is that yesterday I asked him whether or not I should take my name off the university registry, which would force me to face the question of military call-up directly. And he said that since he had only a short time to live, he was not the right person to ask."

"You *should* resign from the university, Valya. It's dishonest to pretend to be a student when you're not really attending classes. It's your duty to resist evil, isn't it?"

Her bluntness annoyed me. "Maybe I don't feel like wasting away in jail? Maybe there is more important work that I should be doing?"

"Perhaps you're a coward."

I was taking this more seriously than she was. She ate as we talked.

"More soup?" She looked up finally.

"Yes, please." I almost said no, just to spite her. But I was starving. One does not eat well at Yasnaya Polyana.

"By their deeds ye shall know them," she said.

In this, and *only* this, Masha reminds me of my mother, who quotes Scripture in the most unlikely circumstances, always drawing on the same half dozen verses she knows by heart. In recent years, I have taken to confounding her by quoting unfamiliar Scriptures back at her to prove exactly the opposite of what she has quoted to me. It drives her crazy.

"Whatsoever the heart commandeth, this must ye do," I said.

Masha looked at me, puzzled. *"Micah?"*

"Bulgakov," I said.

She did not like it when I did the teasing. She poured herself another bowl of soup and paid no attention to me. "You have a high opinion of yourself."

I nodded.

"Let's just hope that God shares your opinion."

I poured tea from the samovar, two steaming glasses, with lots of sugar. She accepted hers, putting the hot rim to her lips, pausing to blow, then sipping.

Footsteps and voices sounded in the hallway.

"Sergeyenko," I said.

"Let's go to my room," Masha offered. "We can talk there. I don't feel like conducting a seminar."

Her frankness always startles me. I feel, by comparison, sly and hollow, a master of deceit. With a tingling in my groin, I followed her down the corridor.

A rickety chair with a lattice seat stood by the dressing table, but it had newspapers piled high on it; I had no choice but to sit beside her on the muslin bedspread. The brownish photograph of an older woman, presumably her mother, was propped on the table.

"Tolstoy got a letter yesterday from a student in Kiev," I said, matter-of-factly. Masha craves little bits of information and gossip, and I feel my ability to satisfy this craving as a source of power over her. Otherwise, with her beauty and supreme self-confidence, she would control everything.

Masha looked at me intently.

"Don't get angry," I said.

"I'm not angry. You're playing a game with me. I don't like that."

"This is no game."

"I won't quarrel with you."

I laughed a bit too ruefully. "You say that, but you quarrel nonetheless. We're quarreling now, aren't we?"

"Valentin, my dear." She sighed. "Tell me about the letter."

"It was an odd letter, really . . . presumptuous."

"In what way?"

"He said that Leo Nikolayevich ought to perform one final symbolic act. He should distribute his property among his relations and the poor, then leave home without a kopeck, making his way from town to town as a beggar."

Masha was awed. Her face tilted upward in my direction, her thin nose razoring the light, which fell into the room through a small north window. Like a magician, ready to dazzle her, I produced a copy of Leo Nikolayevich's response:

*Your letter moved me deeply. What you suggest is what I have always dreamed of doing but have not been able to bring myself to do. Many reasons for this could be found, but none of them has to do with sparing myself. Nor must I worry how my deeds will influence others. That is not within our powers anyway, and it should not guide our behavior. One must take such action only when it is necessary, not for some hypothetical or external reason, but only to answer the demands of the soul, and when it becomes as impossible to remain in one's old conditions as it is not to cough when you can't breathe. I am close to that situation now. And I get closer every day.*

*What you advise me to do—to renounce my position in society and to redistribute my property to those who have the right to expect it after my death—I did twenty-five years ago. But the fact that I continue to live in my family, with my wife and daughter, in dreadful, shamefully luxurious conditions in contrast to sur-*

*rounding poverty, increasingly torments me. Not a day passes that*
*I do not consider your advice.*

*I want to thank you for your letter. This letter of mine will be*
*shown to only one other person. I will ask you to show it to no one.*

I had forgotten that last line.

"You should not have shown it to me," Masha said.

I wished she had been less explicit.

"But what sincerity he has!" she continued.

"Remarkable."

It pleased me that she passed quickly over the fact of my having
shown her the letter.

"He speaks the truth," I said, "even when it's painful to him."

She agreed. I tucked the letter back into my pocket, still regretting
my lack of foresight. I had just been showing off. It seems I have no
moral standards.

"He admires you," said Masha.

"Me?"

"Sergeyenko told me so. He's miserable about it. It's unfair, he
says, that someone like you, who has only just arrived, should enjoy
such close relations with Leo Nikolayevich when so many Tolstoyans,
such as himself, hardly ever see him."

"Leo Nikolayevich treats me well. But he's kind to everyone, even
Tanya's silly husband, Sukhotin."

"Perhaps, but he lets you answer his personal letters. And he trusts
you with the anthology."

"I'm his secretary. I'm sure Gusev had the same privileges. Otherwise, I would be quite useless to him."

"But he also takes you with him in the afternoon. Gusev did not
go with him to Zasyeka Wood."

It is true enough. Leo Nikolayevich takes few people with him on
rides or walks in the woods, yet he often asks me to accompany him.
Occasionally he will take Sasha or Dr. Makovitsky. But almost nobody else.

"What do you talk about when you're with him?"

I told her the truth. "We talk about me."

"Really?"

"It's stupid, isn't it? We should be talking about him, or about his ideas. But he seems so curious about me. He wants to know everything about my parents, about my relations with women, my experience of God—everything."

"What relations with women?"

She tried not to smile, but her eyes shone like quartz crystals. She stirred in me a strange feeling of warmth—like the coals bedded down in a fire pit after a long night's burning.

Without calculation, I moved my hand to her hair and stroked it. It was blond, hay colored, fresh, and perfectly straight. Her eyes, with an emerald tint that recalled the sea, fixed me in their beams. The green irises circled each dark pupil like summer fields around a pond. One could dive into those dark waters easily, and never return.

"I suppose you don't want to talk about the women you have loved," she said. The irony had gone, burned off like morning fog.

"There's almost nothing to tell."

"I don't mean to pry. It's just that I like to know everything about my friends. I'm nosy."

"It's good that you would ask me, but I suspect you'll be disappointed. I've been enamored of many . . ." I hung on the lip of that modifier, speechless.

I would have told her everything—what little there is—but I found it difficult to talk about my past relations. It seemed like a betrayal of this moment of intimacy. I wanted to believe, I did believe, that Masha and I were the only people left on the planet just then.

"I had a lover before coming here," she said. "He was the headmaster of the school where I taught. His name was Ivan."

"Ivan the Terrible," I said. My head was swirling. I thought I might fall off the bed.

"He was married—happily married. This made things difficult for us, since we could only make love at school."

"At school?"

"In the gymnasium, when the girls had left for the day. It was a day school, you see. There were straw mats on the floor. In the gymnasium."

"Ah, I see," I said. But I didn't. My fists clenched, unclenched. Women of Masha's class and rank in society do not allow themselves to be used in this way. She is not a serf.

"He was much older, almost forty," she said. I felt, perhaps unjustly, that she enjoyed telling me, as if my torment gave her pleasure. "There was no future in it, nowhere it could go. I'm much happier here."

I wanted to respond but couldn't. Fortunately, she didn't require a response from me. Her narrative had its own life, which had nothing to do with me.

"My parents suspected that Ivan and I were involved in a dangerous way. I had talked about him rather too freely. Though they detest Tolstoy, they were glad when I left Petersburg. At least in Telyatinki they thought I would not cause them embarrassment."

It was all quite baffling, but I didn't want to appear ignorant. I was, myself, still a virgin. And it seemed ludicrous and unreal that Masha wasn't. In romantic novels, it does not work like this.

"You look distracted, Valya," she said. "Have I upset you?"

"No. I appreciate your frankness."

"You disapprove of me. I see that in your eyes."

"I don't."

She stood up, growing more furious every moment. "I'm sorry I told you all of this. I should never have spoken."

"I'm glad you told me."

"You are a prig, aren't you? A puritan, like Sergeyenko. I should have guessed. Why else would they have hired you? You're a hired man, aren't you?"

"That's not fair."

"I don't care if it's fair. It's true. What is true is rarely fair."

"Masha." I stood up. "I'm leaving."

"Do as you like, Valentin Fedorovich."

She walked over to the window and looked out, sulking. The dusk was coming on fast, its violet color streaking the horizon. The room had a gloomy luster that made everything seem unreal.

"Good-bye," I said.

She stood, silent, looking away from me. I closed the door behind me softly, though inside I raged.

# 13

# SASHA

Once in a while Papa takes me riding with him in the afternoons. He rides Delire, "the Count's horse," as the muzhiks say, which means that nobody else dares ride her. We trot aimlessly along little trails in the forest as branches snap across our faces and bracken thickens into brake; pretty soon you can't tell where you are, but Papa simply presses forward. The more difficult the terrain, the better he likes it.

If a stream crosses our path, Papa will urge Delire on, shouting "Heigh!" like a Tartar and whipping her rump. Delire will jump a small stream or swim a larger one with relish. Once clear of the water, she'll charge ahead, uphill, with Papa shouting. It is impossible to keep up with them.

One day we were galloping past the old iron foundry when Delire stepped into some loose shale, skidded, and lost her footing. Papa pitched sideways off the saddle as Delire crashed on her flank! I panicked, but Papa, without even dropping the bridle from his hand, slipped from the stirrups and landed on his feet beside the whinnying horse.

"That's my girl," he said, putting his face against Delire and whispering in her ear, stroking her long, thick neck.

The horse got back onto her feet, and Papa led her over the shale and remounted. I couldn't believe a man of his age could be so agile. "See that your mother hears nothing about this spill," he said.

Last summer, riding near the Voronka, we passed the little hut we often use as a bathhouse. Soon we came into a small clearing that, in spring, is spread with a bright quilt of forget-me-nots. That day, fat *boroviki* mushrooms studded the field, glistening on their rosy stems, their tops like velvet and their underlining a rich, creamy tan. Papa stopped and dismounted.

"Is anything wrong?" I asked, coming to a halt.

"Right over there," he said, pointing his whip to a deep grassy spot between two lordly oaks. "I want to be buried there."

He looked at me, squinting. I nodded, slowly, keeping my eyes on his. "All right, Papa," I said.

He smiled, and a look of strange satisfaction passed over his old face. I was smiling, too, aware that something of great importance had passed between us.

"Let's go home," Papa said, breaking the spell. "I could use a glass of tea."

He has never again mentioned that incident in the clearing, but I have not forgotten his request. Until that moment, it never occurred to me that Papa could die.

▨ In the thickest part of Zasyeka, Papa's favorite haunt, is a small trail that leads to a spring at the bottom of the woods. A pool of clear water has formed in one spot, and the horses drink there. We call it Wolves' Well. Nearby, a family of badgers live like kings in a dusty hillock. They burrow into deep dens that branch into a maze of connecting tunnels. Papa occasionally brings his favorite dogs—Tiulpan and Tsygan—here; they are crazy for badgers, scratching away at the hillock with a wild hope of unearthing them.

Papa says that writing is like that: you keep scratching away at the dirt, hoping a badger might run out. But it rarely does.

Sometimes, in spring, Papa would come into my room after lunch, saying, "Sasha, would you like to go on a vegetarian hunt with me?" We didn't really hunt as he did as a young man in the Caucasus, where he'd charge like a madman (so he says) through fields teeming with hare, killing as many as sixty in a day. Papa loves bragging about his wayward youth, though it makes people like Dushan Makovitsky or Sergeyenko wince. They want to believe he was always as he is now—as if morality were a gift, bestowed at birth, not something won by hard spiritual work, by the agony of living through sin.

So we'd pull on thick marsh boots that smelled of tar, and I'd race after him across the orchard into the Chapysh and, farther on, into the blue shadows of Zasyeka. Snow, muddy and caked, still clung to the dark sides of ditches. The trees were bare, but the buds would have swollen, turning the woods a washed-out purple. Eventually, we step into a clearing.

"Shush now," Papa would say, putting a finger to his lips.

Sitting on a rock, we'd wait for a long time, trying not to breathe. "Become the woods," he'd say. "You are part of things here."

Then, when you thought nothing was going to happen that day, Papa would raise one of his furry eyebrows and say, "Sasha, look!"

Close by, we'd hear the odd coughing sound of a snipe. It would lift itself into the air, wheeling overhead in great broken rings, then flap across the tips of the trees. Maybe nothing else would come all afternoon, but Papa didn't seem to mind. We'd sit there, silent and happy, till darkness fell.

"It's so peculiar," Papa would say. "Imagine. There was a time when I was fascinated by hunting and killing." He would always say the same thing, and I would always say nothing.

■ This past January, Tanya's stepson, Dorik Sukhotin, was visiting and came down with measles. He was bedded down next to the Remington room in a cot, a somewhat halfhearted attempt to quarantine him from the rest of the family. We were all frantic and did everything to make him feel better. Doctors came and went, pontificating and prattling, while I brought the child sweet things and cool drinks for his fever. Each evening I would read to him from a children's encyclopedia. Dorik recovered, thank God, but before long I found myself breaking out in a rash on my stomach. It spread to my back and arms. Soon I began to cough blood.

Papa grew anxious for me, remembering how my sister Masha had swiftly been taken from us by an illness. Every night he brought me water in a large tin cup, his wrinkled hand trembling. The water would run out of my mouth and down my chin, but I would cover his dear, sweet hand with kisses. And he would sob, taking hold of my hand, pressing it to his beard.

Varvara Mikhailovna almost never left my side. Her soft, full face and chestnut curls were a comfort to me. When Papa left the room, she would climb onto the bed and hold me, rubbing her cheek against mine, so close, without any fear that she might catch my illness.

We had become dear friends. Though we'd met several years before in Moscow, we didn't see much of each other. Our correspondence grew longer and more intimate, and I finally persuaded Mama to let her come and live with us. Secretarial help is always needed at Yasnaya Polyana, and Varvara can type and take dictation.

She has been here for several months now, and we have grown to love each other in the pure love of Christ. We share all fears, all hopes. We touch: hand to hand, chin to chin. We call and respond, alternately, reveling in the flux of real affection.

Now March has come, and the air shimmers with expectation. The midmorning sun on the snow outside is almost too bright to bear, brassy on the windows, filling the house with thick shafts of light. The ice lining the dirt road to our door has begun to melt at the edges.

I'm feeling better, too, though I still cough blood in the morning. The measles have disappeared, but Dr. Makovitsky has raised the specter of consumption. This worries Papa—terrifies him, in fact. But Mama does not trust Dr. Makovitsky, which is pure spite on her part; she insists on bringing these doctors from Moscow. They claim that I must spend at least two months in the Crimea for my lungs. I spoke of this possibility to Varvara Mikhailovna last night as she daubed my forehead with a moist cloth.

"If I go," I explained to her, "Papa will be left alone, and Mama will devour him. He'll be miserable without me. Who would protect him?"

"There is Dr. Makovitsky."

"Mama isn't afraid of him. She treats him like a little boy. She would have free reign over the house. There's no telling what damage—"

"Your father can take care of himself, Sasha. He's far more in control here than you realize. Your mother is the one who doesn't stand a chance."

This was absurd, but I didn't pursue it, turning on my stomach so that Varvara could massage my neck and shoulders.

"I'm frightened, Varvara," I said.

"By what?"

"If I go, I may never see Papa again. He is so frail."

"Leo Nikolayevich has been frail for many years. But he's a tough old bird."

Varvara muttered something about my silliness as she bent down, putting her chin against the crook of my neck. I could feel her warm breath on my skin, her rhythmical exhalation. We do this almost every night now, savoring these quiet moments together. Occasionally we will read a passage together from the Bible or some piece of Buddhist scripture. Bulgakov, at my request, supplied us with a copy of his list of quotations from the great European thinkers and poets, and we read these aloud. I fall asleep thinking of Leconte de Lisle and Sully Prudhomme, dreaming of a warm, sunlit terrace on the Black Sea, where Varvara and I will sit for hours, reading novels, eating oranges, and drinking tea.

But I hate to leave Papa at a time when he seems terribly in need of my support. He needs to feel that I am here, his shield against Mama.

Papa is old, yes, but he is working well on so many projects. There is "The Khodynka," a story, and his introduction to *The Way of Life*. He writes endless letters, too. I don't know why he bothers. Thank goodness for Bulgakov and Varvara, who help him every day by typing into the wee hours.

Papa came into my bedroom this morning, dressed in white. Like a priest.

"My sweetheart, I just spoke with your mother, and we have decided that you must leave for the Crimea as soon as possible. You can take Varvara Mikhailovna with you, for company."

"Do you want me to go?"

He put his thin arms around my shoulders and said that he would give anything not to lose me, but that I must go to preserve my health. He also said that I must not worry about him, and that, in any case, I'd be gone for only a short time.

"It will be summer before you even notice," he said. "Soon we'll all be swimming in the Voronka—like always."

He promised a vegetarian hunt as soon as I came back. He winked, and we kissed, but his eyes had filled with tears. I wondered whether in three months Papa would exist for me as anything but a sharp feeling of sadness, a photographic image on my bed table, a row of books, an empty room.

# 14

# SOFYA
# ANDREYEVNA

It's not that I don't like it here at Yasnaya Polyana. Would I have stayed for nearly half a century if I'd wanted to leave? Yasnaya Polyana was once magnificent—in the days of old Count Volkonsky, Lyovochka's grandfather. *That* house would have suited me fine. But Lyovochka gambled it away. One wing had become a schoolhouse for peasant children—an attempt to put Rousseau's idiotic theories of education into practice. The heart is naturally wicked, as the Scriptures say. The other wing is where I was asked to live. It was barren, with floors of polished oak mixed with dimpled pine and no carpets. The windows had no curtains to subdue the harsh light teeming in from the fields. Except for the odd portrait of an illustrious ancestor, the white walls were devoid of ornament. My husband of only a few days led me into a bedroom that was more like a barracks, without wardrobes or chests of drawers. The miserably hard bed was simply a pad of tightly woven straw, and Lyovochka insisted that we use an old red-leather pillow that had been his grandfather's. I was expected to sleep in felt slippers to keep my feet warm, or to get a pair of bast shoes of the kind worn by peasant women!

I had been through the most trying week of my life. Lyovochka turned up at the church in the Kremlin an hour late for the wedding ceremony, saying he could not find a clean shirt!

After the service, through which I wept like a ninny, we bade everyone good-bye and set off into the future. We went by coach to a little village outside of Moscow called Birulyevo, where we stayed at an inn. Lyovochka behaved like a rabid dog, but I had expected this, after reading his diaries. It took me years to understand why he gave me those diaries. Lyovochka wanted a reader, not a wife. Someone to devote herself to his language, his vision. And now he wants other readers: Chertkov, Sasha, Bulgakov, Dushan Makovitsky. So I am useless.

I feel as forlorn now as I did then, forty-eight years ago, when we drove through the gates of Yasnaya Polyana on a hot, dusty day in late September. I was swimming in my own perspiration, overdressed for the occasion in a blue silk dress. Aunt Toinette, wizened and skeptical, stood on the front stoop with an icon in her hands. The stony look in her eye contradicted her welcoming words.

"She is preparing to suffer," Lyovochka whispered in my ear.

I genuflected before the icon, kissed it, and greeted everyone politely. Sergey Nikolayevich passed around a tray of stale bread and salt. I was eager to get inside, where it was cool. We sat opposite one another in the front hall, and tea was passed around from the antique samovar. It was lukewarm and tasted of burnt metal.

"We are delighted to welcome you," Sergey said. He seemed short of breath and deeply uncomfortable in the presence of his younger brother's new wife—though he would soon enough fall in love with my sister Tanya. Aunt Toinette nodded heavily, looking a thousand years old. I was introduced, one by one, to the three servants who were living behind the kitchen. Only three servants for a house of that size!

That night, after another round of animalistic sex, Lyovochka fell into a snoring slumber, but I lay awake, my nerves tingling, wondering what I had done. Lyovochka woke halfway through the night and shouted "Not her! Not her!"

"Darling," I said, shaking him. "What on earth is wrong?"

"I must have been dreaming."

"About me?"

"No."

"About what?"

"Do I always have to confess my dreams? Is that what marriage means to you?"

I apologized and let him drift back to sleep in my arms. But I know now that, yes, that *is* what marriage is about. Or should be about.

During those first lonely months, I kept thinking about Mama, wondering what the first months of her married life were like. Her marriage was not perfect. Papa was something of a flirt, which did not make life easy. She, of course, had her own flaws. I have since learned, through Lyovochka, about her dalliance with Turgenev, that they were lovers. What a literary family we have turned out to be!

Mama was fifteen when she met Papa. She had been ill for several weeks at her parents' country house in Tula. A mysterious fever had consumed her, and the prognosis was not good. In desperation, her father turned to a famous young doctor from Moscow, Dr. Andrey Behrs, who at age thirty-three was making a name for himself at court. This handsome young doctor was a friend of Turgenev, who had a summer estate in the nearby district of Orel.

Once Papa set eyes on Lyubov Alexandrovna, his heart was no longer free. Her pale skin and dark eyes, her black hair and clean, broad forehead obsessed him. He remained at her bedside for a month, sitting up with her through the night when her fever rose. His courtly manners impressed Alexander Islenyev, my grandfather, though he buckled when his daughter announced, at the end of the doctor's supposedly medical visit, that she wished to marry her physician.

"My dear, he's eighteen years your senior!" he said.

"I love him," she said flatly.

"Impossible!" her mother cried. "You've been at death's door. You're not fit to make such a decision." She had bigger plans for her daughter. A physician was not—after all—a gentleman.

Most horrified of all was my great-grandmother, who said, "I would sooner have Lyubov marry a musician—or die!"

My somewhat indelicate grandmother also pointed out that Dr. Behrs was not a Russian at all; he was German. "Possibly even a Jew," she whispered in her granddaughter's ear.

Mama, typically, would not budge. Her family knew, or should have known, that once she had decided on a course of action the argument was closed.

I don't know exactly what went wrong with Mama's marriage, nor why she took up with Ivan Turgenev, who broke her heart.

"Turgenev was a rascal and a fop," Lyovochka says, all too frequently. "His novels bore me. They are French novels written in Russian." It is not enough for a writer to succeed; his friends must fail.

I talk about the marriage of my parents glibly now, but it hurt me to discover the extent of their misery. At least, during my first lonely months at Yasnaya Polyana, I had the myth of their happiness to aid and abet my spirits. I had the story of their life together, which I told and retold to myself.

Now even that story has deserted me.

# 15

# L. N.

## LETTER TO I. I. PERPER

10 MARCH 1910

Here is a book translated from the German under the title *Horrors of Christian Civilization*. It was compiled by a Tibetan lama who studied at German universities for several years. The title of the book is self-explanatory. Whether it was written by a real Buddhist or someone who used that form as a convention, as in Montesquieu's famous book *Persian Letters*, I can't say. In any case, the book is fascinating and instructive.

Recently Buddhism has become increasingly free from the overlays that have burdened it in the past, just as the Christian world has begun to understand its true essence. Also, one sees more and more people converting from Christianity to Buddhism in both Europe and America.

Apart from the philosophical depth of its teaching, so well explained by Schopenhauer, the moral basis of this teaching strikes me as particularly attractive. I would isolate five essential commandments in Buddhism:

1. Kill no living creature deliberately.
2. Do not steal what belongs to others.
3. Do not capitulate to sexual desires.
4. Tell the truth.
5. Avoid drugging yourself by alcohol or smoking.

One can hardly help thinking what a great change would occur in the world if people knew these commandments and thought them at least as binding as the need to perform certain external rituals.

## LETTER TO V. G. KOROLENKO

26–27 MARCH 1910

I just listened to someone reading your essay on the death penalty. Much as I tried, I was unable to restrain myself—not just from shedding a tear but from actually sobbing as I listened. I can barely express to you my thanks and affection for writing this article, which is marvelous in its expression, its thought, and—singularly—its feeling.

It should be reprinted and distributed in the millions. No speeches at the Duma, no tracts, no plays or novels could have even a thousandth of the impact.

It could have such influence because it stirs a powerful sense of compassion for the suffering experienced by these victims of human insanity; one can't help forgiving whatever their crimes may have been, and (however much one might like to) one can't forgive those responsible for their suffering. Also, your article makes one gape in disbelief at the self-confident ignorance of those who commit these dreadful acts, and at the uselessness of it all, since it's obvious that capital punishment has the reverse effect of that intended, as you show. Apart from this, your article will arouse another feeling, one I have experienced to a high degree—a feeling of pity, not just for those who were murdered but also for those duped, simple, manipulated people—the guards, jailers, executioners, and soldiers who commit such deeds with no sense of what they have done.

One thing that brightens my heart is that an article such as yours unites many readers who are not deceived or perverted. They are united by a single ideal of goodness and truth, and this blazes out ever more brightly—no matter what its enemies may try to do.

# 16

# BULGAKOV

I woke early, startled by what sounded like someone shuffling in the hallway outside my bedroom. Sergeyenko is by nature suspicious, so I wouldn't put it past him to loiter outside my door. He is by now aware that Masha and I have formed an intimate friendship. During meals, we sit together at the narrow pine table in the dining room of Telyatinki, and this is enough to raise suspicion. Nothing is really forbidden at Telyatinki, but there are tacit standards that cannot be ignored.

"Each man is alone with his conscience and his God," Sergeyenko said one morning over breakfast. He did not have the courage to look at me directly as he spoke.

One bright day when the April sun was glistening on the wet grass and the sky was blue as ice, I said to Sergeyenko, "It's a fine day, Leo Patrovich!"

"Indeed," he said. "But we'll pay for it."

Likewise, I said to him one night before retiring, "I'll see you in the morning, Leo Patrovich."

Looking warily at me, he said, "If we're spared."

The atmosphere of general deflation at Telyatinki has become a subject of secret jokes between me and Masha. We tease Sergeyenko in front of the others, asking portentous questions about the meaning of life, begging him to comment on a quotation by the Buddha or La Rochefoucauld, but our teasing occasionally backfires. His impromptu sermons can last for hours.

It amazes me how unself-consciously egotistical people can be. They assume that whatever they say must interest others in the same way it interests them. Leo Nikolayevich is unique, I think, among great men in having a sense of audience. He speaks his mind, but he does not linger unnecessarily over details or digress. Nor, like so many old men, does he repeat himself or talk obsessively about the past.

He gives his opinion freely when asked. Only a week ago I heard him tell a young man who came to Yasnaya Polyana seeking advice on his writing career that his story was without merit. He advised the young man to learn a trade, such as carpentry. The poor fellow was aghast but grateful for such frankness.


■ Masha and I have united against the common enemy: Sergeyenko. But I realized there was still an obstacle between us when I tried to put a spoonful of porridge into Masha's mouth as we stood by the stove. It was my turn to wash up, and she was helping me.

"Please, don't!" she said.

"What's wrong?"

"I don't want that kind of relationship with you. I want to be your . . . friend."

My friend. Of course I am her friend. What did that mean? Romance was not exactly my reason for coming to Tula. I am here to work, to help Leo Nikolayevich. Or so I tell myself.

"Will you be gone all day?" she asked.

"I don't know. What does that question mean?"

"It means I wonder if you will be gone all day. Why does everything have to *mean* something?"

"I will probably not stay for tea today. Not unless Leo Nikolaye-vich needs me for some reason."

He usually works for an hour or two before dinner, after his walk or ride. I don't actually have to stay, but I like being there in case he should want to talk with me. In the past week or so, I have been leaving early. I look forward to returning to Telyatinki as soon as possible, though I had refused to tell myself—until now—that it is because of Masha.

She turned away from me and sat down at the kitchen table with a book. I could not fathom her.

I rode off without saying good-bye and realized, as I approached Yasnaya Polyana, that I was furious. But why? I had no reason to be. No reason whatsoever.

When I arrived at Yasnaya Polyana, Leo Nikolayevich was stand-ing on the terrace at the side of the house, posing for the famous photographers Sherin and Nabgolts, whom Sofya Andreyevna had brought down from Moscow. She was preparing the twelfth edition of Tolstoy's *Collected Works* and wanted a new portrait for the fron-tispiece. I watched as she shouted directions, waving the photogra-phers this way and that. Leo Nikolayevich submitted to these indignities like a schoolboy having his trousers hemmed.

Later, he came into the Remington room, where I had taken over for Sasha.

"You seem tired, Leo Nikolayevich," I said.

His eyes had sunk deeply into their sockets, and his skin had a yellowy, parchment quality. His lips, like thin blue lines, quivered slightly as he hunched beside me.

"I didn't sleep well," he said. "Posing for pictures disgusts me. There are enough pictures of this ragged old man for the press to feed on."

"Sofya Andreyevna is happy about the new edition."

His face tightened. "I wish I had been stricter with her. She is needling me to include that chapter about hunting in *Childhood*. It is a disgraceful piece of writing."

"She thinks it will be popular."

"At my age, popularity is irrelevant. I have to provide an example for other Russian writers. Since I disapprove of hunting, hunting scenes should be cut from my work. At least I'm still alive and can do this. After my death, goodness knows what will happen."

Leo Nikolayevich seemed in a talkative mood, so I withdrew from the typewriter.

"You know, dear boy," he said, "a revolution of sorts has taken place in the public mind. It's quite a recent phenomenon. Russians are becoming more liberal, I suspect. Some years ago, nobody would conceive of hunting as anything but an admirable and manly activity. Now, it's widely considered reactionary. The same is true of attitudes toward stealing. It would never have occurred to people in the past that peasants were victims of the wealthy classes, who in effect stole from those less fortunate than themselves."

"Property is theft," I said, quoting Proudhon.

He knew that I was teasing and liked it. "Valentin Fedorovich, you are a fund of quotations."

He still had on his mind the young author who had come seeking his advice and asked me if he had been too harsh. I insisted he had not.

"I've never denied art, you know," he said. Ever since he published *What Is Art?*, he has been called the enemy of art. "The opposite is true of me, in fact. I consider art a necessary condition of the rational life. But I think that art should contribute to human understanding."

I wasn't quite sure why he felt compelled to go on like this. I agree with him, and he knows that. The empty frivolity of so many French and English and—alas—Russian writers disturbs us both. Perhaps, like many old men, Leo Nikolayevich enjoys restating his positions, which have been won by years of contemplation.

"You see, there are so many writers now. Everybody wants to be a writer," he said, pacing the room. "Look at this morning's mail, for instance. Three or four letters from budding authors. They all want to be published. But in literature, as in life, one must observe a kind of chastity. A writer should attempt only what has not been done before. Almost anyone can write 'The sun shone, the grass was bright,' and so forth.'' His voice trailed off.

"When I wrote *Childhood*, I was convinced that no one before me had portrayed the poetry of childhood in that particular way. But I will say it again: in literature, as in life, one must horde one's bounty. Don't you think?"

I nodded. What could I say?

"What shall it profit a man if he gain the whole world and lose his own soul?" Leo Nikolayevich asked.

I do not intend to lose my soul, I thought. Not for anything.

He abruptly turned and left for his study. I consoled myself that he was lost in meditation. I mean very little in the larger context of his life. He hardly knows me. I have entered his life at the end.

I was left with a moving letter to type on his behalf, a response to a peasant who had written with concern over the contradictions in the count's life. Leo Nikolayevich answered him:

*You ask if I like the life I am currently leading. I do not. Emphatically. I dislike it because I live with my family in ridiculous luxury, while all around me there is poverty and need, and I seem unable to extricate myself from the luxury or answer the needs of the people. I hate this. But what I do appreciate about my life is that I try to do what is within my power, to the extent of my power, to follow Christ's precept and love God and my neighbor. To love God means to love what is good and draw near it. To love your neighbor means to love all men equally as our brothers and sisters. It is to this, and this alone, that I aspire. Since I am approaching this ideal, little by little, though imperfectly, I refuse to despair. Indeed, I rejoice.*

When I finished typing, I went to his study for a signature. Getting no response to a knock, I walked in to find him sleeping with his head on the desk. It was noon exactly. I put a hand on his shoulder and set down the letter so that when he woke he would find it.

Without warning, he lifted his head. "I'm afraid my powers of work exist in inverse proportion to my desire to work," he said. "In the past, I often lacked the desire to work. But now, near the end of my life, I find I have to restrain it."

That afternoon, he seemed much livelier. Goldenweiser, the pianist, arrived with his frowsy wife, cheering the company with his broad jokes and genial manner. Dushan Makovitsky withdrew from the house immediately. His anti-Semitism is quite spectacular in its vehemence, though totally irrational; Leo Nikolayevich has told him so.

Sofya Andreyevna begged Goldenweiser to play, though this was a mere formality. He would have been crushed had she not. The man adores attention, and he does play well—better than Sofya Andreyevna, to be sure.

I hoped that it might be possible to slip away before the little concert began, but Leo Nikolayevich ushered me into the drawing room with a hand on my shoulder. "Come and listen," he said. "You like music, don't you?"

Indeed. Back in Moscow, I had been tremendously interested in opera. I took lessons in singing throughout my boyhood and youth, and at one point went so far as to consider a musical career. The only thing I lacked, it seemed, was talent.

Goldenweiser swayed over the keyboard in a kind of trance, his chin to the ceiling. I was stirred by the performance and watched Leo Nikolayevich as the notes played over his ragged face and his brow loosened; his cheeks were sucked and blown; the white, bushy eyebrows twitched. His eyes blackened, like holes pricked in the visible surface of the world, deepening into eternity. Tears stained his cheeks.

When Goldenweiser had completed Chopin's Étude in E major, opus 10, Leo Nikolayevich sighed. "When a lovely piece of music pleases you, you imagine that you wrote it yourself," he said.

"Chopin considered that étude among his finest compositions," said Goldenweiser. "I am so glad you like it, Leo Nikolayevich."

"If a man came down from Mars and said this étude was worthless, I would dispute him. But there is one thing that worries me. This music would be incomprehensible to the common people." He went on to say that he loved music above all the arts, however, even if it has no social value or intellectual content.

As I rode home through the sharp afternoon light, the stubble fields were yellow and damp, the willows flush with new leaves. I found myself thinking about Leo Nikolayevich. I love him, and I can hardly bear it that he is eighty-two and must soon die. But he would hate knowing that such a thing upsets me. And, of course, I have no reason to be so upset. I am not his son, not even a nephew or, for that matter, a friend of long standing. Yet I feel that God has connected us in some mysterious way, has brought us together for reasons unknown, perhaps, to either of us.

Masha was not at Telyatinki when I arrived, and I felt uneasy about her absence. The prospect of spending the afternoon with Sergeyenko and his merry band did not excite me. I went straight to my room, hoping to get some work done. But I found it difficult to concentrate, thinking first of Masha, then of Leo Nikolayevich in his exhaustion. Life seemed terribly fragile to me, like a shimmering mirage.

I turned my mind once again to the *Inner Chapters* of Chuang Tsu, which Leo Nikolayevich had given me to search. I lit upon this passage:

*The great ones of ancient times slept a dreamless sleep. They woke without fear. They ate simple food, and they breathed deeply. The breath of the great ones rose from their heels, in contrast to the mediocre people of today, whose breath rises from their throats like vomit. When they are filled with lust and desire, their heavenly nature grows shallow.*

*The great ones of ancient times knew nothing of loving life or death. They felt no elation at birth. They felt no sorrow when they entered death. Carefree they went and came. That was all. They delighted in what was given, but they gave it no further thought.*

I am not among the great ones, but I understand what must be done—or not done—to become more like them. I have to give up desire and loathing. I have to delight in what happens, whatever is given. I should not struggle or exert my own petty will.

I knelt beside the bed and prayed to become nothing, to accept life and death, loving neither overmuch, giving myself to the currents of eternal being that moved through me. When I stood, I felt cleansed and whole. A new spirit burned in my heart, as if God had touched me invisibly. The room was bathed in dusky light, with a red—almost peach—glow on the bare walls; I sat on my cane chair and watched it, the simple color of sunset as it flickered against the whitewashed plaster.

The image of Masha's face floated into my head; since it was nearly time for dinner, I decided to look for her.

The door to her room was ajar, and I knocked lightly. She didn't answer, so I pushed it open.

"Masha!" I whispered.

She was not there. I should have turned back, but I noticed a diary on her bed table. It was no more than a few feet away. My heart thudding against my neck muscles, I shut the door. The red ball sun was caught in the window and flared on the little notebook's rough-cut pages. The diary opened to my name.

*Valentin Fedorovich. His soft beard, the smell of his shirt at night: woodsmoke, oil. He is a simple creature, I think, with a decent heart. He does not know himself. He is probably not a true Tol-stoyan, though he imagines that he is. As I do. One lives in hope.*

I could scarcely hold the notebook now, turning the pages with trembling fingers. Sweat fell along my sleeves from under my arms, chilling me, as a particular line flashed from the page: "I may indeed love him. He does not love me."

I do, Masha! I do! This declaration rang in my ears, in the bone of my brow. How can I make her understand that I love her?

I put the diary back where I had found it. One is driven to the edge of immorality by passion, which is why Chuang Tsu recommended against it.

So much for detachment.

"Valya!"

It was Masha. I had just put her diary in place, yet I blushed as if she had caught me with the notebook open on my knees.

"I was waiting for you. Your room was . . . open."

Fortunately, she seemed unconcerned about my presence. She reached up and touched my beard as she passed me, flinging a package on the bed.

"I'll make you a new shirt, Valya," she said. "I bought some lovely blue muslin in town." She unwrapped the material, and I sat beside her on the bed. We fingered the rough cloth as though it was silk.

She was in supremely high spirits, talking of things she had seen in town, her reading, her afternoon conversation with Sergeyenko about Henry George, the American socialist, and the single-tax scheme he has proposed—a favorite subject of Sergeyenko ever since he discovered that Leo Nikolayevich admires George and corresponds with him.

"I've never read Henry George," I said.

"Then you're *really* a virgin," she said.

Once again, I blushed. Masha always manages to tease me about my virginity. I have never made an issue of it. I have committed the act of copulation in my heart many times. My hope, now, rests on purity of heart, of mind, of conscience.

That night, during dinner and throughout our usual discussion in the parlor afterward, I could hardly focus.

"Are you well, Valentin Fedorovich?" Sergeyenko asked, putting a hand on my forearm as I was about to go to bed.

"I have a mild headache, Leo Patrovich. Nothing serious."

"Keep well, my boy. You are doing excellent work with Leo Nikolayevich. He has communicated this to Chertkov, who asked me to pass the word along."

"Tell Vladimir Grigorevich that I am honored."

"I shall. But he also urged me to say that your diaries have not been as detailed as he should have liked. You must remember that it is difficult for him, being cut off. He is hungry for details."

"I will try harder," I said, though I felt disingenuous. Spying on Tolstoy and his family is a disagreeable activity, and I had quickly taken to making things up or filling Chertkov's notebooks with long, boring passages in which I meditate on aspects of Tolstoyan thought.

I took a cup of fragrant linden tea to my bed and, for several hours, sat up in my nightdress, the oil lamp burning on the bed table. I continued to study the *Inner Chapters* of Chuang Tsu, marking passages with a red pencil. At some point I must have fallen asleep. It was past midnight when I realized that I was not alone. Was I dreaming?

"Masha!"

She put a finger to her lips. I had not turned off the oil lamp, and her brow flickered in the yellow light. Her short hair was parted in the middle and fell straight along either side of her head. It was light as corn silk. Her face was a lovely oval, her eyes steady as she knelt above me on the bed. I could hardly breathe.

"Masha."

She sat across my thighs, putting her knees on either side of my legs. They sunk into the mat. She leaned forward slowly. She seemed almost in a trance. As if sleepwalking. Dreaming.

I was afraid of her. What was happening? I put my hands on her narrow shoulders, cupped them in my palms. A flame seemed to burn them as I held her there, almost pushing her away, yet not wanting to. I could not wish for more than was happening to me now. It was a dream, but a dream from which I wanted never to waken.

She was so deliberate, moving over me with a strange, convulsive certainty. A shadow, but palpable. Suddenly her face was close to mine, her lips touching my lips. Our mouths opened into each other, tongues loose and searching. Our teeth touched and clattered like bits of ice.

I breathed her into me, the smell I had come to savor. I drew circles on her back, her neck and shoulders, with moist fingertips. She seemed so terribly slight now, a fantasy, a succuba.

It shouldn't have taken me by surprise but it did when, casually, she sat upright again and lifted her nightdress, exposing her bare stomach, her thighs. She lifted my nightdress, too, curling her hand around me tightly. I turned my head to the side, the pleasure so intense it bordered on pain.

"Is this all right, Valya?"

She looked at me with a peculiar frankness, suspended before me, motionless and beautiful as any piece of statuary from the ancient world. It broke my heart to look at her.

I nodded, and she moved forward slowly but firmly, gathering me into her with ease.

She was so warm, so wet, taking me between her soft, white thighs. With astonishing sureness, she rocked forward, then back. A slow, steady rhythm of attraction and repulsion. When I came, too quickly, I felt that my entire body had been sucked into a holy space, that a lively, understandable spirit had filled me, as I had filled it. Valya and Masha had become, if briefly, more than the sum of their parts. I had obtained union, something like the fabled state of bliss spoken of by Plotinus and Porphyry.

Masha lay heavily on me now, breathing slowly, deeply. Then she curled beside me. The bed is small, but we did not require more room.

When I woke, she was still sleeping, her blond hair against the white pillow, the sunlight blowing through the curtains. I could hear birds in the elm by the window, recent arrivals from the Crimea, perhaps. Or from Africa or Siam. They cackled in the tree, and I began to laugh.

"What are you laughing about, Valya?"

"The birds," I said.

"Do birds always make you laugh?"

"Only when you are beside me, Masha. And we have just made love."

I dug myself as close to her as I could, my bare thighs against hers, our stomachs touching, and I understood that my life could never be the same again.

# 17

# L. N.

**LETTER TO
GEORGE BERNARD SHAW**

YASNAYA POLYANA, 9 MAY 1910

My dear Mr. Bernard Shaw,

I have received your play *The Shewing-up of Blanco Posnet* and witty letter. I have read it with pleasure. I am in full sympathy with its subject.

Your remark that the preaching of righteousness has generally little influence on people and that young men regard as laudable that which is contrary to righteousness is quite correct. It does not, however, follow that such preaching is unnecessary. The reason of the failure is that those who preach do not fulfill what they preach, that is, hypocrisy.

I also cannot agree with what you call your theology. You enter into controversy with that which no thinking person of our time believes or can believe: with a God-creator. And yet you seem to recognize a God who has got definite aims comprehensible to you.

"To my mind," you write, "unless we conceive God engaged in a continual struggle to surpass himself as striving at every birth to make a better man than before, we are conceiving nothing better than an omnipotent snob."

Concerning the rest of what you say about God and about evil, I will repeat the words I said, as you write, about your *Man and Superman*, namely that the problem about God and evil is too important to be spoken of in jest. And therefore I tell you frankly that I received a very painful impression from the concluding words of your letter: "Suppose the world were only one of God's jokes, would you work any the less to make it a good joke instead of a bad one?"

# 18

# DR. MAKOVITSKY

Yesterday the new century arrived in Tula.

I refer to the Moscow-Orel automobile race, which destroyed the peacefulness that one has come to expect from provincial life. The horrid machines—black, ugly things that cough and spit, spewing a pitch of smoke out their backs—came streaking past us as we walked on the Kiev road in the bright morning sunlight.

The drivers recognized Tolstoy, who was unmistakable as he leaned on his stick, with his cloud white beard and bristly eyebrows. This is the problem one must deal with should Fame attach itself like a parasite, feeding, draining one's vital fluids—a frightful prospect that I, happily, shall never have to confront.

The young, Italian-looking men with narrow, cheerful faces and dark mustaches shouted at him, waving their caps, and one of the machines clattered to a halt beside us, frightening Leo Nikolayevich, who shook his head to register disapproval. To make amends, the driver invited us to peer into the mechanism. Leo Nikolayevich is curious about everything. Too much so, I thought, as he peered into the mechanism and flicked a lever with his big finger. The dark machine shook and sputtered, a mess of black, tubular intestines, shiny pistons, whirring belts and fans.

"I wish you good luck in the race," Leo Nikolayevich said, bowing to the driver, who grinned stupidly and bowed even lower.

"It is our honor, sir, to meet Your Excellency," he said. "I have read about you in the papers."

Leo Nikolayevich sighed.

Bulgakov was with us, awestruck as usual. Leo Nikolayevich seems to like him, so I do not interfere. For myself, I avoid the young man whenever possible, though Sofya Andreyevna courts him like a prince, which cannot be a good sign.

Thank goodness I was never young, except in years. Even as a boy, I understood that eternal things are all that count. And I have never wavered in my commitment.

"The machine age is upon us," Leo Nikolayevich said.

"It's disgusting, isn't it?" I responded.

"I suppose I shall not live to see airplanes," he said, pointing to a small group of children who had gathered about us. "But *they* certainly shall. I would rather see them till the soil."

That night, he looked me in the eyes. "Automobiles, in Russia! There are people who have no shoes, and here are automobiles costing twelve thousand rubles! It's filthy!"

I agreed, saying it would lead to revolution, and Leo Nikolayevich nodded. He believes that violent revolutions can only result in chaos, hence in worse conditions for the poor than now exist. This opinion, though correct, does not sit well with the revolutionary types who clog the entrance to his house each morning. No wonder the police lurk about the estate.

The situation at Yasnaya Polyana is desperate. Thank goodness we shall leave tomorrow to visit the Sukhotins at Kochety. Leo Nikolayevich loves his daughter Tanya, even though she has married that fractious bore and abandoned her father's precepts. He is eager to get away quickly, before Sofya Andreyevna returns from Moscow, where she has been indulging herself for several weeks. Delightful weeks for us, I should say. Everyone is much happier when she is away from Tula. Alas, she suspects as much, and is rarely gone. A pity.

We were taken to the station today at half past seven in a troika. I have rarely felt so cheerful, and Leo Nikolayevich seemed alert and well. I checked his pulse several times, and it was normal.

Bulgakov met us at the Zasyeka Station with a small group of Tolstoyans—young Masha, Boulanger, Sergeyenko, and several others. A photographer hovered near us, clicking his contraption. Leo Nikolayevich seemed not to notice. Fortunately, we had to wait only a quarter of an hour before the train wheezed into the dock, steaming from all sides like an overworked horse.

A group of schoolboys emerged from a third-class carriage, shouting, "Count Tolstoy! Count Tolstoy!" We pushed through them with difficulty. Leo Nikolayevich always insists on riding in third class, but today it was full. The conductor led us to a second-class carriage, a situation that clearly upset Leo Nikolayevich, who cannot tolerate a change in plans. We settled on pleasant benches covered with soft, blue cushions, but Leo Nikolayevich insisted that we or the conductor had conspired to seat him in a better carriage. This was simply not true.

At the fourth stop third-class space became available, and everyone was relieved. There are no seats in third class, so we moved a wicker basket near the window for Leo Nikolayevich to sit on and look out. He was so happy that he hummed to himself for much of the journey.

We had brought several newspapers with us, and one of them, *New Russia*, had excerpted a passage from *For Every Day*. This thrilled young Bulgakov, who insisted on reading it aloud. "Suffering and torment," he thundered above the clattering rails, "are experienced only by those who have separated themselves from the life of the world and, not seeing their own sins which have brought suffering into the world, consider themselves guiltless; consequently they rebel against the suffering they bear for the sins of the world and for their own spiritual well-being."

Frankly, I did not understand a word of it. Philosophy has never been my strong suit. I am a practical man.

Leo Nikolayevich said, "This is what I have felt so keenly about myself. It is especially true if one lives a longish life, as I have." After a few moments, he added, "Too long, in fact! It's a great misfortune to outlive one's interest even in oneself."

At each stop we disembarked to walk about the station. An old man gets very stiff between stops, so these ambulations are a necessity for Leo Nikolayevich. There was also the matter of relieving his bladder. I worry when he does not urinate frequently or properly. Infections can be lethal in a man of his age.

At one station, Leo Nikolayevich pointed to a policeman and whispered in my ear, "Look! a typical policeman's face!"

"In what way?"

"Just look at him."

I strolled past the man, pretending to mind my own business. He looked like most policemen: fat faced, full of jowl, but good-natured in appearance. It was a little embarrassing, but Leo Nikolayevich kept staring at me, as if to say, "Well? Was I correct?" I nodded, and he broke into spasms of laughter.

I cannot understand him sometimes.

The conductor behaved badly, spreading word at each stop that Tolstoy was aboard. As a result, voyeurs pushed their noses against the window, ogling. A few would shout, "How are you, Leo Nikolayevich?" and he would remove his hat in response.

At one station, a man rushed up to him and said, "Tolstoy!"

"Not really," he replied. The imp danced in his old, gray eyes.

"Not really?" the man said.

"Not really," Leo Nikolayevich repeated.

The man begged his pardon and withdrew, looking perplexed.

A telegram had been sent to Chertkov, asking him to seek permission from the government to visit Leo Nikolayevich at Kochety. During our last visit there, Chertkov had stayed four versts away, in Suvorovo, which is not in the province of Tula but in Orel. Leo Nikolayevich adored the irony of this situation, which reminded him of the exiled Voltaire, who constructed a castle in Ferney in such a way that his drawing room was in France but his bedroom in Switzerland. I, personally, find such connivances disagreeable. One should obey—or consciously disobey—the spirit as well as the letter of the law.

We changed trains at Orel, where there was an hour's layover. Our baggage was carried to a small room off the first-class buffet, where I heated up some oatmeal porridge for Leo Nikolayevich, who had not eaten anything all day but a bit of stale bread that he carried in his pocket. Asparagus is in season, to my delight. It is especially good for clearing an old man's urine. I asked for a dish of freshly steamed tips; when it arrived, it was nearly time for our departure. I complained to the station manager, who said I could take the dish with me.

Bulgakov led Leo Nikolayevich down the long platform to our carriage, followed by thirty or forty spectators. Leo Nikolayevich sat in the window of the third-class carriage once again, nibbling the slightly undercooked rusks. A young boy pressed his nose to the window, staring more at the asparagus than at Leo Nikolayevich, who insisted that I pass several rusks to the boy through the window. Taking them, the boy scurried off to eat them in private like a dog.

I overheard a man speaking to the conductor: "So the great Count eats asparagus!" He spoke with a contemptuous note in his voice. "Who would have guessed? Asparagus!" he said again.

I wanted to confront the fellow for his insolence, but I decided not to call attention to the issue. It would have been too painful for Leo Nikolayevich, who prefers to ignore slights and insults.

Late in the day we arrived at Blagodatnoye Station, where Tanya stood on the platform, waving her parasol like a figure in a French Impressionist painting. She was beautifully dressed, a real countess. Her father's entire being came alive when he saw her. They embraced like children, with tears moistening their cheeks.

Tanya took us to Kochety, some fifteen versts from the station, in a plush droshky drawn by four black horses. The sun stood on the horizon's edge, red and sharp. We had to shield our eyes.

Though he has often visited here, Leo Nikolayevich seemed enchanted by everything, remarking on the cool, green fields on either side of the road, the well-kept farms, the colorful dresses worn by women in the local villages. As it was Sunday, people were decked out in their finest. Leo Nikolayevich smiled almost continuously, exposing his red gums.

When we arrived at the Sukhotins'—a magnificent house that sits in its own spacious park—Leo Nikolayevich declared that he was going to stay a very long time. "I shall love every moment of it: no passersby demanding five-kopeck pieces, no fugitives from the law seeking counsel, no mothers at war with their daughters. . . ."

I do not actually *like* the hordes of third-rate revolutionaries, fanatics, and fortune hunters who cram the doorway of Yasnaya Polyana each day requesting an interview with "the Count." That he does not banish them all is to his credit. I do not share this largeness of spirit.

We rested before dinner, which was worth waiting for. So many delicious courses, served on English china! Leo Nikolayevich was animated, talking more than eating. I caught a glimpse of the young, carefree count who, back in the 1850s, had dazzled Parisian society with his wit and knowledge, with the sheer force of his character. Here was the man whom even Ivan Turgenev could not withstand.

On our last visit to Kochety, a drawling, simpering woman who was remarkably undeferential to Russia's greatest author had said to Leo Nikolayevich, "Do try to be kind to my son, since he can't bear you. Chat about horses—or something that will interest him. Perhaps he then will forgive you for being so eccentric."

Leo Nikolayevich had grinned and nodded. Later, he claimed that he had enjoyed the woman. "Simplicity on such a grand scale is rare. She has a kind of purity I admire." I did not, myself, see the purity.

Before retiring, Leo Nikolayevich wanted to walk in the park, alone, to "gather his thoughts before sleeping."

"I'll go with you, Papa," said Tanya, taking his arm.

"Let me go alone," he said.

Nervously, Tanya agreed.

"What are you afraid of?" he asked her. "Wolves?"

"You might stumble."

"And the sky might fall!"

She looked mildly sullen.

"My darling, you worry too much about your poor old father. I have already lived a very long time. There is no need to trouble yourself."

He walked off, leaning on a cane, into the cool air.

I sat comfortably in the drawing room with a glass of tea on my lap while Sukhotin nattered on about the rights of landowners and government levies.

More than an hour passed without a sign of Leo Nikolayevich, and it was now dark.

"I suspect that something has gone wrong," Tanya said, breaking our conversation at a convenient point. She clasped her hands in front of her chest like a young matron.

"Not to worry, dear," Sukhotin said, growing red in the cheeks— the effect more of brandy than of panic. "Let me dispatch servants throughout the park. They will find him."

He toddled off to the front hall, where he rang a bell that summoned the household staff. He rattled off orders like an old military officer.

"He has only been gone for an hour," I said.

"He could be dead!" said Tanya. "He might have fallen into the pond!" She began to sob into a red silk kerchief.

"He has probably just had a little fainting spell," Sukhotin said, entering with the bluff self-assurance of a man of inaction. "They'll find him, I'm sure of it."

"He is probably sitting on a bench," I said. "He wanders around Yasnaya at all hours. This is nothing unusual."

But they could not hear me.

Bells rang in the distance, and a brass hunting horn was blown.

Servants scattered throughout the park, crying, "Count Tolstoy!" in a wild chorus that returned in mingling echoes.

When a good while had passed without results, I became afraid that my cynicism would be shown up. Putting on a cloak against the night chill, I set out myself on the least obvious path to the most desirable place. I knew that the large meadow behind a stand of pines was his most likely goal: Leo Nikolayevich likes to emerge into a clearing from a densely wooded area.

In less than half an hour, I found him. He was sitting on a tree stump, humming a familiar folk melody about an old crow that flies off by itself into a dark wood, never to return.

"You've upset everyone at the house, Leo Nikolayevich."

"I have?"

"Tanya thought you were dead."

"She overestimates my good luck."

I sat beside him on the stump, which was vast and moldering. It was not comfortable.

"Why did you come looking for me?"

"They were fussing about you. I was afraid."

"You worry too much, Dushan. You must live as though your life does not matter."

"It's *your* life that matters," I said.

"That's foolish. I don't matter in the least. What matters is the lovely air we breathe. Smell it, Dushan."

I sucked in a breath. Was it lilac?

"I am enjoying myself tonight," he said.

"You are causing trouble."

"Yes, that always pleases me, doesn't it? A sign of vanity. I must pray about that."

"We had better find Tanya," I said, taking his arm.

Once we were inside, Tanya scolded her father. "You must not go out alone, Papa. Not in the dark."

He winked at me. "All right, all right. And I shall try to walk on my feet and not on my head."

"That is not funny, Papa."

■ Another day we sat together in the damp, green park. Leo Niko-layevich took me to look at a flowering chestnut tree that had, for mysterious reasons, caught his attention.

"How marvelous it is!" he said, holding my arm. "It all seems terribly new, as though I were seeing it for the first time. And the birds. Have you ever heard such wonderful singing?" He talked rap-idly, more to himself than to me. "And a little while ago I saw two eagles high above the clouds, and two kites!" It is the geographic setting of Kochety that is most attractive to him.

"If Napoleon had fought in the Novosil district he would certainly have stayed at Kochety," he said. "It is the highest point and has a view on all sides."

Once, when I was walking in the woods with Leo Nikolayevich, he told me about the time he and his brother-in-law, Stepan Behrs, had gone to visit the battlefield at Borodino. He was doing research, pre-paring to write the great battle scenes of Borodino, the scenes that have made *War and Peace* part of the consciousness of Russia.

He spent days tramping those empty, green, rolling fields, picnick-ing in the little copses, sunbathing on the crests of hills, all the while imagining the dead. How many bones had been plowed under? What blood had colored that soil?

Reading Tolstoy's account of that battle, years ago, remains a pri-mary experience of my life. I resolved then to combat violence, es-pecially the insanity of *state* violence. I do not believe that young men should ever die in war. There must always be another solution.

I lay on my back, ill with typhus in Hungary, reading Tolstoy's masterpiece. Though my own life was in danger, I did not care. I did not even notice! I lived with Pierre as he stumbled from cannon to cannon, as he watched the Russian spirit drained and nearly van-quished. I was smitten with Prince Andrey on those fields. The an-guish of the old general, Kutuzov, upon whose shoulders the responsibility for so many dead would lie, was my anguish. Those vignettes, so infinitely personal, live on. They will live on long after Leo Tolstoy is dust.

The afternoon was spent in the cool of Sukhotin's library, modeled on that of an English gentleman, complete with a leather couch from London, a finely tooled desk that had once "belonged to an Edinburgh lawyer," and a pair of George III globes. The bookshelves are crammed with the obvious English, French, German, Italian, and Russian volumes, though I suspect that they have never been opened. Leo Nikolayevich skimmed a number of Parisian editions of the French classics, then settled on Rousseau, his favorite author. He lost himself in a copy of *Émile* until it was time for tea.

"It's fascinating to try to guess what our grandchildren will read," he said later, as we drank a scented Indian tea in the blue parlor with Bulgakov and Tanya. "In my time there was a definite range of classic books, and one knew exactly what it meant to be an educated man. Now there are so many books, one is naturally confounded."

I said that, surely, the one author whom everyone would read in the future was Leo Tolstoy, but he merely shook his head and grinned.

On the sixth day of May, a telegram arrived from Chertkov, saying that he had received permission to visit Kochety. Leo Nikolayevich was overjoyed, though he was able to resist gloating. It is tedious when someone—even Leo Tolstoy—cannot restrain his happiness.

Chertkov arrived midmorning, while Leo Nikolayevich was working in his room. One is normally careful not to disturb him when he's working, but I felt no hesitation that day. He looked up with childlike gratitude, then rushed down the stairs to greet this man whom he refers to as "a dear person and precious friend."

They met on the front steps, kissing affectionately on either cheek. Vladimir Grigorevich paid the driver, while Leo Nikolayevich went inside the front hall and blew his nose. I saw that his face was damp with tears. He appeared quite shaken by the experience, and I felt sorry for him. He is a man of such overwhelming emotions. I understand this, though I rarely experience anything like it myself.

The two friends went up to the bedroom where Vladimir Grigorevich was staying, and they remained there until the bell was rung for lunch.

But, alas, Leo Nikolayevich's euphoria was short-lived. I heard the wheels of a coach outside, dogs barking at the hubs, much shouting and clamor of servants. Out stepped Sofya Andreyevna and her son, the dutiful and boring Andrey. That woman has an instinct for knowing when her husband is about to enjoy himself.

# 19

# CHERTKOV

I thought of England this morning. The early light, soft and gray, had a wet, acidic tang. I stood at the window in my nightdress, watching through the mist, when a bright yellow oriole flashed into sight. Today I would see Leo Nikolayevich. And God had sent this oriole as a harbinger of joy.

I sat down on the bed, trembling. The years in England did much to gird my soul. I read and thought deeply. I made endless speeches on behalf of Leo Nikolayevich. I was greeted warmly everywhere from Southampton to Birmingham and Newcastle. Once, I even traveled into Scotland to address a group of Glaswegian ship builders who had a Tolstoy "study group." Most impressive. One cannot imagine that sort of thing happening in Russia. The only thing I disliked about England, apart from the essentially frivolous nature of the English mind, was the forced separation from my Master.

People are mistaken when they say I love the man. What I love is the Tolstoyan firmness, the call to truth and justice. The lineaments of his prose entangle, embody, render visible the elusive matter of these virtues.

We met at a time when my soul was just awakening. I looked on my life of luxury and privilege with contempt, seeing that I had contributed to the injustice of the world. I had added to its misery by remaining ignorant of what is cruel and unjust.

It was my assignment to a military hospital that alerted me to the truth. I found the hospital crammed, not only with the sick but with political prisoners of various stripes: pacifists, mystics, revolutionaries, Christians who refused to accept the violence of the state, brave men who did not find the tsar's barbarous policies acceptable and dared to say so.

I resigned from the regiment and went to live by myself on an estate in Voronezh owned by my mother. It was a modest country house, with an adjoining farm. I felt marvelously solitary there, but I could not recover my former balance. The world seemed thin as rice paper, so fragile that at any moment "reality"—which now looked like a tragic illusion—might break.

Bleakness overwhelmed me. I wakened each night with sweat beading my face, my breath shallow. I could feel my pulse throbbing in distant parts of my body, sounding in the void of the universe like deadly drumming. I was suffocating, but I clung to life as a drowning man clings to a piece of driftwood.

Both life and death seemed intolerable, terrifying. I shook like an old man, kneeling by my bed there, praying to a God whom I did not trust.

It is not an easy thing to alter the trajectory of your life. People have expectations on your behalf. You come to believe them yourself. When I began to live my life according to new principles, my family and friends dismissed it as youthful folly. Friends and relatives turned against me when I persisted. They said I would end up like the Decembrists, whom I emulated—in Siberia or on the gallows.

My mother and I had tea, once, at a fashionable Moscow restaurant. The luxury of the establishment offended me deeply, and she knew that, which was why she insisted on meeting me there.

"Your father," she said, "would have been crushed."

"By the fact that I have chosen to live according to a set of principles, instead of wasting my time and money?"

"You know what I mean."

"Father is dead."

"Thank goodness. It would have been too awful for him."

"I embarrass you," I said. "Fortunately, what you think about me—or anything—hardly matters."

She affected tears. It was deeply boring but difficult to ignore.

"The fact is that you find my refusal to become a playboy and spendthrift distasteful," I said.

"You are a young man, Vladimir. Someday you will regret the way you speak to me now."

"I daresay you're right, as usual," I said, trying to control my snicker.

"Do as you choose, Vladimir. You will anyway. But remember. You are a Chertkov."

For months, we hardly spoke. But I am her son, after all, and we have in recent years arrived at a truce. She puts my interest in Tolstoy down to "eccentricity," which has given her a way of talking about me to her friends. I let her indulge herself in this fantasy.

Gradually, the Lord has narrowed my enemies to only one person: Sofya Andreyevna. She has never understood. She has not even tried. So Leo Nikolayevich must live in a perpetual state of compromise, preaching poverty and obedience to the will of God while surrounded by every kind of luxury and worldliness. It is no wonder his disciples, upon seeing Yasnaya Polyana for the first time, often retreat in disillusion.

Leo Nikolayevich has talked of leaving her. Indeed, he has often swerved in the direction of abandoning his life at Yasnaya Polyana, a life that has grown more painful as the contradictions become more evident. What he will do, I cannot say. But he must do something.

In midsummer, two years ago, he fell gravely ill. The sickness seemed a combination of spiritual crisis and physical ailment. As I leaf through his diary of that period (which I keep hidden in a strongbox at Telyatinki), I find the tenor of his voice unmistakable.

*2 July 1908*
If I had heard of myself as an outsider—of a man living in luxury, wringing all he can from the peasants, locking them up in prison, while preaching and professing Christianity and giving away small change, and for all his loathsome actions sheltering himself behind his dear wife—I would not hesitate to call him a scoundrel! and that is just what I need that I may be set free from the praises of men and live for my soul. . . .

*2 July 1908, later in the day*
Doubts have come into my mind whether I do right to be silent, and even whether it would not be better for me to go away, to disappear. I refrain from doing this principally because it would be *for my own sake*, in order to escape from a life poisoned on every side.

*3 July 1908*
It is still agonizing. Life here at Yasnaya Polyana is completely. poisoned. Wherever I turn, it is shame and suffering. . . .

*6 July 1908*
Help me, O Lord! Again I long to go away, and I do not make up my mind to do so, yet I do not give up on the idea. The great point is: whether I would be doing it for my own sake if I went away. That I am not doing it for my own sake in staying, that much I know for certain. . . .

*9 July 1908*
One thing grows more and more excruciating: the injustice of the senseless luxury in the midst of which I am living with undeserved poverty and want all around me. I feel worse and worse, more and more wretched. I cannot forget, I cannot help seeing what I see.

Doubtless it was God's will that he should live. Shortly after, we went walking in Zasyeka Wood, he moving very slowly, as when he is lost in thought. It was oppressively hot that summer, the air sticking to the skin like beeswax. I said, "Dear friend, I sense that you are suffering."

He turned to me with his face shining, his eyes glittering like crystals. "I've been thinking a great deal of late, thinking very deeply. And it has become clear to me that when one stands at the parting of ways and does not know which way to act, one ought surely to give preference to the decision which involves the most self-sacrifice."

I understood by this remark that he had chosen to remain with Sofya Andreyevna. Surely nothing could be more painful than that. But I refrained from comment. I have tried, repeatedly, to remind myself that Leo Nikolayevich has devoted himself to Sofya Andreyevna for nearly five decades; he has borne her prattling, her violent temper, the indignities she heaps upon him daily. I thank God that Anna Konstantinovna has never wavered in her devotion to righteousness. She has labored beside me, never questioning the justice of my activity. She understands that a woman's role is to encourage and sustain the intellectual and moral work undertaken by her husband.

As the troika took me through the foggy countryside to Kochety, I recalled a similar morning in 1883 when, fortuitously, I found myself on the same train from Moscow to Petersburg with Leo Nikolayevich. I had, indeed, heard of Leo Tolstoy and his writing before this meeting. Once I saw him across a crowded room in Moscow: his features remained vividly in my head—the ruddy bulb of his nose, the wispy beard, which had not yet turned white.

He was alone on the train, reading, and though I was assigned a different seat, I decided to risk offense and sit across from him. Having only lately read one of his books, I felt confident of my ability to engage him in conversation.

Seeing me, he put his book aside. Our eyes met sharply.

"Count Tolstoy?"

He raised his eyebrows.

I mentioned the reception, which he seemed not to recall. "I am a great admirer of yours," I continued. "Though I take issue with some of the things you have written about the Cossacks." He romanticized them, I suggested. To my surprise, he quickly agreed. I have since learned that Leo Nikolayevich likes nothing better than serious readers who will take the trouble to contradict him.

We swiftly became friends, sharing many ideas and preoccupations, ideals, future plans. Had Sofya Andreyevna not made it difficult for us to continue our relations, there is no telling what we might have accomplished.

From a narrow, personal perspective, I have gained immensely from my contact with Leo Nikolayevich. I treasure the letters he has written to me over the years, especially the one dated 7 November 1884. "I would very much like to live with you," he wrote.

*I wonder if you are perpetually as anxious as when we are together. You can't be like that at home (though—if your letters suggest the truth—you are constantly pressed for time). As you know, I once wrote part of a novel about Peter I, and there was one good thing about what I said—my explanation of his character and evil deeds by the fact that he was simply too busy with building ships, working at a lathe, traveling, making proclamations, et cetera. It's a truism that idleness is the handmaid of discontent with oneself and, in particular, with other people. I would wish, for you, more calm, more idleness. More good-natured, warm, kindly, and self-indulgent calm and idleness. I would like to live with you and, if we are still alive, I shall live with you. Never cease to love me as I love you.*

The directness of the man, the willingness to speak his emotions, his thoughts, clearly and boldly, has never ceased to shock me. I have, indeed, loved him as dearly as one can love another man.

The matter of his will continues to torment us all. The great novels, his diaries, and correspondence remain in the hands of Sofya Andreyevna. Far from seeing that this work receive the widest dissemination among the people, she wants to ensure that it can be published only in the most expensive and, for her, most profitable editions. Alas, she has Leo Nikolayevich cornered, and he cannot see a way around her.

I, however, shall propose that he make me the executor of his work. I can produce it cheaply and distribute it to the muzhiks. This will be the grandest of gifts to the Russian people. *Ad majorem Dei gloriam*, as the Jesuits say.

I felt quite faint with anticipation as the troika wobbled along the muddy road to the front door of Kochety. We had barely come to a halt when Leo Nikolayevich rushed out to greet me, his face full of expectation and love. I was, as ever, overwhelmed by my dear friend's affection, so childlike and unqualified as we embraced, his face wet with tears. Indeed, my driver was embarrassed, turning away from us.

Perhaps those years I spent in England are at fault, but I confess that open displays of emotion unsettle me. Though I tried to respond to Leo Nikolayevich in kind, I shrank from him instinctively.

We went immediately to my room to talk over various publishing projects. Leo Nikolayevich expressed his satisfaction with young Bulgakov, whom I have come to distrust. He has been sending the most idiotic, unhelpful reports from Yasnaya Polyana. He is vain enough to imagine that I should actually want to hear his running commentary on Tolstoyan texts.

Although I tried, delicately, to bring the conversation to the matter of his will, Leo Nikolayevich sensed the drift of my language and emphasized his commitment to Sofya Andreyevna.

"I couldn't do it," he said, his voice faltering.

I put my hand on his shoulder. "I will never ask you to do anything against your better judgment. You must trust me."

"I trust you entirely," he said, standing, putting his arms around me, kissing me on either cheek. "Always, my friend."

I told him that I had recently bought a new house, near Moscow, in Meshcherskoye. It is a lovely, secluded little estate, purchased with an inheritance recently passed on from a distant uncle. I said that he must come very soon to see it, since I have assembled a group of Tolstoyans—young men mostly, from the university—who will live there with me and help me in the work at hand. To my astonishment, he accepted instantly.

"I shall come soon. In a few weeks!" he said. "Perhaps Sasha will come with us. She is doing so well, you know. Recovering in the Crimea. Her doctor has written a most encouraging letter."

The poor, dear man. I held him close to me, and we kissed once more on either cheek. For a long moment, we encountered each other with the rarest intimacy. Then we heard the rustle of carriage wheels, dogs barking, and the shouts of many servants. Soon the shrill voice of Sofya Andreyevna rose above the clatter: defiant, self-righteous, commanding.

"Sonya!" said Leo Nikolayevich, sucking in his lower lip. "She has found us, I'm afraid. I half-expected her."

I touched him on the wrist. "You must come to me alone at Meshcherskoye," I said. "Forbid her to come. Do you understand?"

"That cannot be done."

"It can!" I insisted. "It would be good for her. She doesn't realize it, but it would benefit her marriage. A husband and wife sometimes have to put time as well as distance between themselves to survive."

He looked at me with his sad, large eyes and said nothing. I have to make him understand.

# 2 0

# SOFYA
# ANDREYEVNA

He has betrayed me again. I returned from Moscow with Andrey and discovered that he had stolen off to Kochety. I ran straight to the pond. I wanted to end my life, to make him regret everything he has ever done to me. It was midday, but the world seemed empty. No people. Not a muzhik in the field. Not a bird on a black branch. The air was empty.

I lay on the bank, where the moss is thick as suede, rubbing my face in a patch of grass. Water was seething, rising through the knobby roots of alders, the willows, the black weeds. I listened, hoping to learn something by keeping still. Wondering: Should I die? Must I die?

It is always worst in spring, this feeling that I must die. Worse than in winter, which is bad enough. Snow is mercifully blank. It has no story. It does not jab at me like the blood rose, the gelder rose, the prickly thorn.

My nerves are bad now. Even last week, in Moscow, I burst into tears when a houseguest, hoping to please me, entered the front hall with fresh flowers. "For you, Countess," he said. "Take them back!" I shouted to the man. "I don't want your flowers!"

I wish I were the wind, invisible, circulating without body, without intent.

Lyovochka thinks that I do not love God. That God means nothing to me. But I prayed, at the pond's edge, digging my face in the moss, in a patch of grass beside the moss: "God, my God . . . Why hast Thou forsaken me?"

I rolled onto my back. I let the sun finger my body. I spread my legs to it, the godly sun, its knife, its blade of light. It was hot on my thighs, and I found myself laughing and weeping.

I would not die today. No, I would not die. I would go to Kochety, at once. I would take back my Lyovochka.

I summoned the maids and a driver. Andrey said we would ride through the night if necessary. I would not give Lyovochka time to rewrite the will.

"Papa is not in his right mind these days," Andrey said. "I don't think he is capable of defending himself from those thieves he calls disciples."

I kissed Andrey on both cheeks. I bowed my head to him. He is such a fine son. I wish all my children had turned out like him. He does not play at false modesty, at make-believe chastity, at pseudo-religious piety.

I went to my room to prepare for the journey, but before doing anything I wrote the truth of things in my diary. Otherwise, they will read and believe the diaries of Lyovochka and Chertkov. For all I know, even the parlor maids are keeping diaries. They watch me slyly as I pass, smiling behind my back.

We left for Kochety after dinner. My heart was palpitating the whole way, the pulse reaching extraordinary and life-threatening levels. I broke into tears, off and on, though Andrey was patient. He understands me so well. He knows that there is no moral reason for going along with Lyovochka's schemes for giving our property to the masses, who would not know what to do with it anyway. Chertkov's notions are all calculated to destroy me. And our family. There is nothing more pathetic than impoverished aristocrats.

We arrived just before lunch the following day, having slept badly on the train in cramped sleepers (so much for first-class service!). It was as I suspected. Vladimir Grigorevich was there, wringing his puffy hands. He was standing beside my husband on the steps, gloating over his possession.

"What a pleasant surprise," he said, taking my hand.

"I'm always happy to make you happy," I said.

We stabbed each other with our eyes, taking care not to lose our artificial smiles.

I had barely stepped into the house when Lyovochka and Chertkov began to whisper and sneer like schoolgirls. Like lovers . . .

It's unnatural for a man of my husband's age to cluck and coo over a beastly younger disciple. Whenever I suggest as much, Lyovochka becomes irate, irrational, even hysterical. Whenever I act from powerful and genuine feelings, they call me "a lunatic." When Lyovochka does the same, he is called "a genius."

Tanya's lunch was formal, with waiters in white jackets hovering behind our chairs. Sukhotin presided like an Oriental potentate. "You are looking so well," he kept saying, which made me wonder how frightful, in fact, I must look.

Andrey talked with animation about land resources and the latest measure taken by the government to extort money from the landowning classes, who end up paying for everything—as usual. It is no wonder I have so little money. Count Generosity gives away everything he earns while our estates bring in less each year, partly because of poor management and servants who steal whatever they can lay their greedy hands on. Is it any wonder I get frantic when I think of his giving away the copyrights to his work?

I spoke of the unfairness of these new taxes, too, expecting at least a pleasant nod from my husband. Instead, he sulked, looking up occasionally at Vladimir Grigorevich as if to say, "You're quite right. The woman is intolerable. Just as you said. A bitch."

I don't know why everyone puts up with that man, with his pointy little beard, his reptilian eyes going their separate ways. He dandles his paunch with a fidgety hand as if it were a treasure.

After lunch, my husband spent the afternoon on horseback beside his lover, riding through the woods where nobody could see them—in Prince Golitsyn's park, seven versts from Kochety. I could see them in my mind, like satyrs, scampering about in the dark brush. I tried to banish these images, telling myself how irrational they were, but they would not go away. I could feel my heart racing, my temples pulsing like the throat of a frog.

It began to rain not long after their departure. A damp chill blew through the house, which grew terribly dark. I said to Tanya, "You know, a man of your father's age can easily catch his death of cold." I could think of a dozen cases in point.

"Mama, you fret too much," she said, coldly. "Vladimir Grigorevich is with him. They will surely take shelter in an isba if the rain continues."

"Nobody listens to me anymore," I said.

Tanya refused to notice that I had said anything at all. I realized how blessedly lucky we are that she no longer lives with us. Her pretensions to levelheadedness would be more than I could bear. And she has this accusatory little mouth that puckers up when she doesn't get her way. Who could believe she is my own daughter?

Lyovochka arrived home safely, and I was glad for this, though I had to suffer Tanya's smugness.

That night, he came into my bedroom near midnight. I was reading the Bible, the Book of Ruth, with several candles burning on a table beside my bed.

"Good evening, dear," I said. "Are you unable to sleep?"

He bent close and kissed me. It was not a sincere kiss, but at least he kissed me. I half-wondered if he was going to ask for a sexual favor. At his age, you would think he'd be over such requests. But one never knows with him. There's no goat like an old goat.

"Sit on the bed," I said. "Here." I moved over to make room for him.

I knew something weighed on his mind. He had that stony look that overwhelms him whenever he is about to make a confession or create a scene. It made my stomach flutter.

"Our life together has become intolerable," he said, speaking to the wall. He never looks directly at me when he makes cruel remarks.

"That is pure, foolish nonsense," I said. "We have had some disagreements, but they are no more than any married couple experiences. I love you."

I probably should have said nothing. It is sometimes best to ignore his facetious prattling.

"You and I no longer agree on anything: neither the land question nor the religious question."

"We are not heads of competing states," I said. "We are man and wife. Do we have to agree on such questions?"

"The life I lead is an embarrassment to me and my friends. I am a hypocrite."

"You don't mean a word of that, Lyovochka. That is Chertkov speaking. You are not yourself tonight."

"I don't know how I can continue." His lips trembled as he spoke. I knew it was true.

"Do you love me?" I reached out for his wrinkled hand. It was as cold as marble, and as veined.

"I have never not loved you."

"Come, Lyovochka," I said. "You fill your head with nonsense. Do your duty. God asks nothing more of you. Your duty is, first, to respect your family. There are obligations that come before selfish whims. All you can think about is yourself, did you know that?"

He covered his face with his hands and wept, his shoulders shaking. He seemed like a young child, suddenly, so helpless and without control. It was pitiful. I found myself, to my amazement, weeping, too. We each cried on the other's shoulder.

"There now," I said. "It's not so bad, is it?"

He stared at me, his eyes hollow, red as coals. He shook his head. "It will never work," he said. "I cannot continue."

Slowly, he composed himself and left the room. I said nothing.

I no longer understand my life. I want to die.

# 2 1

# SASHA

I think I could easily have stayed in the Crimea, living beside Varvara Mikhailovna. I had a dream there in which her head was deep in my lap as we lay beside the water, a salt green sea, with waves splattering over low rocks. One night, past midnight, I walked in the fields with her, a hot wind filling our heads, our lungs. The stars fell like snowflakes in the high grass. I told her about my dream, and she hugged me, and we wept. We lay in the grass, shawls drawn up about our shoulders, and slept. When dawn broke the horizon was pink as flesh, a faint wind stirring the field like froth. I was happy.

As the weeks turned, we grew brown in the sun. Our hair cut short like boys', we ran in the sandy woods near the big house that Count Minsky had loaned to us. It was full of servants, and the samovar was never empty or cool. We drank wine, too, a light Bordeaux stored in the count's cellar. It made us feel naughty and giddy.

I recovered my strength as the fever passed. My throat cleared, and my head no longer throbbed. I felt whole again, especially with Varvara beside me. I felt released from a terrible but invisible enclosure.

At Yasnaya Polyana, she would never have felt free to sleep beside me, but there it seemed perfectly natural. Varvara had been sent to look after me, hadn't she? Young girls—children, really—will often sleep together. I daresay it was childish of us. But we enjoyed the silliness. I do not know what Count Minsky's servants thought, but I did not ask.

When I was still suffering from fever, Varvara rubbed my back with alcohol each night before I slept. We soon realized that, even without a fever, back rubbing is a pleasurable activity. I would undress slowly by the fire as it sputtered in the black grate and flickered against the white walls with Varvara watching, nodding, and occasionally smiling. She would hum quietly or, sometimes, sing a Bulgarian folk tune that she loves about two young girls in a field.

Naked, I would walk to the bed and lie on the cool, puffy quilt. It chilled my body, but Varvara's hands were silky and warm. She has a lovely way of kneading the flesh, of finding the muscles to the left and right of the spinal column, of touching a hidden crevice between the vertebrae. She would work the soft flesh of my buttocks, take one thigh, then the other, in her large hands. Her fingers, pressing, seemed to enter my anklebones, to penetrate my arches.

After a long massage, she would collapse beside me and pull the red-and-green patchwork quilt over our heads. We would fall asleep in a short time—a dreamless, wordless sleep in a bed so large it might have been an arctic snowfield (except for the fire between us).

I would have stayed longer if I had not been worried about Papa. I missed him badly, more than I'd have guessed. And he cannot cope easily with Mama, who has grown worse over the years. With reluctance, we went back to Yasnaya Polyana toward the end of May.

Papa had returned the week before from Kochety, where he'd met with Chertkov. He is always buoyant when he has seen or is about to see Chertkov. He loves Vladimir Grigorevich as I love Varvara Mikhailovna. I would never begrudge him this.

Despite Mama, my return home was exhilarating. Papa wept when I came through the door, embracing me for such a long time. He never used to weep so easily. I was afraid for him.

He could think about nothing but going to Chertkov's house at Meshcherskoye in two weeks. Chertkov insists that he continue to ride, but Mama invariably tries to stop him. He wants to think, Papa says. "Think about what?" she asks. "Why can't you think in your house, like everyone else?" We all laugh, except Mama.

I was typing some letters for Papa a few days ago when Mama came barging into the room without knocking.

"Here I am," she said, "an outcast in my own home."

I refused to respond.

"Nobody seems to care that I am sixty-six years old," she continued. "A woman of sixty-six cannot look after this estate. Do you hear me? I'm run ragged. I have no time for myself!" Her whining voice rose to a most unattractive pitch. "I cannot manage it any longer! Don't you see that? Can't anyone hear what I'm trying to say?"

"So who is asking you to do it?" came a voice in the doorway. It was Papa, grizzly and wild. His eyes sputtered like coals stirred by a poker.

"You hate me, don't you? Tell the truth," she said. "In front of your daughter, in God's sight, say exactly what is true!"

The light went out in Papa's eyes, and his whole being sagged. "Go away from here, Sonya. Your nerves will ruin you if you don't. Dushan thinks you need a period of rest." He turned to me. "Tell her, Sasha, how the Crimea helped."

I tried to echo his sentiments, but Mama broke in.

"You'd like nothing better than to drive me away. You want to get rid of me. That's all you can think of."

Papa looked disconsolate. "You always think the worst of me, don't you?"

"I know exactly what to think of you. I think what is true. I'm not ignorant, though you and your friends haven't quite understood that."

"You're mad," he said, and walked away, fuming.

The next day another incident occurred that points up the difference between my parents. Last year Mama hired a young Circassian guard, Akhmet, to protect our property. Everyone knows that Leo Tolstoy lives here, that he is wealthy and generous. Beggars, revolutionaries, students, monks and visionaries, crooks—they all descend on us, and we do need protection of a sort. But Papa hates the sight of Akhmet, who takes his job too seriously and struts about the grounds in a formal black tunic with a sword at his side. He insists on wearing a pompous Persian-lamb cap, which he tilts to one side as if to taunt us. He refuses to let strangers "wander about the Master's property," as he puts it. They daren't even pick wildflowers in Zasyeka Wood.

The man is brutish. I heard from Sergeyenko, in fact, that he has actually molested married women in the village.

The trouble started when Akhmet seized a local muzhik, Vlasov, who had "stolen" a sapling from the wood. Akhmet tied him brutally with a piece of hemp and dragged him on the ground back to the house, where Mama scolded the peasant harshly and said that if he were caught again he would be banished from the Master's property.

Papa unexpectedly stepped into the kitchen, drawn by the commotion. "Do you expect me to stand quietly aside while you mishandle a good friend?" Papa asked her.

"He's a muzhik, dear," Mama said. "You never did understand social distinctions."

"He's a human being, and we have known each other for many years."

Mama objected that Vlasov was caught stealing, and that if everyone thought it possible to steal what they liked, there would be no end to theft at Yasnaya Polyana. "That's just like you," she said. "You want to give everything that we have away. If your grandchildren end up as paupers, it will mean nothing to you. You, of course, never wanted for anything. You have been pampered and protected your entire life, and you don't even realize it."

"Vlasov is free to help himself to whatever he needs," Papa said, barely under control. He pointed to Akhmet with a shaky finger. "And I insist that you dismiss your foolish guard at once." I thought he might swoon.

Later, I found Papa in his study, his head buried in his hands. He was like a world drained of light.

"It's very painful," he said, taking my hand. "Your mother was absolutely right about me. I have lived my life in a glass house, utterly protected, coddled. I know nothing of the world."

"That's foolishness, Papa," I said. "You mustn't pay attention to her."

I kissed him on the head and rubbed his neck.

That day he did not come down to lunch.

Mama looked at me and said, "He is torturing himself and he is torturing me. Why can't he behave in a normal way? Everything with him is hysterics."

In the days that followed, Papa declined swiftly. He would sit in his study for hours at a time, writing nothing. His diary straggled off into incoherent ramblings. One day he came home from a long walk in Zasyeka Wood, his face livid, the sweat standing on his brow. I put him to bed and called Dushan Makovitsky, who took his pulse.

"It is weak, I'm afraid," he said, with the gloom in his voice one expects of Dushan Makovitsky.

Papa had fallen into a deep sleep, his jaw open. He was breathing roughly through the mouth, a slight membrane, a bubble, glistening on his lips. Occasionally, his tongue darted out between his gums.

Mama, behind us, began to cry softly into a scarf.

"Stop it," I said to her. "You'll wake him up."

We kept a vigil at his bedside while he slept. When he woke, an hour later, he said, "I must speak to Vladimir Grigorevich. Ask him to wait for me in my study."

I squeezed his hand, now limp and wet. "He is not here, Papa," I whispered. "He's in Meshcherskoye. You will see him there next week."

What brought about Papa's recovery, I suspect, was the upcoming trip to Meshcherskoye. He simply had to see Chertkov again. And Mama, to my amazement, announced that she was not going with us. She knew Papa wanted a few days of peace beside his "beloved Chertkov."

I began to worry about Mama. She seems so fragile and with-drawn. And Papa worried, too. It was most unlike us.

"We can't possibly leave her here alone," he said. "Of course I'd rather go without her. But this won't do."

"Let me ask Varvara to stay with her. She'll alert us if anything goes wrong. Please, Papa."

It was hard to convince him, but he agreed when Varvara seemed happy enough to stay behind. She does not, herself, find Chertkov's company amusing. "He is a bore," she said. "And he hates women."

The visit to Meshcherskoye, for me, was not the same without Varvara. It's painful for me to separate from her, even for a brief time. But I promised to write every day. Somehow, the thought of being able to write affectionate letters made the separation bearable, even attractive.

The night before we left, I stole into Varvara's room when the house was sleeping and lay my head on her shoulder; I nestled beside her for an hour or more, listening to her breathe, watching the rhythmical swell of her breast like waves cresting offshore, plunging onto shingle, gathering, cresting again. Her hand folded a lock of my hair backward and forward. It was lovelier than sleep.

The next morning we left on horseback, riding to the Tula station in a small pack like a gang of thieves. There were three of us besides Papa: Dushan Makovitsky, Bulgakov, and a servant, Ilya Vasilyevna. Papa led us forward like a Cossack charging into battle.

Papa reined in his horse at the prison in Tula, a small white building with tiny, depressing windows covered with an iron grate. He shook his head.

"Gusev was imprisoned there," Dushan Makovitsky said to Bulgakov, who wants to know everything. Dushan recalled other Tolstoyans who had spent time in that oppressive building, and Papa laughed suddenly, describing the place as his "very own jail."

We rode all day in a cramped second-class compartment, arriving at Meshcherskoye in time for dinner. It is a simple house—unadorned, rather ugly. It's dirty, too. Followers of Papa jammed the hallways, disciples recruited by Chertkov from intellectual circles in Moscow and St. Petersburg, a motley band of young dreamers. Many of them are frauds. But Papa delighted in their company, pouring himself into their midst, chatting freely, answering questions, offering counsel and criticism. Attention, for him, is like sunlight on a plant. He comes alive in the warm rays.

At dinner, as is the custom with Chertkov, we all sat *en famille*, including the servants. But the servants sat gloomily at one end of the table, saying nothing. Ilya would not countenance sitting at the same table as "the Count" and huddled by himself in a dark corner. Papa took him a plate of vegetables, a slice of goat cheese, and a piece of black bread. Everyone watched in awe.

"It is like Christ washing the feet of his disciples," said Dushan Makovitsky in my ear, whose gift for the obvious is spectacular.

During the meal, Papa was asked what to read.

"Disregard all literature written during the last sixty years!" he answered.

"What do you recommend to them?" Vladimir Grigorevich asked. "Pushkin, perhaps?" He was supremely happy, with Tolstoy at his table, his followers about him.

"Yes, and Gogol, too. Gogol is superb. And foreign writers. I recommend Rousseau, Hugo, and Dickens. As usual, most Russians want to read only what is new. They grow quite breathless at the mention of What's-his-name . . . Grut—Mut—Knut Hamsun! They rave about Ibsen and Bjørnson. But to know Rousseau and Hugo only by hearsay, by an entry in the encyclopedia!"

Normally, Papa is keen on looking things up in the encyclopedia. He has the entire Brockhaus Efron beside his desk, and he consults it almost daily. He adores reading about strange countries and customs, packing away bits of knowledge for later use. Long ago he realized that, for the sake of an argument, there is no substitute for facts. You can silence an opponent quickly with the right information.

You can also command the attention of a group by citing statistics and dispensing pieces of erudition. In keeping with this, Papa soon began talking about the island of Formosa, which has interested him recently.

"It's an island that the Japanese have just captured," he explained to the company, most of whom took frantic notes, hoping to catch every utterance in their penciled scrawls. "Imagine! The island is full of cannibals! Eaters of human flesh!" Papa's eyeballs widened like saucers.

"Cannibalism is evil," said Dushan Makovitsky.

Papa grinned. "My friend Trubetskoy says that cannibalism is a kind of civilization, too. Cannibals, you know, maintain that they eat only savages. Most of us, I think, would be included in their definition."

There was a look of mixed confusion and mortification on all faces, though Bulgakov laughed out loud. Too loud, in fact. Chertkov's minions do not dare laugh in his presence.

"Leo Nikolayevich has quite a sense of humor," Chertkov noted with a grimace.


▓ We had intended to stay only a week or so, but Papa showed not even the slightest interest in curbing his visit. He was enjoying himself too much. He began to write stories every morning, completing two in three days. If he were free from the tensions of Yasnaya Polyana, he might well begin writing novels again.

He also finished a preface to his *Thoughts on Life*, a collection of his work assembled by Chertkov, who never tires of that sort of thing. Reading over the preface, Vladimir Grigorevich said, "I like it very much, Leo Nikolayevich. But you should change one phrase. You write about the need for us to cultivate a 'love of God and other beings.' What you mean, surely, is 'a consciousness of God.' "

I did not like Chertkov's presumption. He thinks he understands Papa's work better than Papa. This is one of the things about him that annoys Mama beyond description.

I went riding with Papa and Chertkov one day, and we stopped to visit an asylum. Papa is fascinated by the insane. He says they are closer to God than we are.

Papa noted, "The doctors clearly regard the insane quite objectively, as medical cases, not as human beings for whom they must show pity. They are the material with which they work. I suppose it must be so, otherwise they would become demoralized."

Everyone listened to Papa's observations, nodding eagerly when he was done. I was a little embarrassed by their false attitude.

Papa asked the patients about their religious sentiments. He asked one gaunt, elderly man with no teeth and wild, yellow hair if he believed in God.

"I am an atom of God," the man replied.

My father shook his head in assent, then asked the same question of a fat, oily-skinned woman, who said, "I do not believe in God. I believe in science. God and science cannot exist together."

Papa was taken by the clarity of her remark and asked Chertkov to write it down so that he could record it later in his diary.

That afternoon, before dinner, a delegation of children from the local orphanage came to Chertkov's house with flowers for Papa. He greeted them with affection, kissing the little girls and rubbing his knuckles over the boys' shaven heads. Chertkov appeared from the next room carrying a boxful of photographs of Papa on horseback. He passed them out to the children, who received them in silent gratitude.

"Is this you?" one of the smaller girls asked my father.

"I'm afraid I cannot deny it," he said. He bent to kiss her on the forehead, but she withdrew. "An old man is a very ugly thing," he said.

The next day we received the news that Chertkov would be allowed to return to Telyatinki on a temporary basis. Papa quivered with joy. He wrung his hands, both blood-bright, and shifted from foot to foot like a schoolboy. I liked seeing him so happy.

Chertkov speculated, quite rightly, that this temporary permission will probably be extended indefinitely if he does not publish "inflammatory" pieces. Such strictures are distasteful to him, he said, but he understands the practical need to be close to Yasnaya Polyana and will "behave" himself.

"That's like asking an ass not to brae," Papa said.

Chertkov assumed his usual arctic stare. He can hardly bear it when Papa teases him.

At last the weather grew heavy, with storm clouds swirling in the sky. It was raining hard, a diagonal June rain that turned the garden behind Meshcherskoye into black mud. That night, after dinner, a telegram arrived from Varvara. It startled the entire company: "Sofya Andreyevna's nerves dreadful. Insomnia, weeping. Pulse is 100. Please telegraph."

I felt sorry for Varvara. Mama was putting unnatural pressure on her, trying to pull her into the expanding web of madness that she spins for herself.

Two hours later, as we drank glasses of tea by a fire, a second telegram arrived, from Mama herself: "I beg of you, hurry back. Tomorrow."

I took Papa off by himself into his room. "You must not give in to her," I told him.

"She is unwell."

"She's faking it. She always does this. It's a trick to get you to go home before you're ready."

"I've been here quite a long time."

"A few days! Anyway, Erdenko is coming tonight." Erdenko is the most celebrated violinist in Russia, and Papa cannot resist a good musical performance, even though he disapproves of taking too much pleasure in music.

He wrote a telegram: "More convenient return tomorrow. Unless indispensable."

"I'll send it immediately," I said.

Everyone was pleased with Papa for not giving in. Alas, only a few hours later, a brief reply from Mama was delivered. "Indispensable," she wired.

"You mustn't cave in," I said to Papa. "There will be no end to her demands if she sees that she can force you to come and go at whim."

Papa insisted that she is unwell, not physically but mentally. "She cannot help herself," he said. "It is my duty. I am glad of a chance to do my duty." More to himself than to me, he added, "God help me."

I went to my room and, for the first time in some years, prayed. I prayed for Papa, whose burden grows heavier each day. I sensed that, soon, he would crack under the weight. A man of his age can carry only so much without breaking.

# 2 2

# J. P.

## SONYA: A SESTINA

*On my knees, still praying, by the blackened pond.*
*I watch the moon's bare sickle and the stars*
*that fleck and burn my skin, asking the God*
*of thunder to avenge me now, to cleanse or kill*
*the enemy without, within, to make love*
*blaze like this wild grassfire, searing wind.*

*I feel it rising in the wood, hot wind*
*across the world. It stipples the black pond*
*and wakens what I used to know of love,*
*that whirling zodiac of flinty stars*
*that filled my nights. It's easier to kill*
*now, kill what hurts. To spit at God.*

*What have I come to, railing at my God?*
*Deliver me, O Lord. Let fiery wind*
*rise through my hair. Why should I kill*
*what I love best? I'll float above the pond*

*tonight like moonglow, flaking stars.*
*I'll fill the water, overwhelmed by love.*

*It's what I live for: love, bright love*
*that starts, as always, in the eye of God,*
*then spills through dark, ignites the stars,*
*the fields and forests with its blazing wind*
*and marks the surface of my little pond,*
*a skin of fire. I'd never want to kill*

*what I love best. I may scream* kill
*and kill as Cain did in my heart. But love*
*prevents me, buoys me up. It's like a pond*
*that holds and fills me with the light of God,*
*a love of man. I listen to the wind*
*that scatters, blows, and sparks a billion stars.*

*I'm on my knees still, scattered like the stars.*
*If I am nothing, what is there to kill?*
*I'm piecemeal, pierced, and parcel of the wind,*
*with nothing left to love or not to love.*
*I'm one bright atom in the mind of God,*
*almost extinguished here beside the pond.*

*I'm full of stars and, maybe, full of love.*
*I'll kill whatever in me turns from God,*
*avoids hot wind, the heart's black pond.*

# 2 3

# SOFYA ANDREYEVNA

My chest is so tight I can hardly breathe. At first, I wanted Lyovochka to go to Meshcherskoye. His pulse was sinking. He could remember almost nothing with clarity. I thought the trip to see his beloved would help. Alas, it did. He became well obscenely quickly. It was almost embarrassing to watch him charge to the station in Tula on horseback.

A long absence was not planned. I could have granted him a week or so. But the visit lengthened, and he never said a word about coming back. Didn't he realize how sick I was, with sleeplessness and my rapid heartbeat, my headaches and dizziness?

The bare truth is that my husband, the greatest Russian author since Pushkin, has developed a ludicrous, senile crush on a plump, middle-aged flatterer. As a boy, even as a young man, he was drawn to men. He liked nothing better than his hunting trips. I have talked about this openly, but it makes him indignant. He does not see how foolish it is for a man to love another man. Not only is it foolish, it is sinful in the eyes of God.

Sasha says that I'm fantasizing, but I think Lyovochka would sleep with Chertkov if his conscience could bear it. But it can't. It hovers over him like Father Time, flashing its sickle, making ridiculous demands. He is hounded by Furies, too—demons that pursue him into all corners of his life. It suits him to regard this mania as a visionary religion, but it's nothing more than mental illness.

Religion should be a comfort, not a goad. When I go to the little church in the village, I expect God to calm my nerves. And He does. Otherwise I could not have remained married to Leo Tolstoy for nearly half a century. Nobody could withstand that pressure. It's like living with a tornado.

Chertkov's bitter stare and flabby jowls haunt me when I try to sleep. His smell, his voice, his pudgy fingers—everything about him taunts me, even when he is not here. He would be nothing without my Lyovochka; with him, Chertkov has risen in the world's eyes to the rank of Leo Tolstoy's closest friend, counselor, and publisher. He wears these facts on his shirtsleeves and lapels. "Look at me!" screams from every pore. "I am the beloved of Leo Tolstoy! I am his conscience! His beacon!"

After Lyovochka's death, which cannot be far away, Chertkov will discover who he is. Nobody.

I regard jealousy a defect of character. And I am jealous. I admit it and pray to God for forgiveness. But what does anyone, even God, expect of me? Chertkov has stolen the one thing that has sustained my life for forty-eight years! He has snatched Lyovochka from my arms. My dear, sweet Lyovochka. . . .

Various ways of committing suicide have occurred to me, but I am not the type really. I do not want to die. But I do not want to live like this, either, with the knife of jealousy pushing its hot blade through my heart. This morning I wanted to go to Stolbovo and lie down on the tracks beneath the train on which it was *convenient* for Leo Nikolayevich to return from Meshcherskoye. What irony if the author of *Anna Karenina* should ride home over the pullulating body of his own dear wife! What a story *that* would make for the international press!

I have consulted Florinsky's book on medicine to see what the effects of opium poisoning might be. I do not want a painful death, and death by train sounds dreadful. What if I didn't die instantly? I once saw a dog run over by a heavy cart, its body crushed in the middle of the road. It writhed horribly, trying to drag itself to the edge of the road, bent like a horseshoe. A benevolent muzhik, fortunately, crushed its skull with a large stone, ending its misery. No, that is not for me.

Opium poisoning begins with a feeling of excitement, which soon turns to lethargy. It's a little like freezing to death in the snow. It doesn't really hurt; you just go numb. Eventually, the sky and the earth meet, and your mind becomes your body, and your body turns to air. And there is *no antidote*.

I daresay if I don't succeed in killing myself but do half a job of it, Chertkov will have me committed to an insane asylum. Perhaps then Leo Tolstoy, with his great admiration for the insane, will visit me. Then I shall garner his respect. Not now. I am too sane now. I tell the truth, and it hurts him.

Lyovochka arrived at ten on the twenty-fourth, much later than I wished. It was an act of defiance, of course. Like a little boy who cannot say directly what is angering him. Perhaps without his even knowing it himself, his delay said to me, "See, my dear. You are not so important as you think you are. I do not believe you are ill. But I shall go along with your petty game." Sometimes I feel hatred for him, a black bile that rises in my veins, dragged up through the roots of our ill relations. Sometimes I want to *kill* him.

I wanted to hate him then, but he seemed meek and nervous, frail as a bird, as he sat beside me on the bed, his hand pressed to my forehead.

"Dear Sonya!" he said. "I was so worried about you. Those telegrams had us all frantic."

So. But I did not trust him. He has so often in the past affected great concern when what he usually wanted was sex. Now what he wants is to be let off the hook, to be forgiven for this emotional infidelity he commits repeatedly with Vladimir Grigorevich.

"You want to kill me, don't you?" I asked. "You would prefer that I were dead."

He shook his head. "Nonsense, Sonya. Where do you get such ideas? I don't understand you anymore."

"It's a question of logic, is it? You don't see why B follows A? Is that your problem?"

"You are trying to upset me."

"Do you still love me, Lyovochka?" I asked.

"Yes," he whispered. I waited for him to continue, to expand on this.

He lay down beside me on the bed, putting his broad forehead against my shoulder, and soon we both fell asleep and remained like that through the night. It was altogether strange and caused me to remember our first passionate years together, when it meant so terribly much to feel him beside me, to know that I mattered to him as I had mattered to my father. Once my father went to Paris to attend an international conference of doctors when I was thirteen. He stayed away for three months. And he never wrote me.

The next morning I spoke gently to Lyovochka about Chertkov.

"It is quite insane, darling," I said, nestling beside him. "Everyone is making fun of you."

"Who?"

"Andrey, Sukhotin, even the muzhiks. I heard them giggling in the horse barn one day, and I listened at the door. They were talking about you. Yes, about you!"

"It matters very little what anyone says about me. Let them giggle if they find it amusing."

"I don't find it amusing. I find it sick."

"You don't know what you're talking about," he said, sitting up in bed, kicking back the blankets.

"I know what's not normal. You're obsessed with that man. You hang on his every word, as if God spoke through his mouth!"

"He is a dear friend, and we have much in common." He was putting on his leather boots. "In any case, I do not find it a subject worth discussing. We have been over this ground before, Sonya. So many times. . . ."

"You and that man have nothing in common. He's a sycophant and a pervert. He's just using you, but you can't seem to see it. It may not bother you, but I will not have such a person making a fool of my husband!"

He spat at the floor—I can't remember when he last did that. "Let me alone," he said, "for God's sake!"

I watched as he snapped the door shut behind him, leaving me alone. More alone than I have ever been. I wanted my bottle of opium.

I went downstairs, into the library. I don't know exactly how long I waited there, on my knees like a scrubwoman, trying to work up the courage to swallow the fateful substance. I should have done it instantly.

It was Sasha who found me.

"What idiotic thing is this, Mama?" she said, as if it were nothing. Just Mama on her knees with a little opium in her hands.

"One swallow, please! Just one!" I said, waving the vial before my lips.

She tried to grab it from my hands, but I closed my fists about it. "It's mine! It's mine!" I could hear myself saying, as if someone else were talking.

"So drink it," she said. "Suit yourself."

The ungrateful bitch.

"You disgust me," I said.

I fell on the floor, hardly able to breathe. The vial spilled, and the smell of the opium surrounded me. Three servants lifted me into bed, one of them the ghostly Timothy, whose eyes quiver with the perpetual fury of a bastard. I was examined by Dushan Makovitsky, who kept muttering to himself as if I were not present. He is a nasty little cur.

My husband feigned concern, as he must. He is too cowardly to say outright that he finds me repulsive. But he does. The very sight of me sours his stomach.

"Do you love me, Lyovochka?" I asked him.

"Yes, I do," he said. "Nothing can stop that."

"Then fetch me your diary. I want to read what you're writing about me. I must have the truth."

"What makes you think there is anything to read that concerns you?"

"I want to read your diary," I repeated, coolly. He looked like the sky had fallen on his shoulders. "I have no secrets," he said. "My relations with you are public knowledge. I doubt if there is one muzhik in Russia who does not know everything about us."

The diary was brought to me by a servant, Leo Tolstoy not being man enough to bring it himself. My fingers, twitching uncontrollably, turned the thick pages. It was almost too much to bear. Almost at once the telltale sentence snapped its beak like a prehistoric bird, ugly and devouring: "I must try to fight Sonya consciously, with kindness and love."

I called for my husband, repeating the sentence in my head like a death knell: *I must try to fight Sonya consciously, with kindness and love.*

He stood in the doorway, meek, almost insubstantial.

I glared at him.

"Yes, darling?"

"Why do you want to fight me? What is it I've done to deserve such treatment?"

"I see nothing in what I've written that should upset you."

"Let me see your other diaries. I want to read all your diaries from the last ten years."

"I'm afraid that's impossible." He looked away from me as he spoke.

"Where are they, Lyovochka? Where have you hidden them?"

"I have not hidden them."

"Are they here?"

"No."

"Does Chertkov have them?"

"Please, Sonya. I . . . I—"

"I knew it! He is greedily reading everything you have said about me. This is despicable. Have I not been an honest, loving wife for all these years? Answer me, Lyovochka!"

It began raining hard against the house, the wind blowing in through the curtains. The room grew hot and damp, and the day fell dark.

"I don't mind telling you the truth," he said, after a difficult pause. "Chertkov certainly has them. I gave them to him for safekeeping."

"This is the worst thing you have ever done to me," I said.

My stomach was sick now. I wanted to vomit. I threw off the covers and ran from the bedroom, down the slippery stairwell, out into the rain. For an hour I wandered in the orchard, blind with misery, but nobody came for me. They all hoped I would die. That was just what they wanted, but I was not about to grant them that satisfaction. I came home shivering, wet as moss, and crawled into bed like a child beaten once too many times.

Voices drifted into my room from down the hall. My husband was talking with Dushan Makovitsky. I could faintly make out his words. "The insane are always better at achieving their purposes than the sane," he was saying. "They have no morality to hold them back. They have no shame, no conscience."

The very next day, Bulgakov told me the horrifying news that spelled—in essence—the end of my life. Chertkov had been granted permission to return to Telyatinki to visit his mother. He could stay as long as his mother remains in the province. Indeed, he was already there, plotting and scheming only a few versts from Yasnaya Polyana.

On the morning of the twenty-eighth, while everyone was asleep, Chertkov slipped through a deep mist that stood in the fields, the thick morning mist of midsummer that snags in the pine trees of Zasyeka, that blankets the isbas, a mist like sleep itself, a swirl on the cool Voronka. He came into our house like a thief and woke the kitchen servants, insisting that tea be brought to him in the parlor.

Lyovochka was wakened by Ilya, the servant boy, and he came bounding down the stairwell like a bridegroom on his wedding day. I know this even though I did not see it. Once you have seen the moon, you know what it looks like.

When I came into the parlor, Vladimir Grigorevich bowed with revolting politeness. He remains a dandy, in spite of the Tolstoyan overlays. His britches were made in England, and his red cashmere socks were distinctly un-Tolstoyan. He affected a blue linen blouse—the kind the muzhiks wear to church.

"Good morning, Sofya Andreyevna. I am delighted to see you," he said.

He handed me a note:

*I understand that you have in recent days been speaking of me as an enemy. I do hope this feeling can be attributed to some passing annoyance, caused by a misunderstanding that person-to-person communication will dispel like a bad dream. Since Leo Nikolaye-vich represents, for both of us, what we consider most valuable in life, a substantial, inevitable bond must already have formed be-tween us.*

Feeling lost and stupefied, I went back to my room and wept. Chertkov had doubtless shown this letter to Lyovochka, who would have said to himself, "See! Vladimir Grigorevich is bending over backward to befriend her. He is being generous and openhearted." He cannot see that Chertkov is trying to hoodwink us both.

Three days later, Chertkov walked brazenly into the dining room during the midday meal. My husband became wildly solicitous, as if the tsar himself had arrived unexpectedly. He dragged a chair from the wall for him, offering him anything he might like. "What will it be, my dearest dear, my lovely Vladimir Grigorevich? My wife's heart on a platter? Her kidneys? With salt? But of course, my dear Vladimir

Grigorevich! Whatever pleases you! You would like the estate, is that it? Fine! And permanent copyright on everything I've ever written? Certainly!''

I tried, with difficulty, to sit through the meal, but they had no interest in my company. After the first course, I excused myself by saying that a headache was coming on (it was) and left the room. Upstairs, I settled at my desk to write in my diary. It was July 1. The hottest day yet. In the past, writing in my diary relieved certain feelings. Now, I could think of nothing to say.

Chertkov stayed through the afternoon and remained for dinner. I pretended not to care. Indeed, I was as polite as could be, inquiring after his mother's health, his various projects. I showed interest in his wretched publishing company, the very company that is stealing my children's inheritance. It surprised me that I could remain so cool in the face of such an outrage.

The entire table normally retires to the library for coffee or tea at the end of the meal. Tonight, Sasha furtively whisked Chertkov and her father into the study. I could see that they were plotting. They are always plotting. The whole thing cut and tore at my nerves. I hate it when people lack the courage to tell me what evil deeds they have concocted behind my back. . . .

I tiptoed to the study, where they had shut the door firmly. Lyovochka never shuts his door. It is always ajar, as if to say, "Yes, I am working, but you may knock and enter."

As I listened, my worst fears were confirmed. They were whispering, and my heart stopped when, above the low rustle of language, I heard my name.

My heart caught between beats; I thought surely I would faint when Sasha said, clearly, "Of course, Mama would kill us if she found out." And Chertkov hushed her. They waited, panicky, for a long time, as if listening for footsteps. But I did not move.

When they resumed their whispering, I fled downstairs, where I sat in the parlor with a glass of vodka, burning inside. I resolved to climb onto the balcony where the door, with its venetian slats, might allow me to hear what they were planning. It was information that might be crucial to the welfare of my family.

There is a narrow ledge running along the second floor, and it is possible to slip along the building if you keep your back pressed tightly to the wall. Squeezing through a window, I was able to edge my way along the wall. My weight, unfortunately, is such that the balance was precarious. At several points I swayed forward, almost swooning. Soon I stood exactly outside Lyovochka's study.

I listened at the blinds. Their voices, though hushed, could be clearly discerned through the lathwork.

"I cannot do it," said Lyovochka.

"Papa, I think he is right. You must listen to him. He has in mind only your best interests."

"The interests of the people," Chertkov added. "Which are, of course, identical with the best interests of Leo Nikolayevich."

Here were my enemies, huddled and scheming, inventing their little plots. It was all too horrific. Suddenly I lost my balance; the ground tilted over my ankles, or seemed to tilt, and I shrieked.

"Who's there?" shouted my daughter. Her voice was harsh, bitter, unforgiving.

I went bowling through the latched shutters, flung like a turnkey by the weight of gravity. My skirts fluttered up over my shoulders. I was upside down, peering at the assembled company from between my thighs. "You're all plotting against me!" I shouted. "In my own house, too!"

My husband slumped in his chair, staring ahead weirdly.

"You will kill him, Mama," Sasha said smugly. "But that's what you want, isn't it? You *want* him to die!"

She left me standing there by myself as Ilya, the houseboy, and Chertkov carried Lyovochka out of the room.

When Chertkov returned, he seemed more ferocious than I have ever seen him. The putty of his cheeks blazed like newly fired clay.

I said, "Vladimir Grigorevich, I know exactly what you're trying to do. Don't think that you deceive me for one little moment. I want my husband's diaries back. Return them immediately to this house, where they belong. In the name of God!"

"What are you afraid of?"

"You're the Devil himself," I said.

He looked beyond me to a far corner of the room. "Had I cared to, I could have demolished you and your family. It would have been only too easy, you know. The press is bloodthirsty."

I wish to God my husband could have heard him talking then, the real Chertkov.

"Go ahead," I said. "Ruin us. Tell them anything you like."

"I have too much respect for Leo Nikolayevich to attempt such a thing. You are lucky."

"I detest you, Vladimir Grigorevich." My lips quivered. I could barely contain myself.

"If I had a wife like you," he said, moving toward the door, "I would have blown my brains out a long time ago. Or gone to America."

That night, in bed, I dreamt that my husband and Vladimir Grigorevich were lying on the wet forest floor of Zasyeka, naked, writhing in the dead leaves: an old man, white haired, with a beard of snow, engaged with his fat-faced, oily disciple in an act of monstrous intercourse. They wriggled in the mud like worms.

I woke with a start, pooled in sweat. Trembling, I knelt at the side of my bed and prayed, aloud, "God, dear God. Have mercy on me, a sinner."

# 24

# BULGAKOV

I don't know how long I can allow this double life to continue. In the presence of Leo Nikolayevich, I pretend my private life is beyond reproach. That is, I avoid the subject altogether. He assumes (or I assume that he assumes) that I live according to his principles, since I have vocally supported them and written about them, too, with enthusiasm. But this little deceit, and the nearly invisible contradictions in my life, trouble me.

I do not consider myself immoral. A man must follow his own conscience, and while the Tolstoyans oppose sexual relations outside of marriage (indeed, Leo Nikolayevich has grave doubts about the morality of sex *within* marriage), I find myself more in accord with Plato, who said that one can progress from sexual love to spiritual love. Ideally, one should not have to suffer a split between body and soul.

I do love Masha. My life has changed utterly since we met. But it has become difficult for us to maintain our love at Telyatinki. Sergeyenko hardly speaks to me now. He shuns Masha completely, rudely, and she has become exasperated. Yesterday she spoke of leaving for St. Petersburg, where a Tolstoyan enclave has just been started by a group of her former acquaintances.

"My intent was never to stay here for longer than a few months. When Chertkov invited me to come, he was quite explicit about this," she said.

"Nobody ever worries about that kind of thing here."

"*I* worry about it."

"Sergeyenko ought to be shot."

"You don't mean it, Valya. He isn't nearly so rude as you imagine. You think everyone is shunning us. It's not true."

I could not convince her. She is so imperturbable, so clear-eyed in the face of a storm.

I would spend more time with her if I could, but that has become impossible. Leo Nikolayevich needs me badly at present, and he prefers that I stay overnight at Yasnaya Polyana. He wants me there so that he can escape from the family tensions, I suspect. Chertkov has become nothing less than obsessive lately, coming up with new schemes every week for booklets, pamphlets, anthologies, selections. I doubt the purity of his motives, but Leo Nikolayevich doesn't. He agrees eagerly with Chertkov about everything.

Sofya Andreyevna has been of no help. She discovers plots where none exist. Indeed, she imagines that Chertkov is trying to have her and the children written out of the will, as if Leo Nikolayevich could ever do such a thing.

Chertkov may be something of a prig and a bore, but he is not cruel. On the other hand, without religion to restrain him, I suspect he could be barbarous. There is a peculiar heartlessness in his laugh.

Sofya Andreyevna is obsessed with regaining possession of her husband's diaries. Leo Nikolayevich no doubt writes truthfully about the flux of their relations, but she does not want posterity to have access to this information.

"Can you understand why this bothers me so much?" she asked me last night, as I brought her tea.

"Yes, I can," I said. "But you mustn't think that Leo Nikolayevich would consciously distort the nature of your marriage in his diaries. The truth means everything to him."

"He thinks he's honest, but he doesn't know himself very well. He doesn't realize, for instance, that he loves Chertkov and despises me. He thinks he loves me. But you should see the kind of things he writes about me. These will delight future biographers. They will say, 'Poor Leo Tolstoy . . . dragged down by a jealous, foolish, possessive, and extravagant wife who could not possibly share his lofty intellectual or moral life.' "

"Isn't that Englishman, Aylmer Maude, at work on a biography?" I asked, knowing the answer already. "He is said to be a fair-minded person. He knows you well—and the truth of your relations with your husband."

"He is no better than the rest of them."

I begged to differ, recalling a letter that Leo Nikolayevich had written to Maude only a couple of weeks before. In that letter, he chastised Maude for not appreciating the importance of Chertkov, "the man who for many years has been my best helper and friend." Maude fully appreciates Leo Nikolayevich's overly high estimation of Chertkov. His work will set the record straight on these matters. In fact, Chertkov is terrified of what Maude will write.

Last night, once again, Sofya did her ritual dance, racing from the house, half naked, because her husband would not immediately turn over the diaries. But nobody pays much attention to these wild displays anymore. My impulse was to say, To hell with her. If she drowns herself in the pond, so be it. Life will be easier around here. But I cannot help feeling terribly sorry for her. Her life is made miserable by circumstances beyond her control.

When she did not return for some time, Leo Nikolayevich came into the sitting room, where I was reading, and asked me to search for her. His son Leo said he would join me but insisted his father accompany us. "What right do you have to lie in a warm bed when your wife is wandering the woods, driven insane by your obstinacy?" he asked.

"All right," Leo Nikolayevich responded wearily. "I will go with you."

I split from them to go through the orchard, while they trudged off into the fields. They found her by a stream, delirious, and coaxed her home. It is by now a familiar scene, and very little was said. But I realized that things at Yasnaya Polyana are nearing a conclusion.

The effects of all this on Leo Nikolayevich are painfully evident. His speech is frequently slurred, and he hobbles from room to room with a cane. His writing slowed to a dribble before it stopped altogether. Chertkov became panicky. Tanya was summoned. Her presence becalms the Tolstoy household. Leo Nikolayevich loves her dearly, and he quickened visibly when I told him she was coming. "Wonderful news," he said. "I'm so glad. Thank you, thank you so much!"

It was odd, him thanking me.


▓ "I'm not asking for a great deal, am I? All I want is for Chertkov to return the diaries to me," Sofya Andreyevna said to her daughter Tanya, who had called a family summit in her father's study the morning after her arrival. "If he wants to copy them, that's all right. But I insist on keeping the originals."

"Is there anything wrong with this, Papa?" Tanya asked.

By now the whole subject disgusted him. "Do what you like. Take the diaries. I want peace in my house. That's all I want now. Peace. . . ."

Pleased by his quick concession, Sofya Andreyevna set off for Telyatinki in a droshky. At her request, I accompanied her, aware that Sergeyenko and Chertkov would read my presence as an act of alliance. But I have, by now, given up hope of appeasing anyone.

The day sizzled, and Sofya Andreyevna looked like an empress, her white dress reflecting the sun off its many folds. Everything she does is calculated for effect, and today she was determined to shine. Chertkov's mother—the queen of Telyatinki when she's in residence—

received us ceremoniously, ordering her personal servant to bring the samovar. We were ushered into the bare sitting room, which smelled of floor wax and burnt candles. Sofya Andreyevna looked mildly askance at the books and manuscripts piled on the floor. Chertkov came fluttering into the room, bowing and purring. He understood that a personal visit from the Countess Tolstoy could only mean trouble.

Sofya Andreyevna was left alone with Chertkov's mother, while I was ushered into Sergeyenko's study. Vladimir Grigorevich stood rigidly behind Sergeyenko, a general looking over the shoulder of his field commander.

"Sit down, Valentin Fedorovich," he said, nodding in the direction of a straight-backed chair.

"It's delightful to see you both," I said.

Sergeyenko frowned. "What is going on?" he asked. "Why is she here?"

"We are not her favorite people," Chertkov added. He did not chuckle.

"She feels that Leo Nikolayevich's diaries belong to her, and she wants them back. But she says that you may copy them, if you like. It's the originals that interest her."

"You told her they were here?" Chertkov asked.

"I assumed that you had them with you," I said. "Was I mistaken?"

Chertkov's face crumpled like a piece of paper.

"You may join the ladies, Valentin Fedorovich," he said.

"I hope I didn't make matters worse," I said.

I hated myself for saying that before the sentence had passed my lips. I have been trying, throughout this ordeal, to behave as straightforwardly as possible. When you are dealing with people who are suspicious by nature, you must take care to say only what is obviously true. Speculative remarks only invite further fantasies.

"Go next door and have tea," Chertkov ordered. The remark infuriated me. I did not take this position to be treated like a child.

When Chertkov and Sergeyenko joined us in the sitting room, Sofya Andreyevna stood boldly. "Let me get to the point, Vladimir Grigorevich. I must insist upon the return of my husband's diaries. I do not wish to be your enemy. I am glad that my husband has a friend such as you—someone who understands and shares his ideas. All I want is this little favor—the return of his diaries. If you will grant me this, I assure you that we can be friends. We *should* be friends, as you have said yourself, since we have so many common interests."

I marveled at her self-possession.

"You are very kind, Sofya Andreyevna. And I am glad that you have, at last, honored us with a visit. But I'm afraid I cannot help you with regard to the diaries. I can act only upon your husband's directions."

With this, Sofya Andreyevna bid them all good-bye, harshly, and summoned her driver.

"Are you coming with me, Valentin Fedorovich?" she asked.

Chertkov looked at me impassively.

"Will Leo Nikolayevich be needing me this afternoon?"

"You know better than I."

It had been a mistake to hesitate.

"I'll be back later," I said to Sergeyenko. "After dinner."

"Masha will be delighted," he sneered.

Sofya Andreyevna looked at me knowingly, while Chertkov simply stared, his eyes as narrow as the tip of a pen.

In the droshky, Sofya Andreyevna turned to me coyly. "Have you been keeping something from me, Valentin Fedorovich? I should hope not. We have become close friends."

"It is nothing," I said.

"A young woman in your life is nothing?"

"Masha is a close friend."

"A lover?"

"A good friend."

"That sounds serious."

Friendship is always serious, I thought, irritated by her meddling.

"I didn't mean to annoy you," she said.

"I'm not annoyed."

"You forget that I'm an experienced reader," she said. "I can read your face, every letter. The script is beautifully clear."

Did I blush or merely imagine that my entire body flamed? I said, "My relations with Masha are somewhat painful, just now. I don't really want to talk about them."

"Do you love her?"

"Yes."

"Don't fret, my dear!" she said. "I shall *not* tell the great man." She paused. "I suppose you know about his past. He was a whore-monger in his youth, insatiable. He has hardly ever had much self-control in this regard. Why else would he protest so violently? He doesn't want anyone else to do what he's been doing for sixty years!"

What could I say? Sofya Andreyevna knows far more than I do about the sexual history of Leo Tolstoy, although the general pattern of his life is familiar. He has never troubled to hide the facts of his early life. "I was a sinful young man," he once told me. "Obsessed with sexual longings, overcome by animal desire. Only a long struggle has rid me of these things." That's what he says, though I have noticed his eyes grow lively whenever a young servant girl enters the room.

▓ This afternoon I spent several hours in the Remington room with Sasha, answering letters. Leo Nikolayevich is so upset that he does not even want to sign, let alone revise, our responses. I feel strange, occasionally, as I write letters in his name. It's as though I am Leo Tolstoy. Somehow, the letters don't seem like forgeries. When I write as Tolstoy, I *am* Tolstoy. His spirit, like that of other men and women, is simply a demarcation of the human spirit, which in itself is a de-marcation of the larger spirit, the God-spirit; in death, the demarca-tions end. We become, to use Emerson's phrase, part of the Oversoul.

We touch this God-spirit in daily life, too, during blessed moments, moments of affection, of peculiar insight, of fierce candor. The spirit of Leo Tolstoy is capacious, allowing easy entry. I left Yasnaya Polyana tonight feeling more like Tolstoy than myself.

I gradually reentered the spirit of Bulgakov as I approached Telyatinki. The sun burned on the hay fields, flamed in the elms, and turned the red earth redder under my horse's gallop. I saw Masha standing in the back garden, alone, her shadow long on the grass. My groin began to ache, to swell before I could even see her face.

We said nothing to each other but walked, hand in hand, into the balsam wood behind the house. The forest was like a flame ball, with the sunset shattering through a thousand needles. The ground smelled cool, rich but cool, with its mauve mat of pine.

Standing between the tall and immensely thick trunks of two red pines, we looked at each other for a long time, saying nothing.

But there was something I wanted to say to her. I didn't know how to say it. I was afraid to say it, since once it got said, we were stuck with it. It would either flap there in the wind like a loose shutter, an annoyance, or something definite and palpable would happen.

"I love you, Masha," I said.

The words floated in the air, like a balloon, a bright, shimmering bubble. I waited for it to pop into nothingness, to disappear. For a terrible moment, I felt as though I hadn't said it aloud, that the words had formed, cloudlike, in my head without condensing into utterance.

"I'm glad," she replied.

But there was an aloofness there. She wasn't glad. Not entirely.

"Are you really?"

"If I weren't glad, I wouldn't have said that, would I?"

"It's just that . . . you had to respond."

"I don't have to do anything."

I felt a twinge of panic. Masha has this cool edge, a blade of Damascus steel, which she flashes on occasion.

"Valya," she said. "I don't know what to say. I don't want to hurt you. Do you know that?"

"You hurt me when you say nothing. I dislike it when I can't tell what you're thinking. When I can't seem to find you."

Was she weeping? Slightly. Her eyes caught the evening sun and absorbed its redness. They were watery, as many-sided as a gem. Her blond hair, too, turned a little pink in the strange, beautiful light. I wanted to touch that hair. I let my palm graze the delicate substance. I could feel the roundness of her head, its solid, gourdlike shape, beneath the long strands. I kissed her. I let myself breathe what came before me, the barely fathomable presence of another human being. It seemed impossibly magical. I lifted my hands onto her small shoulders, and I pulled her close.

"I've got to return to Petersburg," she said finally. "Soon."

"For good?"

"Perhaps not."

"I don't understand, Masha . . . now that we—"

"I know that you love me, Valya."

"I do."

"It's difficult for me to respond to you. We've only just begun to know each other."

"That's true, but—"

"You seem young to me."

"I'm older than you are!"

"Our pasts are what matter. I feel like I've lived so many lives already."

"Masha, that's nonsense. Your life is just beginning."

"In other circumstances, I think I'd have been much . . . warmer. I feel my own coolness, and I don't like it. I hate it, in fact. It's not what I mean to happen."

Her honesty overwhelmed me. And the exact, riveting way she spoke. I felt mute, stupid, even silly beside her. I could hardly hope to respond in kind. It wasn't that I couldn't be honest with her. Rather, I had almost nothing to be honest *about*.

"I love you," I said. "You can't go away."

She smiled at me.

"Perhaps I'll go away for a brief while. I can return to Telyatinki whenever I want. I spoke to Chertkov last night, and he was sympathetic. He was actually kind."

Chertkov remains incomprehensible to me. Whatever Masha or Leo Nikolayevich think, I would never trust him.

Masha touched my hair. It was the first gesture from her that I could really take as an expression of natural and unaffected love.

Her head fell against my shoulder.

"I need you," I said.

"I know you do," she said. "I know."

# 2 5

# L. N.

## LETTER TO
## SOFYA ANDREYEVNA

YASNAYA POLYANA, 14 JUNE 1910

My dear Sonya,

1. I promise to give nobody the diary I am writing at this time. I shall keep it with me.

2. I shall ask for the return of my previous diaries from Chertkov, then I shall keep them, probably in a bank.

3. If it worries you that unfriendly biographers will, in the future, make use of those pages written in the heat of the moment registering our conflicts and struggles, I would remind you, first, that these expressions of passing emotion, in my diary as in yours, cannot pretend to present an accurate portrait of our relations. Nevertheless, if it still worries you, I shall happily take this opportunity to say, in my diary or in this letter, what my relations with you were really like and what your life has been, as I have seen it.

My relations with you and view of your life are as follows: just as I loved you when you were young, I have never stopped loving you in spite of the many causes of alienation between us. And so I continue to love you. Putting aside the issue of our sexual relations, which have ceased (a fact that can only add to the sincerity of our expressions of love), those causes were as follows: first, my growing need to withdraw from society, something which you neither would nor could follow me in, since the principles that led me to adopt my convictions opposed yours in quite basic ways. This seems, to me, perfectly natural and I cannot hold it against you. Further, in recent years, you have become increasingly irritable, even despotic and uncontrollable. This could hardly help but inhibit any display of feeling on my part, even cut off those feelings themselves. That is my second point. Third, the chief and fatal cause was something of which we are both innocent: our completely opposing ideas of the significance and purpose of life. For me, property is a sin, for you it is a necessary condition. In order not to have to separate myself from you, I have forced myself to accept circumstances that I find painful. Yet you saw my acceptance as a concession to your point of view, and this only increased our misunderstanding.

As for my view of your life, here it is:

I, a debauched person by nature, deeply depraved in my sexual appetite, and no longer in my first youth, married you, a girl of eighteen who was spiritually pure, good, and intelligent. In spite of my dreadful past, you stayed with me for nearly fifty years, loving me, living a life full of worry and anguish, giving birth to children, raising them, caring for them, and nursing me, without succumbing to any of the temptations that a beautiful, solid, and healthy woman is always exposed to; indeed, your life has been such that I have absolutely nothing to reproach you with. As for the fact that your moral development did not run parallel to mine, which has been unique, I cannot hold this against you, since the inner life of any person is a secret between that person and God, and nobody else can call that person to account in any way. I have been intolerant of you. I was deeply mistaken, and I confess my error.

4. If my relations with Chertkov upset you too much at present, I am willing to give him up, though I must say that to do so would be more unpleasant, even painful, for him than for me. But if you demand this of me, I shall comply.

5. If you do not accept these terms for a quiet and decent life, I shall withdraw my promise not to leave you. I shall simply go away, and not to Chertkov, you can rest assured! In fact, I would lay down as an absolute condition that he must not follow and settle near me. But go I certainly shall, for I simply can't continue to live like this. I might well have continued with this life had I been able to look at all your sufferings unmoved, but I'm not capable of that.

Stop, my dove, tormenting not only those around you but yourself, for you suffer a hundred times more than they do. That is all.

# 2 6

# CHERTKOV

Dr. Nikitin brought the infamous Rossolimo down from Moscow to examine Sofya Andreyevna. Her attempts at suicide have upset the household, and Leo Nikolayevich insists that Makovitsky's advice be followed. Makovitsky puts considerable store in these head doctors, and Rossolimo is accounted the best of them; he has made excursions into the minds of every grand duke and duchess in Russia. Even the Dowager Empress Maria Fyodorovna, an intimate of my mother, has consulted him over a matter of some peculiar dreams. Rossolimo is what he is: an Italian and a mountebank. I distrust anyone who affects a waxed mustache with twirled ends or who dresses like the head-waiter of a Roman trattoria.

Rossolimo examined Sofya Andreyevna for two hours, peering into her eyes with instruments like sextants, tapping her joints with a tiny wooden hammer, asking her improbable questions. Leo Niko-layevich looked on in awe. He has on occasion expressed what I consider an inordinate faith in doctors, but Rossolimo is the limit. Leo Nikolayevich took me aside. "Rossolimo is astonishingly stupid," he said, "in the way of all scientists." I listened intently as he paced the floor but offered no comment. I tread lightly these days. "I don't know why Dushan brought him down here."

"Perhaps they are old friends," I said.

Before tea, Rossolimo talked with Leo Nikolayevich. "I have determined the causes of her mental illness," he said. "The countess is suffering from double degeneracy: paranoiac and hysterical, chiefly the former." He went on to cite the economic, cultural, physiological, and biological sources of her problem, while Leo Nikolayevich drummed his fingers on his desk, yawning violently.

"What about lack of faith? Surely that has some bearing on her condition?"

"Indeed," Rossolimo said. "The want of a fulcrum is often a source of instability."

"A metaphor, Doctor!" Leo Nikolayevich cried. "This is much to your credit."

Rossolimo seemed quite happy now, having been praised by the greatest author in all of Russia. "Indeed, a ship without a rudder is no ship, is it?"

"Certainly not," Leo Nikolayevich said. "Nor is a windmill without the wind."

Rossolimo was not sure what Leo Nikolayevich meant by this, but he agreed that wind is essential for all windmills and quickly changed the subject to hot-air balloons, a topic of some interest to him but none to us. After a big meal, he left Yasnaya Polyana quite pleased with himself.

Leo Nikolayevich has been feeling guilty ever since he signed the new will, but at least he has been brought around. It galls him that the countess still controls the rights to everything published before 1881. He cannot bear that works written for the love of God should be used to support the lavish style of life to which his wife and children have grown accustomed. He is convinced that Sofya Andreyevna's greed on behalf of the family will only increase with the years, and that she is capable of getting her hands on *all* of his copyrights after his death.

Now the complete works of Leo Tolstoy will, upon his death, make their way into the public domain, though I shall edit and reissue everything first. In order to safeguard the will from Sofya Andreyevna's intervention, he has assigned the copyright to Sasha, with strict instructions to let the public have free access to the material. If Sasha—whose health has been fragile in recent months—should die, the copyright devolves on Tanya, with the same proviso.

Leo Nikolayevich came secretly to Telyatinki to revise the will in his own hand, but, maddeningly, a crucial phrase was omitted, one that is needed to ensure the will's validation in a future court of law: "I, Leo Tolstoy, being of sound mind and in full possession of my memory." Our lawyer insisted that this phrase be included, and we could not risk being in possession of a flawed will. So a final draft was composed for recopying by Tolstoy.

Yesterday we met in the wood outside Grumond. Leo Nikolayevich frequently rides Delire in the afternoons, so such a meeting did not draw his wife's suspicion. I did not tell Bulgakov about our plans. He lives in Sofya Andreyevna's pocket, though the poor lad does not realize it. I would prefer to acquire a new secretary, but Leo Nikolayevich admires Bulgakov. "He is headstrong," he says, "but he reminds me of myself when I was younger."

To be sure, I rather enjoy the spectacle of Bulgakov's "friendship" with young Masha. They purr and prance about like kittens. I don't approve, but in the country one looks for entertainment in unlikely places.

"If they wish to conduct themselves like rabbits, they should go live in the woods," Sergeyenko said to me last week, asking me to get rid of Masha. I summoned her with a note. We talked about her future at Telyatinki, and I—somewhat gently—suggested that she spend some time with our new group in Petersburg. She may come back whenever she chooses, of course. I made that clear to her. She is an intelligent girl who speaks and writes several languages, and her usefulness as a translator increases every day.

I was accompanied on our little excursion into Grumond by Sergeyenko, Goldenweiser, and Sergeyenko's new secretary, Anatol Radinsky, to witness the signing. I felt elated by the prospect of victory. It has been a long time coming.

Leo Nikolayevich, who had arrived before us, was nobly seated on Delire with a white hat on his head, his beard visible from the distance and fanning out over a blue linen blouse. As ever, the sight of him took my breath away.

We greeted each other solemnly and dismounted, spreading the will before us on a writing board fetched especially for this occasion. Leo Nikolayevich sat with his legs crossed as he read the will once again, his hands shaking, his lips moving. He held the pages close to his eyes. I was terrified that, at any moment, he might declare the whole thing a breach of faith with Sofya Andreyevna.

"This is an important moment for the Russian people," I said. "They will have the access to your work they deserve."

He looked at me quizzically, then uncapped his pen, an old English one that had been sent by Aylmer Maude, who ingratiates himself by shipping a constant flow of bric-a-brac and mementos. Leo Nikolayevich had remembered to bring a jar of black India ink, which he sniffed before using, pausing to say how much he enjoys the smell of ink! Sergeyenko handed him a blotter and the paper. Meticulously, he began to form the letters, copying everything in his famously illegible hand.

"I feel like a conspirator," he said, looking up.

We all laughed, but the laughs were hollow.

*Get on with it*, I thought.

It was cool, almost icy, beneath those trees. A wind blew up from the woods, carrying a swampy smell. Delire whinnied, rippling her coat, as sunlight flickered across the pages of the will. We heard a strange cry and looked up to see a black-capped kingfisher flash from a branch, a whir of blue and orange feathers.

"A sign," Leo Nikolayevich said.

I spotted a buzzard on a distant limb, but I did not call attention to it.

When he finished copying the will, Leo Nikolayevich signed his name and sighed, pursing his lips. He wiped his brow with the bottom of his shirt. Then each of us signed as witness.

"What a trial," he said. "I hope never to repeat such an act."

"It had to be done," I responded.

We embraced, briefly; then Leo Nikolayevich mounted Delire and rode away. It was not an occasion for socializing.

"It is terrible to see a man of his stature brought to such an impasse," I said to Sergeyenko. "But we did only what was necessary."

Today when I appeared at Yasnaya Polyana near teatime, I learned that a note had just been sent to Telyatinki from Leo Nikolayevich asking me not to come because Sofya Andreyevna was extremely irritable and suspicious. Had I received this note, I would—with deep regret—have acquiesced. I try to avoid direct confrontations with the countess when I can. But I had come, and I intended to see Leo Nikolayevich, however briefly.

Having sidestepped the countess by mounting the back stairwell, I tiptoed along the hall to Leo Nikolayevich's study. The door to his balcony was open, and I went out to greet him. Makovitsky knelt beside him, wrapping bandages about his legs, which have been causing him a great deal of pain. Bulgakov was behind him, reading aloud a response he had drafted on Leo Nikolayevich's behalf to an atheist who had written insisting that God does not exist. It was a surprisingly cogent letter, very much in the style of Leo Nikolayevich. When he finished, Bulgakov said, "May I ask you about love? Perhaps that would convince this man."

I chuckled to myself, thinking of Bulgakov and his dewy-eyed girl from St. Petersburg.

"My friend, I've tried many times to put it into words. Let me try again," Leo Nikolayevich said, with only the slightest trace of weariness. It perpetually amazes me how patient he is, and how simple. He once told me that the Hindus, whenever they greet a man or woman, fold their hands in prayer and bow, acknowledging the divine presence in every human being. Indeed, he treats everyone who enters a room as if he or she were a god or goddess in disguise. It is most annoying.

Makovitsky finished the bandaging and took out his notebook and pencil. He sensed a momentous opportunity.

Leo Nikolayevich cleared his throat and began: "Love is the uniting of souls separated from each other by the body. It's one of the signs of God's presence in the world. Another is the ability to understand one another. I would guess there are countless signs of God, but we tend not to notice them. Still, we apprehend the presence of God through love and understanding, even though the essence of God eludes us. It is something beyond human comprehension, though—I must be emphatic—it is through love that we sense the divine presence."

"But this man is an atheist," Bulgakov said. "I fear he will deny that any presence whatsoever can be detected, either by love or by understanding."

"Yes, that's true. But even if he prefers not to use the word *God*, he will nonetheless recognize his essence. He may call this *bush*, but the essence exists all the same. God can be denied, but he can't be avoided."

I complimented Leo Nikolayevich on his reformulation of a difficult doctrine. As usual, he puts the most complex matters in the simplest terms. It is a great gift, one that has made him the world's teacher.

Soon we gathered on the terrace for tea. Sofya Andreyevna was in a dreadful state—eyes bloodshot, hair unkempt. She looked older than her years and seemed quite shaky. I was unhappy about the pain I have caused her, but I was resolved to stand firm. Morality must not bend to whim.

"Stand when your guests arrive!" she shouted across the terrace to her husband, who had sunk into a wicker chair. He looked embarrassed and stood with difficulty. Makovitsky helped him to his feet, scowling at Sofya Andreyevna, who scowled back. I should at least be grateful to her for ignoring me.

"She is mad," I whispered to Bulgakov, who stood beside me.

A rough-hewn table, covered with a white linen cloth, stood in the center of the terrace. The samovar boiled happily away, shiny as Aladdin's lamp, reflecting the late-afternoon sun. A bowl of raspberries splashed its color, in bright contrast to the tablecloth. I am quite able to enjoy myself in such a setting, but Sofya Andreyevna had cast a pall on the day. We sat in silence.

The lugubrious tea did not ruin my day entirely, however. I rode back to Telyatinki filled with optimism and genial feelings. Everything has been going so well of late. I am living again near Leo Nikolaye-vich, and the will is signed. The only problem is the countess, toward whom I must remain neutral to the extent that this is possible. I only hope that she has similar intentions.

# 2 7

# BULGAKOV

As I entered the dining room for breakfast this morning, Sofya Andreyevna caught my eye. She was alone in the room, nibbling a piece of black bread, with a glass of steaming tea in one hand. There was a plate of goat cheese in the middle of the table.

"Good morning, Sofya Andreyevna. Did you sleep well?" I felt as though I were on stage.

"You have been deceiving me," she said, more calmly than the content of her words might suggest. "You have been conspiring with Vladimir Grigorevich. You know the exact nature of his plots against me and my family, and yet you pretend to be my friend."

"No," I said, but I could see there was no point in protesting.

"I have been talking with the servants. They have heard rumors. And they have *seen* you in the woods, gossiping, making plans, ridiculing me behind my back. Don't think that I don't have my spies, too."

This was so ludicrous that I merely shook my head.

"The worst of it, Valentin Fedorovich, is that I offered you my friendship and counsel, even my love, all quite freely. I expected nothing in return."

"I have not conspired against you," I said. "But I can see that you won't believe me."

"I detest you," she replied, leaving me to eat by myself.

I felt much like the little clerk Shuvalkin in the famous story about Prince Potemkin, chancellor to Empress Catherine II. The empress adored Potemkin, who suffered hideous bouts of melancholic depression. When he was unwell, his rage was so dreadful that he was left to himself, at home, locked in his chambers with all the shutters closed. When he was ready to join the world again, he would emerge from his room as if nothing had happened. And nothing was ever said.

One of these bouts lasted for several months and produced serious problems for the court. Documents requiring the chancellor's signature were piling up, and the empress was becoming anxious. The higher counselors of the court were assembled one day at the palace, discussing the matter, when the little clerk Shuvalkin happened to walk into the room.

"Excuse me, Your Excellencies," he said. "I wonder why you are all so gloomy. Perhaps I can be of service?" Shuvalkin was a man who wished everyone to be happy, especially those above him in rank.

A chuckle spread about the room. Then one of the assembly took pity on Shuvalkin's ignorance and explained the situation.

In a wild flash of ambition, Shuvalkin said, "But, Your Excellencies, if only you will let me have the documents, I will remedy the situation. I have never been afraid of Prince Potemkin."

It was a bold lie, but they believed him. He was given the unsigned documents and sent, with Godspeed, to Potemkin's house.

He arrived at the imposing town house, with its slightly purplish facade of granite, and asked to see the prince on official business. The doorman looked at Shuvalkin with astonishment and said, "I cannot recommend that you disturb the prince."

"I have been sent by the Empress Catherine on official business," he said, exaggerating slightly.

The doorman, with animal fear in his eye, pointed the way to Potemkin's study.

Through corridors carpeted with thick runners from the Orient, past galleries and music rooms, Shuvalkin approached the infamous study. The door was shut. Shuvalkin knocked once, then waited. There was no response. He had read in a book somewhere that opportunity doesn't knock twice and decided, perhaps rashly, to take the plunge. He turned the brass handle slowly. To his astonishment, it was not locked.

Potemkin sat at his desk at the opposite end of the vast, musty room with the shutters closed, the room barely lit. He was sitting in a nightshirt behind his desk, unshaven, motionless. It did not seem possible to little Shuvalkin that the great prince, for whom he had run many errands, could look so poorly. Aware that his time was limited, he thrust the stack of documents under Potemkin's nose.

Dipping a steel-tipped pen from the desk into a jar of ink, he handed it to Potemkin, who took the pen between his stubby fingers but seemed quite ignorant of Shuvalkin's presence in the room.

"Please sign the documents, Your Excellency. The empress's need is urgent."

Potemkin simply stared ahead, the pen in hand.

"The documents are vital, Your Excellency. For the sake of the empress. . . ." It seemed hopeless, and Shuvalkin was about to flee when the prince, rock faced, began systematically to sign the documents. One by one, he turned the pages, signed, and blotted his signature. Soon the entire stack was finished.

Shuvalkin was elated. His career would soar. He imagined himself promoted to chief administrator of the city parks or head of document storage or, perhaps, administrative counsel to Potemkin himself. His heart leaped, and he had to restrain himself from kissing the prince as he gathered the documents in his arms. Wobbly kneed, he said,

"Thank you, Your Excellency. Thank you so very much, Your Excellency." Still bowing and muttering, he closed the door to Potemkin's chambers and ran into the streets.

Back at the palace, he entered the antechamber where the counselors were still assembled. The blaze of triumph was in his eyes as he held the documents before him. "They have all been signed," he said. "Every one of them!"

With amazement, the chief counselor accepted the documents. They were spread on a broad trestle table, and the counselors gathered round. Breathlessly, they bent to look.

The whole group seemed paralyzed. The chief counselor looked gravely at Shuvalkin.

"Is anything wrong?" he asked, stepping forward to the table. It was then he saw that the great Potemkin had indeed signed the papers, but he had signed document after document, in a bold hand, Shuvalkin . . . Shuvalkin . . . Shuvalkin. . . .

Today I was Shuvalkin. I have behaved with fidelity, spoken truthfully to Leo Nikolayevich, to Vladimir Grigorevich, to Sofya Andreyevna. But everyone now considers me a fraud. They see my name on every evil document, but I have not written it there. Still, I must not blame Leo Tolstoy. He is not my Potemkin. God is my Potemkin, teasing me, playing a game that could cast me only in the worst possible light among this household or that of Telyatinki.

I received a letter from St. Petersburg.

*My dearest Valya,*

*Since returning, I have made contact with the Tolstoyans, who have welcomed me. You would be surprised at how much they know about us! Telyatinki fascinates them, and they all want to visit there. Yasnaya Polyana, for them, is Mecca.*

*They know a great deal about you. Rumors fly! They know*

*that Leo Nikolayevich admires you very much, and it is said that you and he spend long philosophical afternoons in the forest of Zasyeka. I assure them that all of this has been exaggerated. . . .*

*Do you think of me? (I'm sure you do.) I think of you. I am quite glad, however, for this period of intermission. I felt your intensity too painfully. It was not comfortable, and it was hurting my ability to respond to you in the way I would like.*

*Let us write letters, lots of letters. I feel close to you now as I compose. Closer than that day in the pinewoods when we touched. Does that seem possible?*

*Let me know what you are thinking and feeling. And let me know what is happening at Yasnaya Polyana. I have been reading* What Then Must We Do?, *which L. N. wrote nearly thirty years ago! Have you read it lately? It once again braces me to work for justice in the world.*

*The inequities of rich and poor must be improved to the extent that they can. I know that you sincerely agree with me on these matters.*

*I wonder when and how we shall meet again. Will I return to Tula? Perhaps. In the meanwhile, know that I value our friendship and look forward to hearing from you often.*

I could hardly breathe. Is it possible that I can live my life without Masha beside me? I have come to love her even more since she left, to yearn for her, to dream about her. I imagine myself beside her in our marriage bed, our children asleep in the next room. I imagine us, like Kitty and Levin from *Anna Karenina*, tending the fields, working the land, enjoying the family hearth.

The possibility, the fear, of having too many lonely years without her stretches ahead of me, and I feel isolated and strangely vacant. God and work with Leo Nikolayevich should be enough to sustain me. But somehow, without Masha, my life seems valueless. I sat for many hours, alone, my eyes blurry with tears, reading and rereading the letter.

My attraction to the idea of marriage is not, however, enhanced by watching the daily struggle of man and wife in Yasnaya Polyana. Last night we had been sitting quietly as dusk covered the pond, watching the barn swallows dart and weave as they snagged fireflies in their tiny beaks. The August evening was dewy and rich. Red light streaked the horizon, the sun having just fallen behind the distant woods.

Shortly after dinner, Sofya Andreyevna came onto the terrace, where I was sitting with Leo Nikolayevich and Dr. Makovitsky. She had a notebook in her hands. Her husband stiffened when he saw her.

"I suppose your friends all know that you prefer men to women," she said, trying to provoke him, embarrassing Dushan Makovitsky so thoroughly that I thought he might crack.

"For God's sake, Sonya," Leo Nikolayevich said. He seemed less angry than weary.

Peace was not her object. "I have been rereading your old diaries," she said. "May I read something to your friends? They are both fascinated by everything the great Tolstoy has said or written—so they pretend."

I hated being privy to such talk, but where was I to go? The normally expressive face of Leo Nikolayevich became impassive. He looked away from his wife.

"Listen to this, friends," she went on. The note of insolence in her voice shocked me. "I copied this from his diary of 29 November 1851. It is quite revealing: 'I have never been in love with a woman. . . . Yet I have very often fallen in love with a man.' " She stopped to let the weight of this passage sink in. "Can you believe it? Now listen to this: 'For me the main indication of love is the fear of offending the beloved, of not pleasing him, or just fear it-self. . . . I fell in love with a man before I realized what pederasty was; yet even when I found out what it was, the possibility never crossed my mind.' "

"So there it is!" shouted Dr. Makovitsky. "He has explained himself. We do not need to hear more of this, Sofya Andreyevna." His bald head twitched as he spoke, the slight dent in his brow going purple with fury.

"I shall continue, Dushan Petrovich. It is all very intriguing," she said. " 'Beauty has always been a huge factor in my attraction to people. . . . There is Dyakov, for instance. How could I ever forget the night we left Pirogovo together, when, wrapped in my blanket, I felt as though I could devour him with kisses and weep for joy. Lust was not absent, yet it is impossible to say exactly what part it played in my feelings, for my mind never tempted me with depraved images.' "

Leo Nikolayevich, looking disgusted, stood and excused himself. I was relieved.

"See what you've done, Sofya Andreyevna? He has been driven from his own terrace," said Dr. Makovitsky.

"He is aware that I have hit upon the truth. Why else would he chase about like a schoolboy after Vladimir Grigorevich? He lusts after the man. He wants to roll about in bed with him, to smother him with kisses, to weep on his breast. Why doesn't he admit it? Why doesn't he just *do* it?"

I fought back a smile. She looked at me scornfully and stomped off. There's a strange passion at work in her heart, but I'm all too aware of knowing very little of what has passed between Sofya Andreyevna and her husband in the past five decades.

Dr. Makovitky asked me to sit with him. "You know, she's been following him in the woods lately, in Zasyeka. And she's been stopping everyone—even peasant children—asking them if her husband has been seen with Chertkov. It's no way for a wife to behave."

Dushan Makovitsky looked shrunken and hurt as he huddled in the chair, alone. He was like a muffin that, having been mixed with too much yeast, expands beyond its natural limits before collapsing into itself. I felt sorry for him, and (for the first time) I liked him. He is terribly innocent and well intentioned, however ridiculous. There is something in everyone that can be loved.

I wanted to ask Dushan Makovitsky what he thought of those passages Sofya Andreyevna had read, but I didn't dare. The idea of Leo Nikolayevich lying with another man was upsetting. I realized that I, too, find men attractive in a way that could easily be misconstrued. I love to see young men haying in the field with their shirts off or bathing in the Voronka without their clothes; indeed, I cannot help but stare at the boy who grooms the horses at Telyatinki with something akin to lust in my heart. I understood exactly what Leo Nikolayevich meant in his diaries, and—once again—his directness and honesty startled me. I would never have risked putting such bold feelings into words.

Bidding good night to Dr. Makovitsky, I went to see if there was something I could do for Leo Nikolayevich before I left.

"What am I to do?" he asked. "In my situation, inertia seems the lesser evil. I must do nothing, undertake nothing. I shall respond to every provocation with the silence it richly deserves. Silence, as you will know, is a powerful weapon." Having said this, he seemed to reconsider. "No, I must aspire to the condition of loving even those who hate me."

"This difficulty between you and your wife can, perhaps, be taken as a challenge," I said. "It might well increase your spiritual sense, bring you closer to God."

He shook his head affirmatively. "Yes," he said, "but she goes too far, too far."

I volunteered to bring him a glass of tea, and he accepted my offer. When I returned, he was sitting in his chair, his boots off. His face, his entire countenance, had softened.

"You must understand that Sofya Andreyevna is not well," he said. "I wish Vladimir Grigorevich could see her when she breaks down, when she shakes and weeps like a scolded child. One can't help but take pity on her. . . . I fear we treat her too severely. She is suffocating here . . . can't breathe . . ." His voice trailed off.

I touched him on the shoulder and noticed a large tear on his cheek.

"I'm terribly sorry, Leo Nikolayevich, I—"

"You are good to say this to me, dear boy," he said. "It is a problem that has been a long time gathering, like a wave at sea. It is about to break over my head. I pray to God for the strength to withstand it."

We kissed each other and said good night.

Back in my room, I found the copy of *What Then Must We Do?* that I had borrowed from Leo Nikolayevich's study. With a sense of growing wonder, I read it till, near midnight, I fell asleep in my clothes.

# 28

# L. N.

—FROM *WHAT THEN MUST WE DO?*

I had spent my life in the country, and when in 1881 I came to live in Moscow, the sight of town poverty took me by surprise.

Country poverty I had known, but town poverty was new and incomprehensible to me. In Moscow one cannot cross a street without meeting beggars, and beggars quite unlike the ones in the country. They don't "carry a sack and beg in Christ's name," as country beggars like to say of themselves. They go without a sack and do not beg. When you meet them, they usually only attempt to catch your eye; depending upon your response, they either ask for something or don't. I know of one particular beggar from the gentry class. The old fellow walks slowly, stooping with each step. When he meets you, he stands on one leg and appears to bow. If you happen not to stop, he pretends that this just happens to be his way of walking, and continues. If you stop, he takes off his cocked cap, bows again, and begs.

He is the usual sort of educated beggar one finds in Moscow.

At first, I wondered why they didn't just ask you plainly. Later I learned something of the situation, but I still didn't understand it.

It seems that in Moscow, by law, all beggars (of whom one meets several in each street, with rows of them outside every church whenever there is a service, especially if there happens to be a funeral) are forbidden to beg.

But I never did find out why some are caught and detained, while others roam freely. Either there are legal and illegal beggars, or there are so many that they can't catch all of them; perhaps as soon as some are caught, others spring up.

Moscow presents all kinds of beggars. There are some who live by it; and there are others, "real" beggars, who have come to the town for some reason and are genuinely destitute.

Among these latter are many simple muzhiks, men and women alike, wearing muzhik clothes. I often meet them. Some of them have fallen ill here and have been let out of the hospital; they can neither support themselves nor get away from Moscow. Some are not ill but have lost everything they own in a fire, or are elderly, or are women with children. Others are healthy and able to work. These healthy ones, begging alms, interested me especially. For since I came to Moscow I had, for the sake of exercise, formed the habit of going to work at the Sparrow Hills with two muzhiks to saw wood there.

These two men were just like those I'd met in the streets. One was Peter, a soldier from Kaluga; the other was Simon, a muzhik from Vladimir. They owned nothing except the clothes on their backs and their own hands. With those hands they earned a tiny sum per day, something of which they were able to save: Peter to buy a sheepskin coat, Simon to pay for the journey back to his village. I was especially keen to talk to them.

Why did these men work and others beg?

On meeting such a fellow I usually began by asking how he came to be in such a state. Once I met a healthy muzhik whose beard was turning gray. He begged. I asked who he was, and he said he had come from Kaluga to look for work. At first he had found some work, cutting up old timber for firewood. He and his mate cut up all the wood in one spot. Then he searched for another job, but nothing could be found. His mate left him, and now he had been knocking around for two weeks, having eaten all he had, and he had nothing with which to buy either a saw or a chopper. I gave him money for the saw and told him where he could find work. (I had previously, as it happened, arranged with Peter and Simon to take on another worker.)

"So, my friend, be sure and go. There is plenty of work for you there," I said.

"I'll go," he said. "Why not? Do you think I enjoy begging? I can work."

He swore he'd go, and I felt he was in earnest and meant to appear.

The next day I joined my friends, Peter and Simon, and asked if the man had turned up. He had not. As it happened, several other men behaved in much the same way. I was also cheated by men who said they only needed money to buy a railway ticket home, but whom I met on the street again a week later. Several of these I recognized, and they recognized me; but sometimes, having forgotten me, they told me the same story again. Some turned away on seeing me. So I learned that among this class there are many cheats, too; but I felt extremely sorry for these cheats. They were a half-dressed, thin, impoverished, sickly group: the sort of people who often freeze to death or hang themselves, as we often read in the papers.

■ When I spoke to the Moscovites about this destitution in their city I was usually told: "What you have seen is nothing! Go to Hitrof Market and visit the doss houses. That's where you'll see the real 'Golden Company.'" One fellow told me, somewhat dryly, that it was no longer a "Company" but a "Golden Regiment"—there are so many of them. The man was right, but he'd have been even more correct had he said that in Moscow these people are now neither a company nor a regiment but a vast army that numbers, I am told, fifty thousand. Old residents of Moscow, when speaking of town poverty, always spoke of it with a kind of pleasure—as if proud to know about it. I recall, too, that when I was in London, people there bragged about London pauperism: "Just look what it's like here!" they said.

I wanted to see this destitution, about which I'd been told; and several times I set out toward Hitrof Market, but each time I felt uncomfortable and ashamed. "Why go to look on the sufferings of people I can't help?" a voice within me said. "If you live here and see all the allurements of town life, go and see that, too," said another voice. And so, one frosty, windswept day in December 1881, I went to the heart of the town's destitution—Hitrof Market. It was a weekday, almost four o'clock in the afternoon. In Solyanka Street I had already become aware of more and more people wearing strange clothes not made for them, and in yet stranger footgear—people with an odd, unhealthy complexion, all possessing a common air, an air of indifference. I noticed one man walking alone rather casually, dressed in strange, incredible clothes, evidently unfazed by what he looked like to others. All proceeded in the same direction. Without asking the way (which I didn't know), I went with them, arriving eventually at the Hitrof Market.

There were also women of the same type, adorned in all sorts of capes, cloaks, jackets, boots, and galoshes, equally indifferent to appearances in spite of the hideousness of their garb. Old and young, they sat exchanging goods of some sort, milling about, swearing and scolding. There were few people in the market. It was apparently over, and most were walking uphill, passing through or past the market, always in one direction. I followed them, and the farther I went the more people there seemed to be, all going one way. Passing the market and following up the street, I overtook two women: one old, the other young. Both wore tattered, drab clothes. Neither was drunk. Something, however, preoccupied them, and the men who met them, as well as those behind and before them, paid no attention to their manner of speech, which to my ears was peculiar. It was evident that, here, people always talked like this.

To the left were private doss houses, and some turned into them, while others went farther on. Having climbed the hill, we came to a large house on the corner. Most of those among whom I had been walking stopped here. All along the sidewalk and in the snow-covered street, people of the same type stood or sat. To the right of the entrance door were the women, to the left the men. I passed both the women and the men (there were hundreds of them), and stopped where the line ended. The house they were waiting for was the Lyap-insky Free Night-Lodging House. The crowd were lodgers waiting for admission. At 5:00 P.M. the doors open, and people are let in. Nearly all those I had overtaken were coming here.

When I stopped, where the lines of men ended, those nearest began to stare at me, drawing me to them by their glances. The tatters covering their bodies were extremely varied, but they all looked at me with the same stare, as if to say: "Why have you, a man from a different world, stopped among us? Who are you? A self-satisfied rich man who wants to enjoy our misery, to kill time, to torture us—or are you that thing which can hardly exist—someone who pities us?" These questions hung on every face. They looked, caught my eye, and turned away. I wanted to speak to some of them but could not decide what to do. Nevertheless, as widely as life had separated us, having exchanged glances I felt that we were similar, that we ceased to be afraid of one another.

Near me stood a fellow with a swollen face and a red beard, in a torn coat with worn galoshes on his bare feet. (And it was well below freezing!) I met his look three or four times, and felt so near him that instead of being ashamed to speak to him, I should have been ashamed not to say something. So I asked where he came from. He answered readily and began talking, while others drew near. He was from Smo-lensk and had come to seek work, hoping to be able to buy corn and pay his taxes. "There is no work to be had," he said. "The soldiers have taken all the work. So I'm wandering about, and, as God knows, I haven't eaten for two days!" He spoke timidly, trying to smile. A seller of hot drinks (made of honey and spices) stood nearby. I called him, and he poured out a glass. The man took the drink in his hands and tried to contain the heat as he cupped his hands around the glass.

While doing so, he told me about his adventures (the adventures or stories told by these men were almost all the same). He had had a little work, but it came to an end; then his purse, with his passport and what money he had, had been stolen, right here in the Lyapinsky House. Now he couldn't get away from Moscow. He said that during the day he warmed himself in the drink shops and ate scraps of bread, which were sometimes given to him; but often they drove him away. He got his night's lodging free here. He was now only waiting for the police to arrest him for having no passport, to imprison him or send him on foot, under escort, back to his native town. "They say there will be a police search on Thursday," he said. Prison or escort home were, for him, the Promised Land.

As he was talking, two or three others from among the crowd confirmed his words and said they were in the same mess. A skinny kid, pale, long nosed, with nothing over his shirt (which had a tear at the shoulder) and wearing a peakless cap, pushed his way sidelong to me through the crowd. He shivered violently all over, but he tried to smile contemptuously at the beggar's speech, hoping thereby to adapt himself to my attitude. He looked me in the eye, and I offered him, too, a hot drink. On taking the glass he also warmed both hands around it, but he had only begun to speak when he was pushed aside by a big, black, Roman-nosed fellow in a print shirt and a vest but wearing no cap. The Roman-nosed man also asked for a hot drink, followed by a tall, drunken old man with a pointed beard who wore an overcoat tied around the waist with a cord and bast shoes. Then came along a dwarfish fellow with puffy cheeks and watery eyes who wore a brown nankeen pea jacket; his bare knees poked through the holes in his summer trousers and knocked together from the cold. He shivered so badly he could hardly hold the glass and spilled the contents all over himself. The rest began to abuse him, but he only smiled rather pitifully and shivered. Then came a crooked, deformed man in rags, with strips of linen tied round his bare feet; then something that looked like an officer, then something that looked like a cleric, then something strange and noseless: all were hungry, freezing, importunate, and submissive, drawing round me and pressing near the seller of hot drinks, who dispatched what he had till all was gone.

One man asked for money, and I gave him some. Another asked, then a third, and soon the whole crowd besieged me. Disorder and a crush ensued. A porter from the next house shouted to the mob to get off the sidewalk, and they submissively obeyed his command. Organizers appeared among the crowd, and they took me under their protection. They hoped to extricate me from the crush, but the crowd, which at first had stretched in a line along the sidewalk, had gathered around me in a circle. They implored me with their looks, begging. Each face was more pitiful, more jaded, more degraded than the last. I gave away everything I had with me, which was not much, and followed the crowd into the Night-Lodging House.

It was an immense building, consisting of four stories. On the top story were the men's lodgings and, on the lower stories, the women's. First, I entered the women's quarters: a big room filled with bunks, arranged in two tiers, above and below. Women old and young—bizarrely dressed, ragged, with no outdoor garments—entered and took possession of their bunks. Some of the older ones crossed themselves and prayed for the founder of this refuge. Others merely laughed and swore.

I went upstairs to the men's lodging. Among them I saw a man whom I had just given money. Seeing him, I felt suddenly ashamed, dreadfully so, and hurried away. Feeling as if I had committed a crime, I left the house and went home. There I entered the carpeted, elegant hallway of my house. Taking off my fur coat, I sat down to a five-course dinner. Five lackeys with white ties and white gloves served me the meal.

Thirty years ago, in Paris, I once saw how, in the presence of thousands of spectators, they cut a man's head off with a guillotine. I knew he was a horrible criminal, and I knew all the arguments written in defense of that kind of action. I also knew his crime was done deliberately and intentionally. But at the moment the head and body separated, with the head toppling into the box, I gasped and realized not with my mind but with my heart and my whole soul that all the arguments in favor of capital punishment are wicked nonsense and that however many people may combine to commit murder—the worst of all crimes—and whatever they may call themselves, murder remains murder. I knew that a crime had been committed before my eyes, and that I, by my very presence and nonintervention, had approved and shared in that crime.

In the same way now, at the sight of the hunger, cold, and degradation of thousands of people, I understood not only with my mind or heart but with my very soul that the existence of tens of thousands of such people in Moscow—while I and thousands of others gorge ourselves on beefsteaks and sturgeon and cover our horses and floors with cloth or carpets—no matter what all the learned men in the world may say about its necessity, is a crime, and one committed not once but constantly. I knew that I, with my luxury, shared fully the responsibility for this crime.

# 2 9

# SASHA

Papa fell asleep over his diaries, and I didn't dare wake him. I glanced at what he had written: "I feel that I should go away, leaving a letter, but I'm afraid for Sonya, though I suppose it would benefit her, too."

My hand was trembling. I turned the page and read: "Help me, O God, universal spirit, origin and point of life, help me, at least now in these last days and hours of my life on earth, help me to serve Thee, to live for Thee alone."

I closed the diary so that Mama wouldn't see. I couldn't bear another bout of hysteria.

Papa, on the other hand, is not hysterical, though Andrey and Leo, my brothers, have been talking in the most distressing way about having a doctor declare Papa feebleminded. What they fear, of course, is the secret will. The disposition of Papa's manuscripts and diaries preoccupies them. They are so money grubbing! Everything they do is calculated to sustain the luxury they adore.

The gloom of it all overwhelmed me, so I went into Varvara's room. She cradled me in her arms, saying, "One or the other will die soon. You can count on that much. Time plays a useful function here."

She is right, of course. The physical effects of my parents' struggle have grown obvious to everyone. Mama's pulse races frantically, while Papa is barely able to cross the room some days. Pale, unsteady on his feet, he is often confused. Somehow, he continues to ride Delire in the afternoons. That horse will kill him if the tension doesn't.

One day Papa told me about an old man who had become weary of life and whose family had grown weary of him. Saying nothing, the man saddled his horse and rode off at dawn into the misty wood-lands, never to be seen again.

"Papa, you would never . . ."

"I can't say what I would or wouldn't do," he replied.

I walked away from this conversation less horrified than awestruck. I felt sure that, whatever came between him and Mama, he would behave in a reasonable manner—even if everyone called him insane.

Tanya, my saintly sister, heard about the latest marital brushfires and decided to visit us. She is like a wandering bucket in search of a fire. But her generally beneficent temper has good effects on the household. Papa seems able to relax when she is here.

"Your sister is so deliciously stupid," Varvara Mikhailovna said to me this morning, over breakfast. "She makes everyone else feel intel-ligent. That's why she is popular."

The current state of siege at Yasnaya Polyana shook my sister up so badly she insisted that we all return to Kochety with her. The atmosphere there is always restorative, what with Sukhotin's genial pompousness and Tanya's ministrations, the tinkle of children's voices, the beautifully kept grounds and French cuisine. Kochety has the additional advantage of being out of Chertkov's immediate range just now, which should increase my mother's sense of well-being.

With very little discussion, everyone agreed to go. Yasnaya Po-lyana has become an emotional torture chamber.

We left for Kochety in mid-August, on a hazy day, in two car-riages. I rode with Varvara Mikhailovna and Dushan Makovitsky in a cramped carriage with four trotters. My parents rode together in the first carriage with Tanya and a couple of servants. Everything went beautifully for three days, with Mama more relaxed than I have seen her in many months. There was not a word of animosity between her and Papa! Then, on the eighteenth of August, an article appeared in the local newspaper saying that the minister of the interior had granted Chertkov permanent residence in Tula.

Mama came into the breakfast room with the paper clutched in her hand like a strangled animal. "I will have Chertkov murdered. Either he dies, or I die. There can be no compromise."

Papa's face turned to chalk. "You all see what I endure," he shouted. "It's . . . impossible!"

Mama glared at him, then fell hard onto the wide-plank floorboards, hitting her head on the molding. A new maid screamed. Dushan Makovitsky hastened to Mama's side and immediately took her pulse.

"One hundred forty," he said. "Not serious." Rather too casually, he slapped her cheeks before putting salts to her nose.

Mama opened her eyes, slightly.

"Sofya!" Dushan said, loudly. "Open your eyes!"

"My chest . . . my chest," she gasped, trying to catch her breath. "I have such a terrible pain. My heart! It's my heart!" She fell back with her eyes closed. Sarah Bernhardt could not have done better.

"Is she dying?" Tanya asked.

"She'll be all right," Dushan said. "It's a mild case of shock."

Mama was carried to her room by two young footmen in uniform, swinging between them like a large hammock. She was propped up in bed, pillows all around her.

I sat beside her with Papa, who smoldered still and volunteered nothing—not a word, not even a sigh. When Mama recovered consciousness, she seemed eerily calm, as radiant as a queen. She asked Papa to promise not to have himself photographed by Chertkov anymore.

"You're like an old coquet," she said. "It upsets the whole family, the way his pictures of you adorn every mediocre paper in Russia. You should have more pride!''

Papa, rather sheepishly, obliged her, saying he would no longer allow Chertkov to photograph him. This appeared to satisfy her, but Papa quickly made matters worse by saying that he did, however, reserve the right to address Chertkov by letter as often as he pleased.

This little maneuver pitched Mama into a turmoil. "Look at the way he insists on having the last twist to every argument!" she said. "It's diabolical!"

The next day she seized me, saying she hadn't slept all night. "All I can think of," she said, quite breathless, her cheeks bright with fury, "is that, from now on, his letters will be full of unfair remarks about me, schemes and frightful lies—all written under the guise of Christian humility. Your father thinks he is Christ, Sasha. That's a sin, you know. A soul can be condemned to hell for that."

"On the contrary," I said, "Papa is extremely humble."

"He's an egomaniac! He thinks he's Christ, and he lets Chertkov play the role of chief disciple. It would be comical if it weren't sick."

Mama lay in bed at Kochety for days, feeding on sweets, drinking tea and chocolate, hunting through her husband's early novels and stories for signs of perversion. In *Childhood* she found a description of a man called Sergey. She called Papa into her room and read the passage aloud to him in her ludicrous, stentorian way.

"How is it that he prefers Chertkov, that obese, balding idiot, to me?" Mama asked one morning as we sipped tea in her dressing room.

"He still loves you, Mama. Why else would he stay?"

She ignored the implications of my question. "I remember when I would be naked, standing by the Voronka, ready to bathe," she said. "And he would surprise me, overtake me. He would roll me into a high patch of weeds, where he would ravish me." Her eyes rolled as she spoke. She appeared quite mad, like Othello just before he murdered Desdemona, his big, white eyes burning in a dark, twisted face.

I did not enjoy hearing this. This was not the sort of thing one said to a daughter.

I could not have made it through these tense days at Kochety without Varvara, who never allowed the atmosphere of deceit and madness to bother her. She is like a running brook beside my field, watering my roots. Without her, I would shrivel.

▦ Papa questioned me about Varvara in a most peculiar fashion one day when I was about to take his dictation. He asked me if I thought I loved her.

"Yes, I am fond of her," I said.

"But do you *love* her?"

"I love her."

He seemed happy to hear this. I am sure he does not think our friendship is ungodly. He is not perverted, as Mama claims; indeed, he realizes that loving men is the same as loving women in all ways but the most technical.

▦ Mama's birthday occurred on the twenty-second of the month. She was sixty-six and looked every minute of it. Papa's birthday came six days later, his eighty-second. It should have been a time of great celebrating, but Mama insisted on rehearsing the old, troublesome issues. One by one, they hammered through them, with Tanya acting as referee.

Papa—who had been battered for days—began this particular round of accusations. We were gathered around the big table at Kochety, when Papa suddenly took it upon himself to say that celibacy and chastity were the two main goals of the Christian life.

"Listen to him!" Mama shrieked. "Leo Nikolayevich, you are eighty-two years old today and still a fool."

Tanya said, "This is no way to speak to each other on a happy day. Let's rejoice as a family and love one another, as the Gospels tell us." She offered everyone a second helping of venison, while Sukhotin passed around a white wine from the Moselle.

But Mama would not be silenced.

"A man who fathers thirteen children insults us when he proclaims the holiness of celibacy. Especially if that man has lain beside God knows how many women—or men. It is disgraceful, Leo Nikolayevich. You shame yourself when you talk like this."

After dinner, I removed Papa from her company. He gripped my arm tightly as we made our way into the long evening shadows, taking a short walk in the park. It was lovely, with barn swallows skimming the trees. The moon pressed its bootheel into the sky's dark sand while, in the distance, a flock of geese could be heard honking as they flew southward.

"They know exactly the way to go," Papa said. "And they don't have to think about it. How I envy them."

We stopped by a little pond full of ducks to sit on a stone bench overlooking the water.

"The pity is," I said, "that Mama loves you."

"What your mother feels for me is not love," he said. "It has the possessiveness of love, but it's something closer to hatred. She wants to destroy me."

This could not be so. Much as I dislike her, I do not think Mama wants to destroy her husband, whom she worships in her twisted way.

"Perhaps not. But her love is being transformed into hatred, day by day." He paused to think. "You see, she was saved for many years from her own egotism by the children. The children absorbed her. But that's over, and nothing can save her now."

Mama refused to stay at Kochety any longer, since everyone (so she claimed) treated her "like a Xanthippe." She continued to view her life as a drama—a tragedy—with herself on center stage. "She doesn't want a family," Varvara told me. "She wants a Greek chorus."

At Papa's insistence, Varvara and I agreed to take Mama back to Yasnaya Polyana. He refused to go himself, thank God. He was enjoying himself at Kochety, playing chess with Sukhotin, walking in the park, reading Rousseau every morning and Pascal at night. He dictated letters and revised proofs sent to him by Chertkov. A brief while apart from Mama would be good for him.

I assumed the separation would benefit Mama, too, but as soon as we got home she became highly agitated. The day after we arrived, she walked into Papa's study in a wild state. Realizing that a number of new photographs by Chertkov and me had been hung on the wall, she dashed them to the floor. Having replaced these by pictures of her own, she sent for a priest, who arrived with his liturgical paraphernalia to exorcise Chertkov's diabolical presence from the room.

We sat in the hall, listening in near disbelief. Then Mama poked her head out, her eyes black as dirt. "I don't care what your father does, Sasha. He can make everything over to Chertkov, if that's what he wants. It won't matter, because I shall break the will. Your brothers will stand behind me, and so will the tsar!" She throbbed like a chicken's disembodied heart.

Varvara assured Mama that Chertkov had no such evil plans.

"The man will stop at nothing," Mama replied. "He wants to destroy me!" She decided to return to Kochety at once.

The next few days were dreadful. Back at Kochety, Mama refused to eat any solid food. She would sit at meals, sulking, while Papa hovered meekly, imploring her to nibble. "Just a piece of black bread, my love," he would say. It was so pathetic that Sukhotin, who is normally pacific, lost his temper. Livid, he rose, leaning on clenched fists at the head of the table. "For God's sake, Sofya Andreyevna!" he said. "Do you know what you're doing? Your only claim in life is as Leo Tolstoy's wife, don't you know that? If he leaves you, history will say it was your fault. And, I swear to you, they will be right!"

Papa's head sagged. He realized that the situation was unbearable and put a hand on his wife's shoulder and sighed.

I saw tears on Mama's cheeks now, a look of unbearable sorrow pooling in her face.

She left that day for home—a merciful gesture on her part—asking her husband to follow in a few days. She wanted them together at

Yasnaya Polyana, however, for their forty-eighth wedding anniversary, on the twenty-third of September. He could hardly not agree.

On the morning of the anniversary, Mama came down from her bedroom dressed in a white silk dress, a childlike smile on her face, as if their marriage had been half a century of inexpressible bliss. I confess, she looked radiant. Varvara Mikhailovna and I both complimented her.

"Tell your father to put on a clean shirt," she said. "I will ask Bulgakov to take our picture on the front lawn."

With reluctance, Papa put on a white linen blouse and his best leather boots—ones that he had made himself a couple of years ago and reserves for what he calls "state occasions." He brushed his hair and beard carefully.

Husband and wife of nearly five decades had a cup of hot chocolate before going outside for the picture. It was a warm day for late September. Though it was not yet noon, the sun burned with an almost lurid brightness, and the heat stood, quivering, on the recently mowed fields—the last cut of the year. Bulgakov was assigned the role of photographer because he supposedly has a knack for it.

Mama thought that a grand, stately photograph of herself and Papa appearing in all the newspapers would put to rest what she called the "persistent rumor that there is marital strife between us." Papa could hardly refuse to be photographed beside her, since he lets Chertkov take his picture at the slightest whim. I doubt that any man in history has been more photographed than Leo Tolstoy.

I put a screen behind the anniversary couple, as Bulgakov directed. He was being "professional."

"The screen will concentrate the sun's rays on the photographic subject," Bulgakov said. Varvara Mikhailovna and I giggled behind his back, while Dushan Makovitsky frowned.

Papa squinted into the sun, haggard and distracted.

"Please try to smile, Leo Nikolayevich," Bulgakov said.

Papa forced a meager smile.

Bulgakov put his head under the camera's black hood, holding the rubber pear to one side. "A little to the left, please. . . . There! Now smile. . . ."

Mama, of course, looked like heaven on a dish. She stealthily slipped her arm around her husband's waist and cocked her head toward his shoulder. She wanted the world to see the Perfect Couple. But nothing would alter Papa's mood.

The shutter clicked, but when Bulgakov attempted to develop the pictures, two featureless ghosts appeared on the strong-smelling paper. Varvara Mikhailovna said, "The camera knows what is really there."

They tried again the next day, with better results. Afterward, I took Papa aside. "You should never have let her talk you into that photograph. It was dishonest."

"You are much like your mother," he said. "Full of anger."

He should never have spoken to me like that. But I realized his situation made it impossible to behave rationally.

Before lunch, I went in to take his dictation. He was sitting on the couch and looked up like an old spaniel. "It's not your shorthand I need, Sasha. It's your love."

Intense love, pity, and sadness rushed from my heels up my spine and broke in a full wave over my head. "I need you so, Papa," I said, falling to the floor. I wrapped my arms around his knees and wept.

"What a dear girl," he said, stroking my hair. "So dear, I love you. So dear. . . ."

The next day Papa put the photographs taken by me and Chertkov back on his study walls. That afternoon, Mama lost her mind.

Varvara and I had been invited to visit a friend for a few nights, and we left after breakfast. That same afternoon, Papa went off into the woods on Delire. When he returned, he discovered that Mama had gone into his study with a cap pistol and fired shots at Chertkov's pictures before tearing them up—the servants recounted the whole sordid tale in scrupulous detail, as always. When Mama saw Papa in his study, she rushed at him with the same pistol and fired several times at his head before racing back to her room.

Varvara and I were immediately sent for by one of the servants. When we returned, Mama pretended that nothing had happened. "You silly girls, what brings you back so quickly? I suppose your hostess was dull."

I lost my temper. "You're crazy and you'll kill us all."

"Is that what you think?" She began to enumerate her sufferings, but it was too much for Varvara Mikhailovna to endure.

"Be still, for once!" Varvara said.

Mama looked bitterly at my friend. "I have tolerated you for a long time, a very long time, Varvara Mikhailovna," she said. "But I am going to have to ask you to leave us for good. You and Sasha act like tiny children, milling about, pecking and cooing at each other. You disgust me, both of you. The presence of my own daughter I must accept. But you!" She pointed a crooked finger at Varvara and shook it. "I will not have *you* in my house!"

I wanted to bash her to the floor. Instead, I slammed the door and went to Papa's study and told him what had happened. He suggested that Varvara and I go to Telyatinki for a few days until Mama's temper cooled.

Today, before breakfast, I rode off beside Varvara Mikhailovna with a few loosely packed bags and my parrot. Even Chertkov's company seemed preferable to that of a woman whose entire life was now a sustained note of hatred streaked with self-pity.

# 3 0

# L. N.

## LETTER TO GANDHI

KOCHETY, 7 SEPTEMBER 1910

Your journal, *Indian Opinion*, arrived, and I was delighted to find out that so much has been written there by those who practice nonresistance. I would like to share with you my thoughts upon reading this material.

As I grow older, and now that I feel so vividly the approach of death, I want to tell others about things that move me in a special way. I want to talk about what seems to me of extreme importance, especially what is called nonresistance (but which is really nothing more than the teaching of love unsullied by false interpretations). The fact that love, which is the striving of human souls toward unity and the activity that follows from this striving, is the highest law of human life is sensed by most people in the depths of their souls (we see this most vividly with children)—sensed, that is, until the world snags them in its false teachings. All the great prophets—Indian, Chinese, Jewish, Greek, and Roman—have proclaimed this law. But I think it has been expressed most cogently by Christ, who stated explicitly that the Law and all true prophecies hang on this one supreme law. Having foreseen the possible distortions of this law, Christ pointed out the dangers threatening those who live according to more worldly interests; specifically, he mentioned the danger of letting oneself defend worldly interests by force (that is, returning a blow with a blow, reappropriating by force stolen objects, etcetera). Christ knew, as does any reasonable person, that the use of violence is incompatible with the basic law of love, and that once violence is tolerated, the inadequacy of the law of love reveals itself and repudiates it. Christian civilization, so brilliant on the surface, was founded on this obvious, strange, occasionally conscious but mostly unconscious misunderstanding and contradiction.

In essence, once resistance was allowed to exist side by side with love, love could no longer continue as a fundamental law. The only law that survived was the law of strength—the power of the stronger over the weaker. This is how, for nineteen centuries, Christians have lived. I grant that, at all times, people have mostly been guided by violence as they sought to organize their lives. The only difference between Christian civilization and the others is that Christianity has expressed this contradiction clearly. At the same time, while Christians accept this law, they disregard it in their private lives. Hence, Christians live a contradiction, basing their lives on violence while professing love. This contradiction continued to grow as the Christian world progressed, and it has reached new heights recently. The question now becomes this: either we recognize that we don't follow any religious or moral teaching and are guided by the power of the strong, or we recognize that all our taxes have been collected by force, and that our institutions (our courts, our police, but—above all—our armies) must be abolished.

This past spring, during a Scripture examination in Moscow, the teacher, a bishop, asked the girls being examined about the commandments, especially the sixth one. When the right answer was produced, the bishop routinely asked a further question: Is killing always forbidden by the Scriptures? The poor girls, corrupted by their mentors, had to answer "not always." Killing, they had been taught to say, is allowed in time of war and for the execution of criminals. Alas, when one of these poor girls (this is a true story, told to me recently by an eyewitness), after giving her answer, was asked the routine question about whether or not killing was always sinful she replied, blushing nervously, "Yes, it is always sinful." When questioned further, she pointed out that even in the Old Testament killing was forbidden; she added that Christ, in the New Testament, had even forbidden the perpetration of evil against one's brother. In spite of his renowned eloquence, the bishop was silenced, and the girl walked away victorious.

Yes, we may talk in our journals about the successes of aviation, about complex diplomatic relations, about clubs, inventions, alliances of all kinds, or about so-called works of art, yet still ignore what the girl in Moscow said to the bishop. However, we must not do that. Everybody in the Christian world knows this—knows it more or less vaguely—yet knows it. Socialism, communism, anarchism, the Salvation Army, the growth of crime, unemployment, the continuing luxury of the wealthy classes and the destitution of the poor, even the rate of suicides—all register this internal contradiction, which must be solved, and, of course, solved in the sense of acknowledging the law of love. And so your work in the Transvaal, at what seems to us the other end of the world, is the most central and important of all tasks now being done in the world, and not only Christians but all people will inevitably take part in it. I think you will be glad to know that this work is also rapidly developing in Russia in the form of refusals to do military service, a movement that grows every year. However insignificant the number may be among your people or ours who practice nonresistance, they can all say boldly that God is with them. And God is more powerful than men.

In recognizing Christianity, even in its distorted form as professed today, and in recognizing at the same time the necessity for armies and arms to kill in wars on such an enormous scale, governments express such a crying contradiction that sooner or later, probably sooner, they will be exposed. Then they shall put an end either to Christianity (which has been useful to them in maintaining power) or to the existence of armies and the violence they support. All governments—your British and our Russian included—feel this contradiction keenly; as a result, they attack those who practice nonresistance all the more vigorously, out of a feeling of self-preservation. Governments know where the enemy lies, and they keep a close eye on their own interests, aware that their very existence is at stake.

# 3 1

# BULGAKOV

It has been awkward for me here, living between two worlds. I still have a few friends at Telyatinki, mostly among the servant boys and drivers, but Sergeyenko and Chertkov have abandoned me. Since Chertkov came to live here again, the situation has grown even less tolerable. He is a crude, manipulative ideologue and, worse, a bore. On the other hand, Yasnaya Polyana is no longer the comfortable place for me it briefly was. Sofya Andreyevna has become skeptical of my intentions. She doesn't understand that my first loyalty must be to Leo Nikolayevich, that I try to do what serves him best. Her attitude toward me goes to extremes: either she treats me as a traitor or she behaves as she did yesterday when I passed her in the hall. "It's a godsend having you here with us, my dear. Did you realize that?" she said.

"If that's true, I'm pleased to hear it."

"It's much less tedious when you're here. Even Leo Nikolayevich feels livelier in your presence. And you are so tactful! A walking miracle of tact!"

It occurred to me that she was teasing, but she was not being entirely false. The problem with Sofya Andreyevna, always, is her manner of expression. Like many people, she has no control over her tone. A myriad of conflicting feelings cross in her head and mangle her nuances. You have to guess at what she really means.

"I should also say that you seem evasive," she said. "Are you evasive?"

"There's no way to answer that without implicating myself."

"Hush!" She put a finger to my lips. "No excuses. You're better than that. You are simply trying to keep the peace around here—a perfectly Christian thing to do."

"You do understand me, don't you?"

"I hope that in sixty-six years I have learned a little something, dear Valentin Fedorovich. I am to be pitied for what I haven't learned, perhaps."

I saw here a glimmer of the great person she might have been, given other circumstances. The situation of life here is not conducive to sainthood, especially for a woman in Sofya Andreyevna's position. She is torn, like me, between two points of the compass.

Through all this, I remain impressed with Leo Nikolayevich. He cannot be flattered. A few days ago, I walked down by the Voronka and came upon the bathhouse used by the family in summer, an endearing little structure made of clay and wattles. There is one plastered wall on the outside, on which visitors to the estate have inscribed their comments. I copied them in my notebook:

1. *Down with capital punishment!*
2. *May the life of L. N. be prolonged for as many years again.*
3. *In token of a visit to Count L. Tolstoy, a man with an intellect as large as a lion . . .*
4. *Come, all you who have grown weary in the struggle. Here you shall find peace.*
5. *This hallowed hut was visited by a student of the Moscow Geodetic School.*
6. *A humble pilgrim offers his respect.*

7. *An admirer of the Count, now and always.*

8. *Glory to the great one, glory!*

9. *No one, not even Tolstoy, knows the truth.*

10. *After long dreaming, we have at last visited the genius of the human mind.*

11. *"Those born to crawl cannot fly." What can I write? All look pale compared to you.*

12. *M. Bolsky was here.*

At her request, I gave Sofya Andreyevna a copy of these remarks, and she placed it on the piano in the sitting room, where Leo Nikolayevich would see it. Passing through the room, he said gruffly, "What is this?"

"Comments, my dear. Mostly about you. Bulgakov copied them from the bathhouse wall."

He picked up the paper and skimmed the comments. His lips moved slightly as he read.

"Not interesting," he said, dropping it on the piano.

Biryukov has been visiting. One of Leo Nikolayevich's most ardent disciples, he is being prosecuted by the government for possession of certain banned texts by Tolstoy. The trial begins in four weeks, and he may be sent to prison for as much as eighteen months. This is an enormous source of pain to Leo Nikolayevich, who is reluctant to have anyone suffer on his behalf.

This afternoon he went for a long ride on Delire and returned looking haggard. He said he would go to his room for a nap—not his usual habit.

We waited for him to sit down to dinner, but when he hadn't emerged from his room by seven we began eating without him. Sofya Andreyevna ladled out the soup, a hot chicken broth with fat carrots floating in it, then excused herself to check up on her husband. It was unlike him, she said, to miss a meal. None of us spoke, though we continued to eat. It is always nerve-racking when an old man does not appear on time.

Sofya Andreyevna came back wringing her hands. It seems that when she went in, he was sitting up on the edge of his bed. He looked pallid and claimed he was not hungry and would simply go to bed without dinner. His pulse was slightly rapid, and a fine sweat beaded his forehead and made his cheeks appear slick.

"Do you think he's all right?" asked Sergey. He, like his sister Tanya, was visiting for a few days, drawn home by the crisis between his parents. They all imagine it's possible to do something.

"His eyes looked vacant," she said. "I think he's about to have an attack."

After a few sips of broth, she stood again. "I must go to him."

When she left, Sergey and Tanya exchanged a look of annoyance. Why couldn't she let the poor man rest?

Their mother reappeared with a ghastly look. "Go quickly, Dushan Petrovich! He is unconscious, and mumbling—God knows what is wrong!" She crossed herself several times and knelt on the floor.

Everyone leaped from his place at the table, following Dushan Petrovich, who had run from the room as soon as he saw the flash of fear in Sofya Andreyevna's eyes.

The bedroom was dark, though a candle glimmered on the small bed table, its flame nearly extinguished. Leo Nikolayevich lay on the spread, his jaw quivering. He made queer, inarticulate, lowing sounds. Everyone stood by, dumbfounded.

We watched as Dushan Makovitsky undressed and covered him with a wool blanket. The old man's eyes were closed, but he struggled to talk, his brow contracted, his cheeks blown. He began to work his jaws as though he were chewing.

"He will probably sleep now," Dushan said. "You might as well finish your dinner. I'll stay with him."

"No, I'll stay," said Biryukov. This was unexpected. But he feels intensely loyal to the man; for his sake he would endure prison.

"Call me if there is any change," Dushan said. "And take his pulse every five minutes."

We descended quietly into the dining room and resumed our meal.

Hardly a word was said. I don't think we had quite finished dessert when Biryukov came rushing into the room shouting for Dushan Makovitsky.

Once again, we raced upstairs. Leo Nikolayevich had gone into convulsions, though by the time we reached the bedroom they were subsiding. Still, his legs twitched violently and his face appeared distorted by pain; the edges of his lips were drawn upward in a grimace. His fingers opened and closed mechanically like the mandibles of an insect.

Dushan Makovitsky gave orders like a military captain: "Hurry! Go down and get hot-water bottles for his feet. We should put a mustard plaster on his calves, too. And coffee! Bring some hot coffee!"

Amid the commotion, Dushan remained cool and dispassionate, a scientist through and through. Sofya Andreyevna stood with her back against the wall, praying, her eyelids red and swollen, half-closed.

Awhile later, covered in plasters and cold packs, Leo Nikolayevich sat up in bed with our help. The worst seemed to be over. He was trying to speak.

"Society . . . ," he said. "Society concerning three . . . concerning three . . . make a note of this."

"He is delirious," Dushan Makovitsky said.

"Must read!" Leo Nikolayevich declared, abruptly. Then, in a low, phlegm-clogged voice: "Wisdom . . . wisdom . . . wisdom."

What a grievous and unnatural thing to witness, a man of luminous intelligence reduced to blather. Nevertheless, even in his confusion, his central concerns as a human being boiled to the surface of his brain's caldron.

Without warning, the convulsions started up again, a succession of seizures that racked his entire body, as if he'd been struck by bolts of lightning. After each seizure, he lay shaking, trembling, sweating.

Dushan Makovitsky held down his shoulders during the worst convulsions, while Biryukov grasped his legs. Following orders, I massaged his calves whenever the writhing stopped. He suffered five attacks in a row, the fourth being especially violent, tossing him crosswise on the bed. We could barely restrain him.

When the worst appeared over, Sofya Andreyevna knelt by the bed and clutched his feet. "Dearest Lord, not now! Don't let him die now!"

Tanya put a hand on her mother's shoulder and said, in a kindly way, "Let's go downstairs, Mama. He should rest now."

"You don't understand," Sofya Andreyevna said. "If he dies, you will lose a father. But I will have killed a man."

Her words drilled through the dark.

"You must all go down," Dushan Makovitsky said. "I shall keep watch over him myself."

Leo Nikolayevich was not ready to die, however. By ten o'clock, he had nearly recovered, though he didn't try to stand. He sipped tea and asked that Dushan Makovitsky read to him from the Gospels.

I listened, quietly, at the door.

"A new commandment I give unto you, that ye love one another." The words sang in my heart, they were so beautiful, so perfectly simple. "By this all men know that ye are my disciples, if ye have loved one to another."

Leo Nikolayevich echoed Dushan in a hoarse, low voice.

Now I lay in bed awake, unable to relax. It had been harrowing to observe the signature of death on that dear, wrinkled face. As always, my thoughts turned to Masha in Petersburg. I lit the candle on my table and wrote a letter to her:

*I find myself wrestling once more with the old formulations. Is the soul really a separate entity? Is the body a vessel? I do not know, but—having seen dear Leo Nikolayevich in such a condition—life seems even more mysterious to me now, so fragile, evanescent. And precious. We pass, so briefly, from the unknown to the unknown, our days on earth like petals on a bough.*

*I think of you, Masha, even now, as I sit at this wooden table in the middle of the night. My thoughts return to you at odd times. Our friendship is like a chink of light in an otherwise dark wall. It's as if, somehow, I have you with me always. Here again the mystery of time and space confounds me, upsets me. Your soul,*

*I dare to think, has linked itself to mine, and the space between us is somehow irrelevant. I don't believe it exists. I actually believe I have you here beside me when you're not. Am I foolish to think such things?*

*I keep thinking, however, that only love could lessen the terrible rift between mind and body, between spirit and flesh, that torments me. I can't imagine what it means to say that today I am a young man in the flush of youth, that tomorrow I will be old and alone, that the next day I shall be dust in the earth. If there is no love in the world, no enduring spirit in man, then I am nothing now, our affection is nothing, and we might as well both be dead.*

*But as soon as I write that, I feel the deep hunger for God that makes me aware that God exists. By God I mean the World Spirit, the sense of the Eternal, the hovering blaze or mind that informs and, in a way, creates the world around us. We are each of us a small God, and the love we engender between us can only increase the Godness within us, enlarge the circle of affection we can share, the breath of spirit.*

*You will, I hope, forgive my expostulations and philosophizing. It is horribly late, and language runs away from me. I am tired now, can hardly think. Tomorrow, I shall write again. Write to me. I miss you. I love you.*

## 3 2

# SOFYA ANDREYEVNA

"Mother, you're jealous of him," Sasha said to me yesterday. "That's the problem."

Where is that girl's mind? Of course I'm jealous of him! Why should I share him with vagabonds and mountebanks, money grubbers and frauds? Yet I must try to ensure that he is not continually upset. The tension will kill him. It is my duty, as his wife, to see that he lives in a calm atmosphere.

The day after Lyovochka's attack I told Sasha that she and Varvara Mikhailovna could return home. It was killing her father to have his little briar rose removed from him. And there was no telling what plots she might hatch with Chertkov once removed from my view. So I made a spectacle of myself, standing on the wooden steps at Telyatinki, begging forgiveness of my daughter and her friend. They appeared genuinely dumbfounded. I loved it.

Sasha is a sentimental girl, the kind who weeps over the death of a toad; she burst into tears at the sight of me, and we embraced like long-lost sisters. Even Varvara Mikhailovna, who has the sensitivity of a granite monument, shed a few lightly manufactured tears and hugged me.

"A family gathering!" said Chertkov, dripping poison as he stepped from the shadows. Light glanced from his slick, bald forehead. He was redolent of scent—a womanly affectation appropriate to a man of his Greekish ways.

"It is good to see you, Vladimir Grigorevich."

"Always a pleasure, to be sure."

"I would like you to visit us tomorrow. Will you come for lunch?"

He thanked me without a trace of his usual irony, a marvelous performance.

The offer was rash, however. I should have known better. He contaminates the ground he walks on. And there is the matter of habit. If the idea were planted that he could visit us without difficulty, he would turn up every day.

When I heard the approach of his carriage, my pulse began to race: 142! I peered out the window of my bedroom with binoculars. Lyovochka stood on the front steps, happily waiting to receive his disciple. I had asked him not to embrace the man. That is more than I can bear. But he could not hide the joy on his face; he looked like a young bride who has just spied her lover in the distance. A disgusting thing for the servants to see!

How I managed I shall never know. With all my strength, I maintained a cool civility, inquiring after his mother and wife, inwardly counting the minutes till that scoundrel was out of my house. When he had finally gone, I begged Lyovochka to make this the last time I had to endure that malevolent presence. He unexpectedly agreed to write to Chertkov and his wife, suggesting that this experiment in reconciliation was premature. Some time must pass before they attempt another visit.

I suppose Lyovochka was unwilling to make my life harder because he feels guilty. A few days ago, I discovered a secret diary in his boot. I've said nothing to him about the diary, but he must realize it is missing. The wording is cryptic, but it confirms my suspicion that he and Chertkov have entered into an unholy contract to steal his copyrights from the family. This comes just when I have had an offer from Prozveshenye, one of the most sturdy publishing firms in

Russia, to purchase all the rights to Lyovochka's work upon his death. And they have offered one million rubles! Enough to sustain the Tolstoy family—all twenty-five grandchildren included—for life!

I went into Lyovochka's study with the letter from Prozveshenye, but he waved me aside.

"Don't concern yourself with such matters," he said. "They are of no importance. I do not write for publishers. I write for people."

He was beyond arguing with, so I was forced to write an explicit letter to him on the fourteenth of October:

*You ask about my health every day with an air of compassion, Lyovochka. You ask how I have slept with such apparent concern in your voice. And yet, each day, you drive fresh nails into my heart, shortening my life and subjecting me to unbearable pain. Nothing I do seems to ease this pain—you should know that. It was the decision of Fate that I should learn about this twist, this corrupt deed you have perpetrated by depriving your numerous offspring of your copyrights (I might point out that your partner in crime has not done the same kind of thing to his family). . . .*

*The government that you and your friends slander and criticize in your pamphlets will now legally take the bread out of the mouths of your heirs and give it to some rich publishers in Moscow, while your very own grandchildren will starve as a result of your vanity and sin. And it is the government, again—in the form of the State Bank—that will receive Tolstoy's diaries for safekeeping, a mere ruse for keeping them from your wife. . . .*

*I am horrified, aghast, to think of what evil may grow up out of your grave, and in the memories of your children and grandchildren.*

I put this letter on his desk in the morning. Just before lunch, my hands trembling, I knocked at the door of his study. I wanted his reaction, in person. This is too important an issue to leave to chance.

He told me to come in.

"Lyovochka," I said, feeling like a schoolgirl on a visit to the headmaster. "I wonder if you have read my letter."

"I have."

I waited beside him, my hands folded in front of my apron. "Do you have anything to say to me?"

He looked up at me with disdain such as I have never seen before on his face. His nostrils appeared, like a bull's, to flare.

"Can you possibly leave me in peace?" he asked.

I implored him to think about his family, to reconsider whatever he had done to adjust his will, to listen to reason. But he sat impassively in his chair, casting a pall across the room like a bare electric light.

"Are you finished, Sofya Andreyevna?"

"I am," I said. I could see that, in all ways, I was. Whatever love may have lived between us was dead.

We spoke not a word to each other that day. The following morning he left home before breakfast, on horseback. This was most unlike him. I realized he must be heading to Telyatinki, so I set off, on foot, for Chertkov's house.

At the entrance to the estate, I hid myself in a low ditch. I lay there all day with binoculars trained on the house. I did not see Lyovochka's horse anywhere, or catch a glimpse of him. Twice I saw Chertkov come and go, which made me wonder if, indeed, Lyovochka had gone to Telyatinki. Perhaps I had been mistaken?

When darkness began to fall, I set off, weary of heart, back to Yasnaya Polyana. By the time I got there, my temples throbbed. My feet burned. I felt dizzy and nauseated.

I sat on a wooden bench, beneath a tall pine, for an hour or two. Stars speckled the sky above me, and I felt I was looking into infinity. I said, in my heart, *I am all yours, God. Take me. Take me.* I wanted God or oblivion. I wanted to count myself among the thousand stars.

I might easily have sat there forever had not Ivan, the coach driver, seen me.

"Countess? Is that you?"

"Ivan," I said. "It's me."

"Are you all right?"

"I am quite unwell, Ivan. Help me."

He took my hand and led me home, like an old mule back to the barn.

Lyovochka was still awake, sitting on his bed, reading by candlelight. I don't know why I did this, but I told him exactly what I had done that day, how I had waited in the ditch, frantic, till nightfall. How I had asked, prayed, even begged, for death.

He listened carefully, then said, "Sonya, I am extremely tired of your whims. What I want now is freedom. I am eighty-two years old, and I refuse to let you treat me like a child. I will not be tied to my wife's apron strings!"

"What does this mean?"

"It means that, from now on, I shall feel perfectly free to write to Chertkov, even to meet with him when I feel it is necessary. I cannot play this game any longer."

"You can't do this to me," I said.

"Wait and see," he said.

The next day, Lyovochka seemed determined to prove his independence. He sat in the garden drinking tea with Novikov, a muzhik he admires for reasons I cannot fathom. Right in front of me, Novikov said, "You ought to see how we treat our women in the village! When they get out of line—swat!" He slapped his thigh with a flat palm. "A woman has to be ruled with a stick! It's the only way to keep them quiet."

Lyovochka, apostle of nonviolence, began to laugh uncontrollably. "We have a good deal to learn from the muzhiks," he said. "This is quite wonderful. Lovely!"

I left them to their ridiculous conversation.

That afternoon, Lyovochka decided to prove his manliness by resuming gymnastics. As a young man, he would hang upside down from a bar in his study, terrifying the servants. "It brings blood to the brain," he used to say. Now he attempted to hang upside down from a wardrobe, which has some iron hooks that fit his bootheels. But his weight, of course, brought the whole thing down on top of him.

"You're like a child," I told him. "You can't be trusted."

Furious more with himself than with me, he locked his study door until dinner. At seven, he came down and ate in silence.

▓ It is almost November, and I am sad. The weather grows worse every day: windy and cold, with rain like pellets, sometimes a dust of snow. I walk in the woods each morning with my dogs, Marquis and Belka. We follow the same ruts in Zasyeka Wood that Lyovochka uses when he goes riding in the afternoons. I can't believe he still insists on riding. At least he is willing to let Dushan Makovitsky ride behind him. A few days ago he took a frightful spill, and came home covered with black mud. But I said nothing about the incident. It would only have upset him.

Miss Natalya Alexevna Almedingen arrived yesterday. An elegant woman, she edits a magazine and writes popular books for children. Quietly, she has been talking to me about the deal with Prozveshenye (whom she apparently represents). They are desperate to get Lyovochka's copyright. If I can induce him to sign a statement, even a tentative, noncommittal statement, this will be useful. I must stop Chertkov while there is time.

We have other visitors, as usual. There is the talkative Gastev, who comes full of gossip, and Lyovochka takes it in quite eagerly. Tanya is here again. And Sergey, who plays chess with his father twice a day. I wonder how I tolerate these crowds.

Everything has been going well for a little bit, so I was saddened when I discovered that Bulgakov had taken a letter to Telyatinki this morning. Sasha made a note of this, and I found the note on her desk in the Remington room.

"Who was the letter for?" I asked her.

"Galya," she said.

Why was my husband writing to Chertkov's wife? I went straight to his study to ask him.

"You sent a letter to Galya Chertkova this morning," I said.

"Perhaps I did. It should not concern you." He hunched over his desk, continuing to work.

"What was it about?"

"I forget," he said. "Old men forget things."

"Please, darling. You needn't treat me like a child."

"I simply don't recall what was in that letter."

"You're lying to me."

He squirmed in his chair. I had him now!

"Let me see a copy of that letter," I said.

"Never!" He stood up, looking like Jove himself, his fists full of lightning. He would have struck me dead if he could have.

"There was a time when you would never have screamed like that," I said. "A time when you loved me."

He withered into his chair. I saw before me an old, sick man— the ghost of the man I love, that I have loved more than life itself, for nearly fifty years. Why doesn't he know this? Why can't he feel the presence of my love?

"I wish you would leave me alone," he said. "I want to be alone."

"You *are* alone, Lyovochka. We are both alone. We have been alone for some time."

"I must go away."

"You have already gone," I said. "I live alone here."

I left in control, but as soon as I stepped outside the study I had to brace myself by leaning with my back to the wall. My legs could barely hold me. My *life* could barely hold me.

"Lyovochka," I said, muttering into my fingers. I shook all over. I waited for his hand to touch my shoulder. For his big shadow to loom, to cover me as night covers the fields. To be led to my bed, to be held, to be loved.

But he never came.

He will never come again.

# 3 3

# BULGAKOV

Last night I slept in my little room at Telyatinki, which always reminds me of Masha. I see her in every object in the room, feel her presence. I want her beside me, touching me. I read and reread her letters, and I feel guilty. It is all wrong to have come to Yasnaya Polyana to work with Tolstoy but to find myself dwelling compulsively on my relations with a woman.

This separation, though painful, has made me vividly aware of my need for her. I can see the world more freshly through her eyes. Everything that happens to me takes on a delicious tint because of her.

Lately, I have found myself in greater sympathy with the Tolstoyans, partly because it is so difficult to remain intimate with Sofya Andreyevna. She has grown testy and suspicious, more so than ever.

Chertkov floats on air nowadays, smelling victory. Even so, his brittle relations with Sofya Andreyevna worry him, since they prevent easy access to Leo Nikolayevich; he talks incessantly about "mending fences" with her so that he might spend more time with the Master before he dies.

I think Chertkov underestimates the intensity of her feelings about him. She does not merely dislike him. She loathes him.

This morning, shortly after breakfast, I was summoned to the dining room in Telyatinki. Chertkov was seated on a high stool, looking radiant. Like a bride before the wedding. The atmosphere in the room was prickly and tense.

I bowed to him, more emphatically than necessary.

"There is news," he said. "Astonishing news, in fact."

I felt my stomach muscles tighten.

Chertkov maintained a cool demeanor. "Leo Nikolayevich has left," he said. He plucked each word from space as if with tongs, laying them on a bone china plate. "He left this morning, with Dushan. Nobody knows where they have gone."

This came like a death in the family after a protracted illness. In such cases, one regrets the loss but is also relieved.

"Go to Sofya Andreyevna," Chertkov said. "Find out what you can, and report to me later in the day."

I set out immediately for Yasnaya Polyana, arriving at about eleven; Sofya Andreyevna had only just awakened, having passed a sleepless night. Her eyes were puffy and red, her cheeks swollen, as if she had already been crying for several hours. But panic animated her now. She and Sasha and I converged, breathlessly, on the second-floor landing.

"Where is he, Sasha?" Sofya Andreyevna spoke with a rare intensity. "Where is Papa?"

"He has left home."

"What do you mean, 'left home'? When?"

"Last night."

"This is impossible, Sasha!"

"I'm telling you what happened, Mama. He is gone. I have no idea where. Nobody has."

Sofya Andreyevna staggered backward, her mind a million leaves whirling in a dark wood. "He is gone," she repeated, testing the words.

"Yes. He is gone," Sasha said.

"Has he gone for good?"

"I think so."

"Alone?"

"With Dushan."

Then she became solicitous. "Darling Sasha, now tell me. Where has your father gone? I'm sure you know. You mustn't play games with me . . . not now."

"I have no idea where he went. He said nothing specific. But he gave me a letter." She handed the letter to her mother.

Sofya Andreyevna tore at the paper, holding her breath. She read it slowly, moving her lips:

*My departure will grieve you. I am sorry about this, but please understand and believe I cannot do otherwise. My position in this house has become intolerable. Along with everything else, I can no longer abide these luxurious conditions. What I am now doing is what old people have commonly done—leave their worldly life behind to spend their last days in peace and solitude.*

*Please understand this and do not attempt to follow me, even if you discover my whereabouts. This would only worsen your position and mine. It would not change my decision.*

*I am grateful to you for your honest forty-eight years of life with me, and I ask you to forgive me for everything I am guilty of before you, as I, with all my heart, forgive you for what you may be guilty of before me. I advise you to adjust to the new conditions of life you will face on my departure, and to bear me no ill will.*

*If you wish to write to me, tell Sasha. She will know my whereabouts and send me anything I need; but she cannot tell you where I am, since I have made her promise to tell no one.*

The letter, dated 28 October, was signed in the usual scrawling hand.

Sofya Andreyevna's face began to quiver, her cheeks like sheets drying in the wind, cracked and blown. The muscles in her neck, like cords, stood out boldly now, as if trying to maintain the balance of her immense head. Her shoulders began to shake. Within a moment, she drew up her floor-length dress and ran down the stairs, howling, out the front door. From the window, we caught a glimpse of her streaking across the lawn.

"She's heading for the pond!" cried Sasha. "Go after her!"

Following directly in Sasha's path, I squinted into the sun and saw Sofya Andreyevna's figure, a large, gray blur, disappear into a stand of beeches. She ran faster than I could believe was possible for a woman of her age and size.

A couple of servants raced behind me. There was Semen Nikolaye-vich, the cook, and Vanya, the fat manservant, who ran on spindly legs that barely held him up. I saw Timothy, too—the bastard son—with his toothless grin, waving from a tree.

Sofya Andreyevna had by now passed the beeches and was headed through a grove of lime trees toward the pond. Sasha was behind me, shouting, "Don't run so fast!"

But it would not do to linger. Sofya Andreyevna was nearing the pond. I could just see her in the distance, her white calves flashing.

Suddenly, Sasha passed me, huffing like a steam engine, her skirts wheeling in the sun. Now she was shouting, "Hurry! Hurry!"

Sofya Andreyevna stood on the planks by the bathhouse where the women bend to wash the linen. She turned, saw us running toward her, and rushed out onto the wooden bridge. But the slats were slippery, and she fell hard on her back. She clawed at the surface with her red hands, to no avail, and rolled off sideways into the black water.

Sasha was well ahead of me now, approaching the bridge at full tilt. She had managed, while she ran, to tear off her thickly knit wool sweater. But the mossy slats toppled her, too, and she skidded onto her backside. By the time I reached the bridge, she had scrambled to her feet and jumped into the pond ahead of me. I kicked off my boots and followed, jumping feet first into the icy water.

Water is a strange dimension, one that alters the geometry of movement. It makes space and time seem oddly irrational. I seemed to experience a thousand images and thoughts in the brief moments after I hit the water and before I spotted Sofya Andreyevna floating with her cheeks puffed like the gills of a tropical fish.

The distance between me and Sofya Andreyevna seemed infinite, and I felt dizzy now, my skin tingling, my breath short. The murky water was bitter, having been chilled by several terribly cold nights.

Sofya Andreyevna suddenly bobbed to the surface like an otter, face up, about ten yards away. She looked dead already, with water trickling into her open mouth, then slipped completely under once again.

Sasha, who can barely swim herself, was thrashing about not far away, trying to reach her mother without success.

"Get back to the dock, Sasha!" I shouted.

"Help!"

I reached for her hand and helped her back to the wooden dock.

"She's drowning!"

"You mustn't try to help!" I said. "I can manage!"

Though we were face to face, I was shouting.

Pushing away from the dock, I made a sharp plunge in what seemed like the right direction and, after an impossibly long time, perhaps ten or fifteen seconds, touched Sofya Andreyevna's head. Snarling my fingers in her long hair, which had come undone in the water, I dragged her back to the bank, rolling her large body up along the margin of the pond. She was black with mud, her eyes closed, her tongue lolling between her teeth.

"She's dead!" Sasha was crying. "My mother is dead!"

Vanya, the overweight manservant, was beside Sofya Andreyevna now, and he seemed to know what to do. He turned her over on her stomach and pushed some water from her lungs with his knees, astride her like one hippo mounting another. She lay there in silence, in what I imagined was agony, a great, dark slab of a woman. In a few moments, she was breathing normally, her eyes closed. Life had returned to torture her for another while.

When she was able to stand, we led her back to the house, stopping to rest every few minutes. At one point she fell sobbing to the ground, saying, "Let me die here! Let me die! Why must you all rob me of my death?"

Finally, Vanya and I made a seat with our hands and carried her to the house. She was shuddering throughout, and her lips were dark blue. Before we even got her into bed, however, she told Vanya to go immediately to the station to inquire what train her husband had taken.

She fell into a kind of stupor and slept for an hour, but when she woke she began beating her breast with a stone paperweight. We took away the paperweight as well as the penknife on her desk and the vial of opium in her dresser drawer.

Sasha, who seemed quite unstable herself now, sent to Tula for the psychiatric doctor who had helped Sofya Andreyevna during previous crises. She also summoned the Sukhotins by telegram.

When Vanya returned with news of the train Leo Nikolayevich had taken, Sofya Andreyevna wrote a telegram, which she addressed to Train Number 9. It said, "Dearest Papa: Return at once, Sasha." She had told Vanya to show it to no one, but—thank goodness—he showed the telegram to Sasha (since, like most of the servants, he is loyal to Leo Nikolayevich and dislikes Sofya Andreyevna). Sasha let the telegram go but sent with it one of her own telling her father to ignore all telegrams supposedly from her that were not signed "Alexandra." Sasha enjoys these little deceits. She is not unlike her mother in this regard.

I sat in the Remington room with Sasha throughout the long afternoon. She told me frankly that she didn't know where her father had gone. Indeed, his remark in the letter to her mother had puzzled her. He had told several people, including her, that he would probably visit his sister, a nun at the Shamardino, in the province of Kaluga. This was, as he put it, "on his way." But where he planned to go after visiting Shamardino was anyone's guess.

Having talked to Sasha and several of the house servants, I was able to piece together what happened last night.

Near midnight, Leo Nikolayevich had been awakened by the sound of rustling papers in his study. It was Sofya Andreyevna, who was looking for concrete evidence of a new will. This was the last straw. A few hours later, he knocked quietly on the door of Sasha and Varvara Mikhailovna, who share a small room on the same floor.

"Who is it?" Sasha cried.

"It is I."

Sasha opened the door and found her father with a candle in his hand. He had a look of resolution in his eyes.

"I'm leaving immediately, for good," he said. "But I need your help."

Dushan Makovitsky had already been roused and was packing for himself. He would accompany Leo Nikolayevich on his final journey.

They huddled in Leo Nikolayevich's room, trying to decide what he must take.

"Only the essentials!" he kept saying. "I can take nothing that isn't absolutely necessary." These included a flashlight, a fur coat, and the apparatus for taking an enema.

The packing done, he went to the stables to harness the horses himself. On the way, in total darkness, he fell into a thicket and lost his hat. He returned, hatless, demanding his flashlight. Sasha began to worry that he was not sufficiently well to travel, but she said nothing. Her father had made up his mind to go.

Adrian Eliseyev, the coachman, had been summoned by Dushan Makovitsky, and he went to the barn with his master to harness the horses to the droshky. Filya, a postilion, lit a torch to ride ahead of the droshky, since it was a starless, moonless night and they could barely see the road.

"Everything was ready to go," Sasha told me, "when Papa asked for a moment by himself. He walked to the front lawn and stood for a long while looking up at the house where he was born. I thought, briefly, that he might change his mind and go back to bed. Suddenly, he knelt in the wet grass, bowing low to rub his fingers in the blades. Then he kissed the ground and rose. His past life was behind him now."

Sasha and Varvara Mikhailovna helped him to the droshky, having exchanged a tearful farewell, and Adrian drove them off to the Ya-senki Station, where Leo Nikolayevich and Dushan Makovitsky took the eight o'clock train for all points south.

This was the beginning of a new life for Leo Tolstoy. Of that much, everyone was sure.

# 3 4

## L. N.

**DIARY ENTRY**

I lay down at half past eleven and slept till three. Then, as on previous nights, I heard footsteps, the squeaking of doors. I had not before bothered to look, but I did so now and found a light under the crack in my study door. I heard the riffling of papers. It was Sofya Andreyevna, searching my study, probably reading things I had written. The day before she had insisted that I not close my doors, and she kept her own doors open, so that my slightest movements could be detected. She wants my every word and movement to be known to her instantly, to be under her control. When I heard her this time, closing the door, walking down the hall, I felt the deepest sense of aversion and rage. I don't know why, but I could not restrain myself. I tried to fall asleep, but that was impossible now. I tossed and turned, lit a candle, then sat up.

My door suddenly opened. It was Sofya Andreyevna, who said, "How are you?" She was surprised, she said, to discover a light. My fury increased. I checked my pulse—ninety-seven.

I could lie there no longer, and suddenly I made the final decision to leave home. I am writing her a letter and am beginning to pack only what is necessary in order to leave. I woke Dushan, then Sasha—they helped me. I shook at the thought that my wife would hear and come out to check on us. There would have been scenes, hysteria, and—afterward—no getting away without an upset. At six o'clock everything was packed, somehow, and I went to the stable to tell them to harness. (Dushan, Sasha, and Varvara finished the packing.) It was still night—pitch dark. I missed the path to the barn, stumbled in some brush, fell, lost my hat, then made my way back to the house with difficulty. The others came back with me. I trembled inside, fearing pursuit. But, at last, we drove off.

At Yasenki Station we had to wait an hour, and I fully expected my wife to appear at any moment. At last we took our places in the railway carriage and the train lurched forward; my fear evaporated, and pity for Sofya Andreyevna rose in my breast. Still, I had no doubts about what I had done. Perhaps I am wrong and merely seeking to justify my behavior, but it strikes me that I have saved myself—not Leo Nikolayevich but that something of which there is sometimes a spark in me.

The journey beyond Gorkachev to Shamardino took place in a crowded, third-class carriage full of working people. It was all instructive, though I took it in quite feebly. It is now evening, and we are in the monastery at Optina.

29 OCTOBER 1910

Slept badly. In the morning was surprised to see Sergeyenko. Not understanding what news he brought me, I greeted him cheerfully. Then he told the terrible story. Sofya Andreyevna, having read my letter, gave a cry, ran outside, and threw herself into the pond. Sasha and Vanya fished her out.

Andrey is home. They have all guessed my whereabouts, and Sofya Andreyevna has insisted that Andrey come to fetch me home. I expect his arrival today. A letter from Sasha has arrived. She advises me not to despair. She has called in a mental specialist, and she expects Sergey and Tanya. I was very depressed all day and feeble. Went for a walk. Yesterday, I managed to add a note to my speech on capital punishment.

Drove to Shamardino. A most consoling and happy impression of Mashenka, my sister, and her daughter, Lizanka. On the journey, I puzzled over ways of escape for me and Sofya Andreyevna from our situation, but I could think of nothing. I must concentrate only on how to avoid sin.

# 35

# LETTERS

## FROM SERGEY TO L. N.

Dear Papa,

I write because Sasha says you would like our opinion. I think Mama
is mentally ill and in many respects irresponsible, and I believe it was
necessary for you to separate. You should have done so long ago.
However, this situation is painful for you both. I also think that if
anything happens to Mama—and I think nothing will—you should
not blame yourself. I believe you chose the right way out. Forgive the
frankness of my letter.

## FROM ILYA TO L. N.

Dear Papa,

I feel I must write to you at this painful time. I want to tell you the
truth, and I know you prefer that I do so.

Sasha will inform you of what happened after you left, how we all assembled at home, and what we discussed and decided. Nevertheless, I'm afraid that her explanation will seem one-sided, so I am writing, too. We chose not to judge your actions. A thousand causes exist for every action, and even if we could know all of them, we could still not correlate them. Needless to say, we have no desire to, and cannot, attach blame to anyone. Yet we must do what we can to preserve Mama and calm her. For two days now she has eaten nothing and drunk only a mouthful or so of water in the evening. She says there is no reason for her to live, and her state is so pitiful that none of us can speak of her without weeping. As ever, in her case, there is much affectation and sentimentality, but at the same time there is so much sincerity that her life is genuinely in peril. That is my opinion, and, for truth's sake, I offer it bluntly. I realize that your life here was difficult, but you regarded that life as your cross, as did those who know and love you. I am sorry you choose not to bear that cross to the end. You have both lived long lives and should die becomingly.

Forgive me if, by chance, it seems to you that I speak harshly. Be sure that I love and understand you in many things, and that I wish only to help. I do not ask you to return here at once, since I know you cannot do that. But, for the sake of Mama's mental health, it is important that you keep in close touch with her. Write to her. Give her the opportunity to strengthen her nervous system, and then let whatever God decrees happen as it will! If you wish to write me, I shall be very glad.

**FROM ANDREY TO L. N.**

Dear Papa,

Only the very best of feelings, such as I mentioned at our last meeting, oblige me to say what I think about my mother's condition.

Tanya, Sergey, Ilya, Mikhail, and I have gathered here, and however much we consider the matter, we have been unable to think of any way but one of protecting Mama from herself, though I think she will eventually kill herself no matter what we do. The only way to prevent it is to put her under constant supervision. Of course, she would never submit to it. The present situation is an impossible one, since we cannot abandon our own families and work to remain at our mother's side. I know you have finally decided not to return, but as a conscientious duty I must warn you that by this final decision you are killing our mother.

I know how heavy the burden has been for you during the last months, but I also know that Mama is mentally ill, and that living together has, in these late years, been unbearable for you both. Had you summoned us to speak with Mama, so that you might not separate for an infinite period but amicably in the hope that her nerves would calm, we might not have experienced this dreadful suffering that we share with you both—even though you are far away. As to what you said to me the last time we met about the luxury surrounding you, it strikes me that since you have endured it up until now you might have sacrificed the last years of your life for the sake of your family and put up with it awhile longer.

Forgive me, dearest Papa, if my letter seems too full of advice, but I feel how painful and sad things are for you and Mama, whom I find it impossible to look at without anguish.

## FROM TANYA TO L. N.

Dearest, most precious Papa,

You have always suffered from too much advice, so I won't give you any more. Like everyone else, you have to act as best you can and as you consider necessary. I shall never condemn you. Of Mama, I will say only that she is pitiable and touching. For her, either fear or power is necessary. We try to calm her, and this seems to help.

I am exhausted and foolish. Forgive me. Good-bye, my friend.

## FROM L. N. TO SERGEY AND TANYA

4:00 A.M., OPTINA. 31 OCTOBER 1910

Dearest Sergey and Tanya,

Thank you very much, kind friends, true friends, for your sympathy in my grief and for your letters. Your letter, Sergey, gave me special pleasure. It is brief, pithy, clear, and—above all—generous. I can't help being afraid of everything and can't free myself from a feeling of responsibility, but I had not the strength to act otherwise. I am also writing to Mama. She will show you the letter. I wrote, after thinking it over carefully, what I was able to write.

We are just leaving here, but we do not yet know where we're going. You can always reach me through Chertkov.

Good-bye, and thank you, sweet children. Forgive me for causing you to suffer—especially you, my darling Tanya. Well, that is all. I must hurry to avoid what I most fear—that your mother will find me. A meeting with her now would be terrible. Well, good-bye.

## FROM L. N. TO SOFYA ANDREYEVNA

OPTINA. 31 OCTOBER 1910

Dearest Sonya,

A meeting between us, still more my return at this time, is impossible. It would be harmful for you, as my position and ill health would become even worse than they are because of your agitation and irritability. I advise you to reconcile yourself to what has happened. Try to settle down in your new situation and, above all, attend to your health.

If you . . . I cannot say love me but at least do not hate me . . . you should try to understand my position to some extent. And if you do that, you will not only not condemn me but help me find peace and the possibility of living some sort of human life. Help me by controlling yourself, by not wishing for me to return right now.

Your present mood reveals more than anything else your loss of self-control, which makes my return unthinkable at present. Only you can free me from the suffering we endure. Try to channel all your strength toward pacifying your soul.

I have spent two days at Shamardino and Optina, and now I am leaving. I will mail this letter on the road. I shall not say where I'm going, since I consider our separation essential for us both. Don't think I left because I didn't love you. I love and pity you with all my heart, but I can't do otherwise than as I am doing. Your letter was written sincerely, I know, but you are not capable of carrying out what you say. What matters is not the fulfillment of any wish or demand of mine, only your equanimity and calm and reasonable relation to life.

As long as that is missing, life with you is unthinkable for me. To return to you while you are in such a state would mean to renounce life. And I do not consider that I have the right to do that.

Farewell, dear Sonya, and may God help you! Life is not a jest, and we have no right to throw it away on a whim. And to measure it by its length of time is also unreasonable. Perhaps those months that remain to us are more important than all the years we have yet lived, and they should be lived well.

# 3 6

# SASHA

I traveled to Shamardino with Varvara Mikhailovna just two days after Papa. Chertkov told me exactly where to find them.

All day we felt free, Varvara and I, riding in a second-class carriage with the golden sun of October glazing the stubble fields on either side of the train as we rode southward. We would lunge through a deep pine forest, full of shadows, then burst onto open plains. We would rise over small hills, descend into valleys, then pass beneath rocky cliffs. We both sat tensely in our seats, upright, gazing at the wonder of creation.

When I think of the world's great beauty, I am saddened by humankind. We have nothing to match it. Our souls are dirty, soiled by greed, by hatred of differences.

Occasionally Varvara would reach across the seat and touch my hand. It moved me to tears. There is such love between us. It makes the bright world all the more blazing.

I had brought with me a cache of letters from my brothers, from Tanya and Mama. I had not, of course, read them, but I knew they would cause Papa a good deal of pain. What he required now was release. It seems we cannot let him die in peace.

Near dusk, we arrived at the white-walled nunnery at Shamardino, where my aunt now lives. She is an Orthodox Christian who adheres slavishly to the letter of the law, but she and Papa have remained on excellent terms. We went straight to my aunt's narrow cell. I hardly recognized her. A dried-out little fig of a woman in a dark habit, she was taken aback when I entered.

"A family conference?" she said, with only a whiff of cynicism.

A nun should never be ironic, and she knew that.

"Where is my father?"

"Sit down, my dear," she said. She pointed a crooked finger at Varvara Mikhailovna. "And you, sit. Who is this young woman you have brought with you?"

I introduced my aunt to my companion, who looked fresh and fine in a peasant dress with yellow embroidery on the neckline. Her dark hair shone in the candlelight.

"Alexandra Lvovna!" cried Papa, who stood frozen in the doorway.

"Papa!"

We embraced tightly, and he wept. I knew at once that he was glad to see me.

"And you, Varvara," he said, cupping her chin in his hand.

He studied her like a bronze statue, then turned to me. "I hope your mother has not accompanied you?"

"She is at home. But she is suffering."

Papa shifted awkwardly from foot to foot.

"There was nothing else you could do."

"I know," he said. "Nevertheless, if something happens to her, it will sadden me. She is still my wife. One can't avoid a sense of responsibility for things. . . ."

"She wants you back. You must know that."

He shifted again, uncomfortably. "I have found an isba to rent," he said, his eyes fixed on the floor. "It's a pleasant little hut within the sound of church bells. A good place to end my days, Sasha. I shall read and think and, perhaps, even write a little."

"Mama will find you. She will drag you home."

Varvara Mikhailovna squeezed my wrist. Enough.

"You're right, I'm afraid," Papa answered. "We must leave before she finds us here."

A servant passed in the hallway, and my aunt called to her for tea. "Sit down," she said to us. "This useless chatter upsets everyone."

Papa bent to kiss his sister on the brow. "I cannot stay, though I would like to."

I gave Papa the letters, and he took them reluctantly and went back to his room to read them.

Later that night, we sat about in Papa's room, planning our next move. A fire in the stony hearth gave off the sweet odor of peat.

"If we are to go," said Dushan Makovitsky, with his penchant for truisms, "we must know where we are going."

"Excellent, Dushan Petrovich," Varvara said, though I was the only one in the room who caught her sarcastic undertone. "Let us go somewhere."

Papa seemed quite eager to discuss possible routes. It was suggested that Bulgaria or Turkey might be good destinations—nobody would know us there, and the climate would be tolerable. I wondered, however, if we might not need passports to cross the border. Why not settle in the Caucasus? There are several Tolstoyan colonies there, and they would be only too flattered if Leo Tolstoy himself chose to pass his final days among them.

We had been debating the pros and cons of the Caucasus for a while when, unexpectedly, Papa began to speak in an angry voice. It was quite unlike him. "No! I cannot stand these projections, these ridiculous plans. Let us go . . . anywhere will do. We need no plans."

Papa has always avoided plans, preferring the spontaneity of a butterfly. He likes to point out that Christ himself was against plotting the future.

"I am very tired," Papa said.

"Let me take you to your bed, Papa."

I led him to a cot in the small room with whitewashed walls and a vaulted ceiling. The bed table had been laid out just like at home, with a candle, some matches, a notebook, and sharpened pencils. He likes to be able to make notes in the middle of the night if he should awaken with an idea or want to record a dream.

He lay down gingerly. He was so exhausted he did not even want me to remove his boots, though I covered him with a rough wool blanket, since the room was very cold. He was asleep before I left, snoring through his wrinkled mouth. It worried me that his breathing was so uneven.

I slept in a room with several other women and Varvara Mikhailovna. It was a peculiar, disorienting experience. The room smelled of beeswax and disinfectant. A filthy cat slept under my cot, making my eyes itch. An old woman coughed in her sleep like a goat on the hillside. I was freezing.

Somehow, I managed to fall asleep. But Varvara Mikhailovna woke me at four, pricking the bubble of my dreaming with her sharp words.

"Wake up, Sasha! We're leaving. Your father wants to go while it's dark. He thinks Sofya Andreyevna is closing in."

I hated the cynical note she had been adopting. "It's not possible," I said.

"You frightened him last night. He thinks your mother is planning to follow you. He won't be convinced otherwise."

"This is insane. Papa can't stand this kind of shifting about."

I saw Dushan Makovitsky in his nightdress, standing in the doorway with a candle. He had come to wake us and was waving frantically. His feet were bony and bare.

The road to the station at Kozelsk was full of ruts and runnels. Parts of it had been washed away by a recent storm, and there was a lengthy detour through a farmer's turnip patch. Though the station was only nine miles away, it took hours to get there. The droshky we had borrowed from the nuns seemed barely to hang together.

Papa groaned as the wheels rattled over each bump, and I knew now that he was dying. The glaze of his eyes frightened me. He seemed already to have abandoned the life of this world, though he had not yet entered the next one. I wanted to weep but restrained myself.

We took the first southbound train from Kozelsk, aiming vaguely for my cousin's estate near Novocherkassk. Denisenko is fond of Papa, and they have recently been in correspondence. Papa seemed to approve of this plan, even though it would take at least twenty-four hours to get there.

"Leo Nikolayevich is well enough for such a journey?" Varvara asked Dushan.

"He's in reasonably good shape," he said.

Dushan Makovitsky is an optimist, as I am. We wanted very much to push straight through to Novocherkassk, if possible. But Papa looked ghastly when we got to the station, his eyes clouding over, his hands trembling.

"Are you sure you're able to travel, Papa?"

He looked at me askance, hurting my feelings.

"Do you feel well enough, Leo Nikolayevich?" Dushan asked him, taking his pulse. "There is no point in damaging your health."

"We have to go, Dushan. I have no choice."

"Pulse—seventy-six. Excellent," announced Dushan, as if my father's health were his invention.

"I think we should stay here," said Varvara. "Sofya Andreyevna will not follow. Tanya is with her."

But the decision had already been made, and Papa was not going to change his mind.

"Please get me the newspapers," he said. Whenever he begins a journey by train, he buys all the papers.

Dushan Makovitsky bought the papers, but I could see by his dour expression that something was amiss.

"Read the headlines," he said, pointing to the front page of one paper. It read: TOLSTOY ABANDONS HOME! WHEREABOUTS UNKNOWN! Another paper said: SAGE OF YASNAYA POLYANA TAKES FLIGHT!

Papa leafed through them and shook his head. "They know everything," he said. "It's no use."

Everyone in the railway car was yammering about the headlines, embarrassing Papa. A dapper fellow behind us in an English waistcoat said, "He's given her the slip. Good for him!" His friend, a slightly older man, gave a wink and said, "She wasn't giving him what he wanted, eh?" They both giggled like schoolboys. Papa's face took on the impassive but depthless quality of stamped tin. He clenched his fists.

"It's Leo Tolstoy! That's him!" a man shouted.

Dushan Makovitsky ran to quiet him, but it was too late. Everyone in the carriage instantly realized that Tolstoy was there. They had all seen his picture in the newspapers, and he does not resemble many people, with his white beard and wild, snowy eyebrows. I looked back at the men who'd been gossiping about him so gaily and enjoyed their panic. The older man, in particular, looked as though he'd been caught naked in the Winter Palace by the tsar himself.

"Be sure your sins shall find you out," Dushan whispered in a voice just audible to the men.

I saw Varvara Mikhailovna wince, and I pinched her. Dushan saw the pinch and blushed. He muttered something, but I ignored it. I love to embarrass him.

As word spread through the train that Tolstoy was aboard, crowds gathered in the passageways at either end of the carriage. Curiosity seekers kept passing us in the aisles, gawking at the most famous Russian in the world. I was oddly proud of being the daughter of Leo Tolstoy just then, but I felt protective, too. I hated their insolence, their scummy faces, the incessant leering and pothering. Who did they think they were?

I asked the conductor to control the crowd, and he agreed to help, bowing and saying, "Yes, Your Excellency. Anything you wish, Your Excellency." This particular address seemed out of place in a rather scrubby, second-class carriage; anyway, I object to such forms of subservient behavior, although the man's solicitude was useful for the moment.

I heated some barley soup for Papa over an oil stove at the back of the carriage, with Dushan, who had become rather talkative. He likes it that Papa is a famous man.

"You should have seen the fuss on the way to Optina," he said. "Everyone gathered around him in the railway car, asking questions about God, about the proper form of government, about taxes. You should have seen your father! He stood in the center of the carriage and lectured for an hour about Henry George and his theory of the single tax. A man who had just left his home of eighty-two years! And he'd had no sleep the night before, either. Not a wink. He's remarkable. A remarkable man."

This story puzzled and mildly upset me. Was Papa so detached, so unemotional, that he could focus on a theory of taxation in the midst of the most stressful time of his life? Was he superhuman or . . . inhuman? On the other hand, he can be so lovable, so considerate. He responds directly, unpretentiously, to all who address him, house servants or heads of state. When he looks at you with that flinty stare, you daren't say a thing you don't mean.

We gave Papa the barley soup with a bit of cracknel Dushan had brought along, and he seemed grateful. He sat in the sun that pushed itself through the train window and lay, as if sourceless, on the shiny metal floor. Afterward, he fell asleep, in spite of the rattling and swaying of the carriage, the whining of the rails, the stench of soot that blew back from the engine. I covered him with a blanket, letting him curl up on a seat by himself.

At one station, two men got on the train who looked as if they were on a mission of no good. They stood at the back of the carriage, stealing glances at us, pretending to smoke and talk to each other. I grew suspicious and called the conductor.

"Yes, Your Excellency?"

"Those men . . . see them?"

"I do, Your Excellency."

"Who are they?"

"Policemen, Your Excellency. For your protection."

Papa unexpectedly sat up, confused and ill. "Where are we now?" he asked, loudly.

Dushan ran to his side. "It's all right, Leo Nikolayevich. Everything is fine." He eased my father back onto his side and took his temperature. It was 102.5!

"Dushan!" I cried.

He seemed shaken, too. "He will be fine. Everything will be fine," he said. But I could tell by the squint of his eyes that he did not believe a word of this.

Papa reached out for my hand. "Listen to Dushan, darling. I'm feeling much better now . . . just need a little sleep." He scarcely had the strength to squeeze my wrist.

I bent over Papa and began to weep. I couldn't help it. The smoke in the carriage was so thick, and there were so many strangers crowding around us. It was horrid. Even Varvara Mikhailovna seemed distant, lost in a mood I couldn't fathom. She had been testy, impatient, even bitchy, throughout the day. I did not see how we could possibly make it to Novocherkassk.

Two, perhaps three, hours later, Dushan whispered to me that Papa's fever was rising. He was quite panicky now. Pretending was of no use.

"We can't go on!" I said.

Dushan shook his head. But what could we do?

The train lurched and made the familiar screeching sounds of metal rubbing against metal. A small, dusty station drew up beside our window: Astapovo.

"This will do," said Dushan. "We can spend the night here, if need be. Your father is too sick to travel. He wants complete rest, perhaps for several days." He bit his top lip, which was quivering now. I think, at that moment, he saw his beautiful dreams of Turkey, Bulgaria, or the Caucasus dashed.

Several men stepped forward to help Papa from the train, while Varvara and I followed.

"I'm sorry, Sasha. I really am," Varvara said.

"About what?"

"I feel . . . confused. I don't know what I'm doing here."

"We love each other, don't we? You are my old friend. I need you."

She put her arms around me. "Am I horrible?"

"Yes. You're horrible," I said.

Hand in hand, we followed Papa and Dushan Makovitsky. Papa took each step with infinite premeditation, holding on to Dushan's arm for balance. To be carried now would seem to admit defeat.

He sat on a wooden bench beside the station, holding a cane between his legs. His head slumped to his chest. His cheeks were slightly damp.

Dushan went to speak with the stationmaster, who had a house nearby where, we hoped, Papa could rest for a few days. It was a small cottage with a bright tin roof; its mud-plaster walls were painted red. It was only fifty or so steps from the tracks—which meant it would be noisy—but it was set in a little garden.

"Leo Nikolayevich will be comfortable here," Dushan told us. He seemed confident again, to my relief. "The stationmaster says we may have his guest room for as long as we should need it. There are no inns nearby, so we're lucky he is generous. The rest of us can sleep in the station itself, in the waiting room. He will find cots."

I watched Papa stagger into the tiny house—no bigger than one of our toolsheds at Yasnaya Polyana. I don't know why, but I could not stop myself from crying, even though Varvara Mikhailovna squeezed my hand and pressed my head against her shoulder.

It seemed that we had come to the end of the world.

# 3 7

# DR. MAKOVITSKY

We should doubtless have stayed at Shamardino. My professional judgment may well have been impaired by enthusiasm for our project. I regret this.

Leo Nikolayevich lies ill in Ozolin's house.

It was frightful to see him walk from the train. The immense weariness of each step! Muzhiks lined the path to the door, aware that something magnificent and terrible was taking place. Everyone knew it was Leo Tolstoy. They removed their hats and bowed as they would in India, where a Holy Man is respected.

Leo Nikolayevich thought he was back at Yasnaya Polyana. "Where is my blanket?" he asked when he lay down in the tiny room. That blanket with the key design has adorned his bed since childhood.

He was shuddering now, so we covered him with thick quilts provided by the stationmaster's wife. He soon fell into a phlegmy drowse, his head awkwardly slumped to one side.

"Will he live, Dushan?" his daughter asked me.

I did not know what to say. "If it is God's will."

She sat on a chair beside his bed, and I thought she might weep. I do not like to see anyone weep.

I took his pulse. It was ninety-three. Given his condition of sleep, I found this ominous. I saw, too, that he was experiencing minor convulsions, which secretly worried me. It was the beginning of a difficult time. His fever remained steadily high, though at least it was not climbing. His left lung, which is often inflamed, exhibited a distinct wheeze. I feared the onset of pneumonia.

The stationmaster's wife, who is a gentle, round-faced soul with masses of dark hair shot through with snowy white and pulled back in a bun, brought us kasha and oats. We drank tea from her samovar, glass after glass. They are respectful, straightforward, simple people who understand the significance of having Leo Tolstoy here; indeed, they seemed quite chuffed that he should be using their guest room. I kept thanking them, for all of us.

It was too bad that Sasha did not thank them herself. She is a child, really, and does not understand about politeness. Quite frankly, she has a selfish streak that has always troubled her father. Varvara Mikhailovna is even worse. The two of them would try the patience of a saint. It has required stamina this past year to watch them giggling and pinching each other and holding hands. Their physical attachment has become an embarrassment, although no one mentions it. I shall not be the first to address this issue.

When Leo Nikolayevich woke, he motioned for Sasha. He wanted her to take dictation. A telegram to Chertkov. "I very much want to see him," he said, and we agreed to summon him. "But not the others!" he added. "Tell no one else where I am."

"You mustn't trouble yourself," I said. "Every precaution will be taken."

"I'm so grateful to you, Dushan. So very grateful." He seemed teary-eyed and pathetic. I turned away.

That night, once more, he drifted into a scramble of thoughts, confused especially about his whereabouts. But soon he fell asleep, the first truly deep sleep since arriving in Astapovo. He had only a few convulsions.

The next morning he was greatly improved. His pulse was normal, and so was his temperature. It appeared that he might really survive this crisis and that, soon enough, we'd be in the Crimea or Bulgaria or Turkey—somewhere bright and warm, where Leo Nikolayevich could think and work and pray in unobstructed privacy.

He sat up in bed, remarkably cheerful, chatting amicably with everyone. He wanted to discuss the various projects under way, and we did so for nearly an hour. He had not lost interest in the world.

Sasha asked him about God, thinking that during his delirium he might have realized something different from what he has always thought. Inwardly, I scoffed at her. But he was kindly, as ever, and answered her query with his usual directness. "God is the eternal whole of which each person represents a tiny part. We are the manifestation of Godness in time, in space, in matter." She wrote this down, as did I.

Leo Nikolayevich raised a finger. "Another thought for you, Sasha. God is not love, but the more love there is in man, the more is God made manifest in him, and the more truly does he exist."

"Doesn't this make the existence of God arbitrary?" I asked him. He shook his head. "Nothing is arbitrary."

I thanked him for his statement.

We reminded him that he had asked for Chertkov the night before, and he grew anxious about how Sergey and Tanya would feel about this. He asked Sasha to write the following:

*Please do not hold it against me that I have not summoned you along with Chertkov. You know that he bears a special relation to me, having devoted his life to the cause I, too, have served for much of forty years. That cause is dear to me, and I strongly hold it to be essential for all men, including you both. . . . Farewell. Try to comfort your mother, whom I love sincerely.*

"You may give them this note after my death," he said, when suddenly he began to weep. It was most unlike him.

All day, Ozolin's three young children played in the next room, sang songs, whistled, and shouted. A delightful smell of boiling cabbage issued from the kitchen, with much clanging of pots and laughter. I worried that this would disturb Leo Nikolayevich, but he said he liked the commotion and told me not to disturb them. "We are guests," he said. "We must respect their family life."

At four, he was overtaken by chills. He crawled back beneath the covers again, a cold sweat on his brow, his jaw quivering. I took his temperature: 103.5. Soon he began to spit bloody mucus into a pan.

I took Sasha aside in the next room. "I recommend that we summon Dr. Nikitin from Tula. He knows a good deal more than I do about pneumonia."

"I should telegraph Sergey," she said. "He will see that Nikitin gets here quickly."

Sasha went swiftly to the station, a ghostly whiteness on her face. It is well known that pneumonia is desperately bad for elderly people—or good, perhaps. It's often referred to as "a friend to old men" because it removes them from the scene of present misery.

I sat up beside Leo Nikolayevich all night, taking his pulse and temperature at intervals. It was torturous. He had an unquenchable thirst, and he cried out several times to God to ask for death. He was like an old ship beating through a storm, its straking loose, sails torn, the bowsprit broken.

I was relieved when dawn came and Leo Nikolayevich was alive. I took myself outside for a breath of air while he snored, having fallen into a deep sleep at last. I felt exhausted, too, with cramps in my intestines. I held on to the railing to avoid toppling over.

The station was empty at that hour. As I sat by myself on the platform, I studied the silvery tracks that trailed off into infinity. It occurred to me that the life of the body and the life of the soul are like these tracks, running parallel into the visible future. We like to imagine a meeting point, a junction where the earthly body joins a heavenly one. But this is an illusion. The body rail, somewhere, at a definite point in time, stops. The spirit rail continues, perhaps to infinity. Who can say?

Kneeling at the bench, I prayed for the Tolstoy family and for my own soul. And I felt, deep inside me, that I was not alone.

When Leo Nikolayevich woke, an hour later, he took his own temperature. It was 104.3.

"Not a good sign, Dushan," he said.

"You'll be all right," I said.

"You needn't lie to me, my friend," he said. "But I understand how you must feel. Remember that you are my doctor, not my angel. Whatever happens, it is not your fault."

A fit of coughing took him by surprise, and he shook violently. I gave him a glass of water.

"All will be well," he said. "You are quite right."

I looked at the floor. It was foolish of me to address him like a child.

"This is it," he said. "Checkmate."

I looked up at him, and he was smiling.

# 38

# CHERTKOV

I rejoiced when Leo Nikolayevich left Sofya Andreyevna. Everyone assumed that I was behind his departure, although this was untrue. Reporters from Moscow and Petersburg, from Paris and London, were in touch with me from the outset. But I told them, at first, the truth: I did not know where he had gone. I told them that Tolstoy wanted to escape. He did not want publicity.

But the cause needs publicity. In order to prevent Sofya Andreyevna's side of the story from dominating the press, I prepared a statement on the reasons for Tolstoy's flight. For moral consistency, he had no choice but to leave, it explained.

The telegram from Astapovo, which requested my presence, moved me terribly. I was breathless and strangely elated now. My work had not been in vain.

I left at once, arriving on Tuesday in the little railway station, having traveled through the night to his bedside. Sergeyenko accompanied me.

My heart leaped when I saw Leo Nikolayevich, the weary, shrunken, but still beautiful face, a blanket drawn up beneath his chin. He was feverish, flushed, and exhausted, but he greeted me with tears and embraces. "It is you!" he kept repeating. "I can hardly believe you're here, at last. Thank you, Vladimir. Thank you."

The stationmaster asked if I was his son.

Leo Nikolayevich nodded eagerly. "He is my son," he said. "I have no other son who has understood."

We drank a glass of tea and talked about his departure from home. The business of Sofya Andreyevna is all quite impossible. Being out of her mind, she would pounce on us as soon as she learned of her husband's whereabouts. That much was certain.

"I don't know when she'll come," Leo Nikolayevich said. "But she will come. I know it."

"She will not bother you," I said.

He seemed to relax when I said that, and I determined to keep her away from him. She will not make his death a miserable one.

As I feared, we did not have to wait long for the wretched woman. Sometime in the early afternoon Ozolin appeared and asked Sasha and me to step outside. Leo Nikolayevich was dozing, luckily.

"A telegram has come from Tula," he said. "The Countess Tolstoy has hired a private train, a first-class train! She will arrive in Astapovo after dinner."

At once I called everyone together in the waiting room of the station: Sasha, Varvara Mikhailovna, Dushan, Sergeyenko. All agreed that Sofya Andreyevna must not be allowed to see her husband. In his condition, it would kill him.

"Mama would drag him back like a sack of beans, dead or alive," Sasha said.

"We must form a protective circle around the stationmaster's cottage," I said. "Sofya Andreyevna, and her dreadful offspring—I refer to the odious ones, Ilya and Andrey—must be prevented from invading his sickroom."

We could be grateful for one thing, that young Leo was in Paris. He is a liar and a bully, and Lord knows how he would have tried to thwart my plans.

That evening, before dinner, Sergey arrived. But I felt strongly that he should not be admitted to his father's bedside—not now.

"I *shall* see my father," the boy insisted, standing boorishly in the doorway.

"It's all right," Sasha said. "He can go in."

I saw no point in resisting. Consenting would give me leverage later on, when I might need it.

Leo Nikolayevich was, as I suspected, confused and upset by Sergey's arrival.

"How did you find me, Sergey?" he asked, in a whisper of panic.

"I was passing through Gorkachev," Sergey replied. "And I happened upon a conductor who knew where you were. It was sheer luck, Papa!"

Leo Nikolayevich seemed to realize that a game was afoot, and that he had to play his part.

To my surprise, he seemed eager to get news from Sergey about his wife and Yasnaya Polyana. I realized, sadly, that he still yearned for his past life.

After dinner, his fever shot up and he became delirious. Near ten, he fell asleep.

"What do you think, Dushan?" I asked in a low voice.

"It is almost over," he said. "It would be dishonest to say otherwise."

██ Sofya Andreyevna's dark blue train arrived at midnight and was put on a sidetrack. She rode in a luxurious carriage with several servants, a nurse, and miscellaneous children and their spouses. It was a ludicrous spectacle, worthy of the countess in all respects.

Dushan Makovitsky went to greet her, saying that both he and Dr. Nikitin agreed that nobody else could see her husband at present. His unwavering approach paid off: Sofya Andreyevna accepted his argument, agreeing to remain in the train until Leo Nikolayevich was stronger.

"Sometimes," Sergeyenko whispered to me afterward, "a warm wind blows from the north."

No other accommodations were available, so the private train became a makeshift hotel.

Dr. Nikitin didn't arrive until the next day, but Sofya Andreyevna didn't know this. He examined Leo Nikolayevich and said that his heart was weak and that the left lung was indeed infected. Nonetheless, it was a good sign that the fever had dropped to 100.9 and was holding steady. Pneumonia was by no means the final diagnosis, he said, since he could hear rattling in Leo Nikolayevich's chest. With pneumonia, the lung—or lungs—fill up with fluid. Instead of rattling, one hears an ominous silence.

Leo Nikolayevich was alert now and delighted by this report; he huddled in a cushioned chair with a blanket around his shoulders and his legs on a stool. He seemed eager to talk.

"Let me explain to you my view of life, Dr. Nikitin, so that you will understand why I left my wife, and why, even if I'm too old for such a thing, I feel I must continue this journey."

We sat back, astonished, as he delivered a miniature lecture on his philosophy of life: concise and well articulated. I could not have done better.

"It would be ill-considered of me to recommend anything but prolonged rest," Dr. Nikitin said. "Your resistance is low."

"How long, then? A week?"

"Two weeks—at least. A month would, in fact, be safer."

"Impossible! My wife would certainly find me in so much time. That must not happen." He turned to me. "Vladimir, you understand why this must not happen, don't you?"

I assured him that I did, but I told him he must not worry. Hadn't Sergey just explained that Sofya Andreyevna was reconciled to her new life?

"Do you expect me to believe this?"

"I do," I said. "There is no reason to believe otherwise."

He looked around the room, skeptically, then settled back, tucking his chin into the blanket we had wrapped around him. "I'm terribly cold," he said. "There is a draft somewhere."

At midday, Goldenweiser arrived from Moscow with Gorbunov, our publisher. I had wired Goldenweiser two days before, but I did not expect to see him in Astapovo. I knew, as did Leo Nikolayevich, that he had an important concert date in Moscow, at the Academy. Some weeks ago we had been discussing the possibility of surprising him with an appearance at the concert. Leo Nikolayevich, though gravely ill, remembered the date of the concert and scolded Goldenweiser for canceling it.

"I could not have done otherwise," Goldenweiser said. "How could I play in public with you lying ill in a distant place?"

"Nonsense," Leo Nikolayevich said. "When a farmer is plowing his fields, he does not leave those fields, even if his father should be dying. The concert is your field. You should not have left the plow."

Leo Nikolayevich then turned eagerly to Gorbunov to discuss future publications of *The Intermediary*. He was going to finish a book called *The Way of Life* when he settled in the Caucasus or wherever, he explained. He had taken extensive notes already, some of which remained at Yasnaya Polyana, and he hoped we could retrieve them. I assured him that this was no problem. Sasha backed me up, saying she knew which notes he referred to and would help.

Leo Nikolayevich lay back, closing his eyes. He continued speaking, but his voice grew weak.

Suddenly the face of Sofya Andreyevna filled the small glass-paned door of the sickroom. That fat, distorted face, her tomatolike cheeks and nose, pressed against the glass. Her eyes grew wide.

Sasha leaped from her chair, startling her father, who caught a passing glimpse of Sofya Andreyevna before she was pulled away.

"What!" he shouted. "Who was there?"

"The stationmaster's wife," Sasha said. "She wanted to come in. I told her you were sleeping, that you were not to be disturbed—"

"It was Sofya Andreyevna!"

"You're imagining things," she said. "It was Ozolin's wife."

"That's true," I said. "It was not your wife. She is at home, as Sergey told you."

"If Sonya should want to see me, I could not refuse her," Leo Nikolayevich said. "But it would kill me. I know it would kill me."

"There is no possibility of that," I said. "She is at home."

Fortunately, he was too sick to argue. He accepted our remarks, though again I wondered if he didn't know the truth. To prevent further intrusions, we put a blanket over the glass, telling him that the stationmaster's friends were curious and would disturb him further if we didn't block the pane.

"Sasha," he said, his voice trembling, barely audible. "I must dictate another letter."

"Yes, Papa." She took up a pad on her knee.

"Send this to Alymer Maude in England: 'Dear Maude—On the way to a place where I hoped to be alone, I was taken ill. . . .' " He tried to continue, but Sasha couldn't hear him; his voice dissolved in a loose gargle of phlegm.

"You can finish later, Papa," Sasha said. "After you've slept."

I saw in his face the intense frustration of a man for whom human communication had been everything. He could hardly bear it.

Sasha fastened tightly onto her father's statement that a meeting with his wife would kill him. Rather cruelly, I thought, she rushed to the blue train to convey this sentiment. I followed to make sure Sofya Andreyevna believed it.

"Have you told him that I nearly drowned myself in the pond?" her mother asked.

"He knows everything," Sasha said.

"And what did he say?"

"He said that if you killed yourself, it would upset him horribly, but that he could not have acted other than he did."

"Do you know what this train is costing me?" Sofya Andreyevna screeched. "Five hundred rubles!"

Sasha replied that she didn't care if that ridiculous train had cost her the entire Tolstoy estate, whereupon Sofya Andreyevna became frenzied, accusing me, then Sasha, then her husband, of every sort of perfidious act. I could hear her screaming from the train, "Liar! Liar!"

Later, in a calmer mood, she implored Dushan Makovitsky to give her husband a small embroidered pillow that she had brought with her from Yasnaya Polyana. It was a favorite of his, she said. He would rest more easily with it tucked gently beneath his head.

Makovitsky is sentimental about such things and, stupidly, brought the pillow into the sickroom and set it on the bed. Leo Nikolayevich noticed it right away.

He said, "Where did that thing come from?"

"Your daughter Tanya is here. She brought it," Makovitsky said. The idiot!

"Tanya! Let me see my daughter," he said. "Where is Tanya?"

Tanya, shaking and tearful, was led into the stationmaster's cottage by Sasha. She embraced her father and wept on his shoulder.

"Where is your mother, Tanya?" he asked.

"She remained at home."

"How is she? Is she going to come here?"

Tanya's eyelids quivered. "I don't think so. . . . I don't know, Papa. There is no way to—"

"To what?"

Tanya could hardly speak. Her father reached for her hand and told her not to worry, that he would be fine in a couple of days. "Ask Dr. Nikitin," he said. "It's just a rattle in the left lung. That lung has always been a problem."

Tanya is hopelessly weak in character. And her sweetness is cloying. As Varvara Mikhailovna once said, she has the patience of old wallpaper.

Leo Nikolayevich called for his diary, whereupon he wrote in a wobbly hand:

*Horrid night. Two days in bed, feverish. They say Sofya Andreyevna . . . The third of November, Tanya. Sergey came last night. I was extremely moved by his visit. Today, the third, Nikitin,*

*Tanya, Goldenweiser, Gorbunov. And so my plan . . . Fais ce que dois adv . . . It's for the good of others, I hope, but mostly for myself.*

He rarely used French anymore—not like others of our class. But he chose a good proverb: "Do as you must, no matter what happens."

Outside the cottage, it had become a circus. A reporter had found out about the visit to Shamardino, and he'd traced our whereabouts. The otherwise forgettable town of Astapovo became famous. Word spread like smallpox through the journalistic community, which feeds and survives on gossip. At first, a trickle of reporters joined us. Before long, the numbers swelled to a small throng, culminating with the arrival of Pathé newsmen, who carried cine cameras for shooting newsreels to be broadcast throughout the world. Now every train brought a fresh load of cameramen, copy editors, reporters, typists. The telegraph office was jammed, and Makovitsky was reduced to giving regular press conferences, announcing Tolstoy's pulse and temperature, projecting the state of his health for the next few hours.

Mounted police arrived by order of the government, who feared, I suppose, a revolutionary uprising. They overestimate us greatly.

The railway people felt obliged to erect a large tent for the reporters and set up a dozen rows of cots. It was like an army camp, except for the sounds of typewriters clacking and cameras clicking. The Ryazan-Ural Railroad Company contributed a number of sleeping cars, which arrived this morning, and an unfinished warehouse was prepared for yet further platoons of gawkers, hangers-on, and so-called members of the press. If Leo Nikolayevich did not die, there would be hell to pay somewhere. . . .

Sofya Andreyevna, for once, had an audience commensurate with her ego. She preened before the camera and supplied an endless stream of printable lies. She told them I was keeping her from her dying husband, so everyone assumed I must be a devil of the first rank. I should have expected this, but it was shameful of her all the same.

In any case, we succeeded, day by day, in preventing her from disturbing the tranquillity of Leo Nikolayevich, who at least pretended to believe he was alone in the country, surrounded by a circle of friends who sympathized with his view of life. He appeared happy, even serene, whenever the fever dropped and he could speak.

On Thursday morning, he said to Sasha, "I think I will die soon, but perhaps not. How can one know?"

"Try not to think, Papa," she told him.

Her remark pricked him in the wrong place. "How is it possible not to think?" he said. "I *must* think!"

Much of the time when he was conscious, I sat beside him and read passages from *For Every Day*, focusing on important chapters of the Gospels, the Upanishads, and the *Analects* of Confucius. Leo Nikolayevich often asked for something from Rousseau, too, though I tried to dissuade him from this old habit. He also insisted on Montaigne, another atheist. I could not understand this wish, either, but I acquiesced.

That night, Leo Nikolayevich suffered a number of small convulsions. He shook from head to toe, briefly; all the while his right hand held an imaginary pencil and scribbled on nonexistent paper.

Varvara Mikhailovna came noisily into the room, and Leo Nikolayevich startled. "Masha! Masha!" he cried, then sank back into a stupor. He has never recovered from the death of his beloved daughter Masha. It hurt Sasha's feelings that he would cry Masha's name with such ferocity and obvious pain of loss.

On Friday, his condition worsened. The eminent Dr. Berkenheim, a specialist in lung cases, arrived from Moscow, and he did not conceal his opinion.

"It is the end, I'm afraid," he said.

"It can't be!" Sasha said. "You're quite wrong about this. His fever is down."

But the fever was not down. It had been 103.6 for two days. The pulse became unbelievably rapid in the afternoon, so that we thought his heart might burst. Dushan Makovitsky was frantic, since he considered himself personally responsible for his patient's pulse rate.

Dr. Berkenheim had brought with him an arsenal of modern medicine: oxygen balloons, digitalin. But Leo Nikolayevich, distrusting modern medicine and its gadgetry, refused treatment.

His condition fluctuated hour by hour. He was perfectly coherent during dinner, ordering us about, discussing *The Intermediary*. By eight o'clock, he was delirious, calling to his long dead Aunt Toinette.

Tanya reappeared, and he said to her, "So much has fallen upon Sonya, my dear Sonya. She can't stand this. It will kill her."

"Do you want to see her?" Tanya asked. "Shall I call her?"

Everyone stiffened. What had got into her head?

Fortunately, her father said nothing. He looked at us, confused, and slumped into his pillow. His mouth sank into his toothless gums like a yeasty loaf of bread collapsing into itself.

Two more doctors arrived from Moscow, Dr. Usov and Dr. Shurovsky. Andrey and Ilya had summoned them. Incompetent hacks, they huddled in one corner and discussed the situation in pseudoscientific gibberish with Makovitsky, who looked painfully confused.

When Leo Nikolayevich saw them, he whispered to Tanya, "So this is it. The end. And it's nothing."

We stood about, stock-still. I was reminded of the time he almost died at Gaspra, nine years ago. Leo Nikolayevich had gone there to recuperate in the warm Crimean sun. He got worse at one point, and when it looked as though he might die, Sergey asked if he wanted to see the local priest, who had been begging for a final word with "the Count." Leo Nikolayevich replied, "Can't they understand that even on one's deathbed, two plus two is still four!"

Now Sasha hovered beside him, adjusting his pillow, smoothing the starched linen sheets, giving the blanket a tuck or tug.

"My darling," he said. "You waste too much effort on an old man whose life is gone. There are many people in the world in need of your attention."

"Shush, Papa," she said.

Sofya Andreyevna, Andrey, and Ilya stood outside the cottage, a circle of hate, demanding entrance, but Dushan Makovitsky held them off like a brave lieutenant. He said that Leo Nikolayevich is much better today, that his temperature had dropped. Somehow, he managed to persuade them to return to their train.

Leo Nikolayevich grew delirious toward evening, and the Muscovite doctors insisted on giving him camphor injections, which made his body writhe, briefly, and relax. They put an oxygen balloon—a hideous modern contraption, a torture chamber—over his face. I had to turn my head.

We had trouble, too, with the Church. Leo Nikolayevich symbolized a challenge to their bankrupt dogmas. The Church has mesmerized the people, urging them to follow the tsar's armies into an endless succession of futile battles. It was obviously in their interest to report that Leo Tolstoy, on his deathbed, had recanted and died in the arms of Mother Church.

A telegram came from the Metropolitan of St. Petersburg, begging Leo Nikolayevich to repent. Soon a tedious monk called Father Varsonofy arrived on our doorstep. A comose little creature, his black beard flecked through with white, he reeked of garlic and wine. At first, he pretended to feelings of great sympathy for Tolstoyan ideas, then he tried to wheedle us into letting him see Leo Nikolayevich. "I only wish to *see* him!" he cried. We told him this was impossible, so he approached Sofya Andreyevna, as if that would improve his chances of an interview! Then Ozolin told me that the bishop of Tula himself had been dispatched to Astapovo by the archbishop of Moscow. Such nonsense.

Sasha handed me a note the monk had written to her. It is a remarkable piece of deception, penned in an ornate hand:

*You should be aware that the count told his sister, your aunt, that he wished to speak with a representative of the Church for the sake of his soul's everlasting peace. He deeply regretted that this wish could not be granted while he was at Shamardino. I beg you, dear lady, with all respect, to inform him of my presence in Astapovo. I will be happy to see him, if for only a few minutes. Should he not want me to bear his confession, I shall return immediately to Optina and let God's will be done.*

I dropped his note into the fire, where it spread its wings slowly before it burst into orange flames.

I recalled a passage from Leo Nikolayevich's diary of 1901, written in Gaspra during his illness: "When I seem on the edge of death, I want to be asked if I still see life as a continuous progression toward God, an increase of love. If I have no strength to speak, and the answer is yes, I shall close my eyes; if the answer, alas, is no, I shall look up." It occurred to me that I should ask him that question now, but it did not seem worth the risk.

My dear Leo Nikolayevich seemed close to whatever lay behind the papery veil that separates us from Eternity.

On Saturday evening, his lips turned stony. Blue spots emerged on his cheeks, on his ears and hands. He began to choke, calling in a raspy voice to his doctors, "I can't breathe!"

They gave him further injections of camphor oil, though he continued to object.

"Foolishness . . . foolishness!" he shouted in a hoarse whisper. "Stop the injections. . . . Let me be, for God's sake!"

Nevertheless, the injections helped. Again, he seemed much calmer almost immediately and sat up in bed. He called for Sergey.

"My son," he said, as Sergey knelt beside him, his ear close to his father's lips. "The truth . . . it matters so much to me . . . the way—" His voice broke, exhausted by the effort, once again, to formulate the truth, to command the whip of language.

He fell asleep, looking quite blissful, at 10:30. I ushered everyone but Makovitsky out of the room.

Perhaps for the first time in his life, Dushan Makovitsky wept.

# 39

# SOFYA
# ANDREYEVNA

After four days of silence, eating nothing, drinking only a little water, I wrote to him:

> *Don't be afraid, my dear one, that I shall come in search of you. I can hardly move, so weak have I become. I would not force you to return, not for anything. Do what you think is best. Your departure taught me a lesson, a dreadful one, and if I do not die as a result of it, and you come back to me, I shall do anything I can to make things easier for you. Yet I feel, in my bones, that we shall never meet again. . . . Lyovochka, find the love that's in you, and know that a great deal of love has awakened in me.*

I needed a way to end, a way that would signal my affection, which has never ceased, not for a second: "I embrace you, my darling, dear old friend, who once loved me so much. God keep you, and take care of yourself."

I slept badly that night, in spite of weariness beyond description, dreaming of Lyovochka and our life together. The next morning, before dawn, I went, again, to my writing desk, holding an old portrait of myself and Lyovochka to the candle, watching the flame bring life and color into the ghostly cheeks of ancient silhouettes.

I tried to make a few sentences that would touch him, yet the accusations began to tumble out, and I realized that this would only alienate him further. It was just no use.

A servant knocked on the door while I was writing. She had a telegram from a man called Orlov, a reporter from *The Russian Word*. "Leo Nikolayevich ill at Astapovo. Temperature 104."

He was dying!

Duty presented itself. I realized I must go to him. He would want to see me, wouldn't he? Hadn't we lived together all these years? Hadn't we brought thirteen children into the world? I did not doubt that, in the end, he would want me near him. He would want to hear and receive my confession, as I would hear and receive his. Whenever he was ill, he was like a child, thirsting for my attention. And I granted it, as I would grant it now, even if he insisted on mocking me, on making public ridicule of our marriage, which had lasted nearly half a century.

I traveled with Tanya, Ilya, Mikhail, and Andrey, taking a nurse, the psychiatric doctor who has been looking after me in the past weeks, and a few servants. One never knows what will happen on such journeys, and it is better to be prepared. We made our way to the station at Tula in several carriages. We had hurried to catch the morning train, but we missed it, obliging me to hire a special train, which cost five hundred rubles!

All day and well into the evening we rode southeast, arriving late that night. As we neared the station where my husband lay dying, I could hardly catch my breath. I felt like an important actress in Moscow who was about to make her farewell appearance to a packed house. I formed a dozen perfect sentences in my head for Lyovochka. His old, soft hands would touch my hair once again, as always. The curtain of death would fall across his eyes. And I would die, too. Affection would never waken in my breast again.

But the horrid facts hit me when I got to Astapovo. Lyovochka was surrounded by his followers, his fanatics, and they would not let me through to him. Sergey had arrived from Moscow on an earlier train and came to us like an ambassador from an enemy country, addressing the family circle like a pompous little prince. He is my own son, but I hated him. It would "kill" his father if he saw me, Sergey said. Was I hearing him correctly?

I was too weak, however, to do otherwise than obey these men, who would force their will upon me now as they always had. Does a woman ever have a chance? Did I ever have a chance with Lyovochka, who used me like an old cow?

Day after day he lay dying, while I lay mostly awake. Now and then the miracle of exhaustion released me, briefly, from my pain. But I could always hear my heartbeat ticking noisily in my temples, in my wrists. My mind was tortured by visions, images of hell.

All the while the cinematographers recorded my grief. The whole world saw but never understood my sorrows.

"Turn to the right, Countess," cried the wretched cameraman Meyer. "Show us your eyes, Countess." I can still hear them, can see them cranking their machines, my Furies.

Once, as I passed the stationmaster's cottage, I found no guard at the door. Boldly, I walked in, whereupon I saw him—my dying husband—writhing in the narrow bed. I saw his white beard and hair, his bleached eyebrows, white against the white sheets. A blur of whiteness, the image of death. Death and blight!

"Lyovochka!" I called, but somebody was pulling me backward as I spoke, like Eurydice, back into the hell of my loneliness.

A telegram arrived from the patriarch of St. Petersburg, asking my husband to repent, but Chertkov refused even to show it to him. They kept from him, too, the Abbot Varsonofy, who had come from the monastery in Optina.

On the Lord's Day, Sunday, Sergey woke me just after midnight. I had been dreaming of a day in June, decades ago, when Lyovochka and I went running in the woods. We sat in a bright clearing, surrounded by wildflowers, and ate venison and bread and drank wine. He told me that he would never leave me, that I was his life, that he could not live without me. He pushed me back in the buttercups and daisies; he lifted my skirt, tore at me with his big hands. And he pushed through me with his indomitable spirit. He raised the fiery sword of love, and he seized me. I gave myself wholly over to his rude and flashing soul.

And now this.

"Mama, wake up!" Sergey said. I could smell tobacco on his breath. "He will not last the night. You may see him now."

Still in my nightdress, shaking, I followed my son through the double row of journalists.

"Is he dying, Countess?" a man shouted in French.

I brushed them all aside.

"Let me see him!" I screamed at Chertkov, who stood, a stony barrier, in my path. "You pig! Let me through!"

"You must be patient, Sofya Andreyevna."

What had I been doing? Had I not been waiting for days in a stuffy railway car while they conducted a party around the bed of my dying husband?

I stooped beneath Chertkov's outstretched arm, and he did not try to stop me.

Lyovochka lay on the bed, empty of himself. His face was blue in the dim light, his nose sharply chiseled. I felt his forehead: it was damp and burning. He was moving his lips, but there was no sound. Not even a whisper.

"Forgive me, my darling!" I said, as I knelt beside him. I held his hand, so lifeless and strange.

He startled, slightly, and began to gasp. He could not breathe.

"Please, my darling, forgive me! I have been foolish. I am not a wise woman—you know that. . . . I am a selfish woman, yes. I have never been able to show you the love I feel. You must believe me, Lyovochka! You must understand! Please! Please!" I was speaking too loudly, but I was not shouting.

Sergeyenko dragged me backward from the room.

"Control yourself, Countess." He looked at me coldly, having pushed me onto a chair in the adjoining room. A crowd circled above me, like vultures, waiting to tear at my flesh, to feast on my remains.

"I want to speak to my husband," I said, sobs sputtering between each word.

They had given him morphine against his will, I soon discovered. And further injections of camphor oil, for his heart. It was all barbarous and cruel.

Later—hours later—Dr. Usov persuaded them to let me sit by his bed, provided I did not speak loudly.

Near dawn, Dushan Makovitsky held a candle to my husband's face. Lyovochka grimaced and turned. He began to twitch and groan.

"Have a drink, Leo Nikolayevich. Wet your lips," said Dushan, holding a cup to his mouth. He drank a little, and fell back, sighing.

I cried, "Lyovochka!" But he could not hear me.

His breathing grew slow, then fitful.

His consciousness widened, like circles on water, each ripple farther from the old center.

Abruptly, Dr. Usov cried, "First cessation!"

I knew what was coming now, the moment that I had imagined and replayed for years. I pressed Lyovochka's right hand tightly to my cheek. It was hot, coursing with blood. He was still alive, my Lyovochka. "I know you don't believe it, Lyovochka, but I'm sorry. I have been callous and didn't listen to you. Can you possibly, possibly . . ." I could not control my sobbing now, and Sergey reached for me, tried to comfort me, but I swept with a hand at the boy's face, and Sergeyenko grabbed me with his big hands and pulled me back.

I damned him, and I damned Chertkov, too. They had kept my husband from me, as they'd kept him from God's vicar, the abbot, who'd pleaded with me, for the sake of my husband's eternal soul, to let him talk to him, if only for a minute or two.

Dushan Makovitsky stepped forward now. "A quarter to six," he said.

What did he mean? I could not understand, even as he closed the eyelids of Leo Tolstoy, shuttered the eyes that would never again look to the light, crave the light, invent the light.

They had kept me from saying good-bye to my Lyovochka. They had done this to both of us. And now, it was over.

"I am sorry, Sofya Andreyevna."

The voice came, strange and soft. It was Chertkov, who stood over me, a hand on my shoulder.

As dawn fluttered at the curtains, teasing and mocking, I saw it was finished—the end of the world as I had known it. What happened from now on could never really matter. Never.

# 4 0

# L. N.

—FROM *THE DEATH OF IVAN ILYCH*

Time did not exist for three days, while he fought hard to resist the black bag into which a hidden, invisible source was stuffing him. He fought like a condemned man fights his executioner, even though he knows that no escape is possible. He knew that each moment, in spite of his resistance, he drew closer and closer to what most horrified him. He was in agony because of that black bag, that black hole, but it was worse because he could not simply slip in. What held him up was the feeling that his life had been a good one. This self-justification buoyed him up, kept him from progressing, provoked his anguish more than anything else.

Suddenly a pressure struck him in the chest, on the side, then constricted his breathing. He slipped into the black hole, hit bottom, and found it shining. What had occurred was like the experience of being in a railway carriage when one thinks it's moving forward but it's really going backward, then one suddenly realizes the truth.

"So, what I've experienced thus far was not the 'real thing.' No matter. But perhaps I can make it the 'real thing,' perhaps. But what *is* this thing I want?" Ivan Ilych asked himself, then grew still.

This happened near the end of the third day, an hour before he died. At that moment, his son crept softly into the room and approached his bed. The dying man continued to cry and flail his arms. One hand touched the boy's head. The boy grabbed it, kissed it, and began to weep. At this moment, Ivan Ilych slipped through and saw a light, and it came to him that his life had not been what it might have but that the situation was not beyond repair. "Yet what *is* the real thing?" he asked himself and grew still, listening. Then he felt someone kissing his hand. Opening his eyes, he saw his son. He felt sorry for him. Then his wife entered the room and approached him. She looked at him softly with an open mouth, with tears on her nose and cheeks, with despair on her face. He felt terribly sorry for her.

"Indeed, I'm making their lives miserable," he said to himself. "They pity me, but it will be better for them all when I die." He wished to say this but had not strength to speak. "But why speak? I have to *do* something," he thought. He glanced at his wife and motioned to her to remove their son.

"Take him away . . . I'm sorry . . . for him and you." He would have liked to have added, "Forgive me," but instead "Forget" came out. He was too feeble to correct himself, however, and didn't worry, since He would understand who had to know what he meant.

Suddenly it dawned on him that what had been weighing him down and would not disappear was vanishing, all at once—from two sides, ten sides, everywhere! He grieved for them and wanted to comfort them. To free them and himself from this anguish. "And the pain?" he asked himself. "Where is it now? Where are you, Pain?"

He waited, anxious, for its return.

"Ah, it's still there. Well, so what? Let it be."

"And death? What is death?"

He tried to locate his accustomed fear of death and could not. Where was death? What death? He felt no fear because death did not exist.

Instead of death was light.

"So, that's it!" he cried. "What joy!"

This all happened in an instant, but the significance was lasting. For those around him, his anguish stretched out for another two hours. A rattle invaded his chest; his wracked body trembled. Then the rattling and wheezing ceased.

"It's finished," someone said who stood beside him.

He heard this comment and repeated it in his soul.

"Death is finished," he said to himself. "Death is no more."

He sucked in quickly, broke off in midbreath, stretched out, and died.

# 4 1

# BULGAKOV

As he lay dying, I spent my days at Telyatinki. I wrote in my diaries—
trying to remember everything I could about our last days together—
and I worked on an essay about Tolstoy's early years in the Caucasus.
In 1854, in Sevastopol—having come from Odessa by ship in early
November—he had spent some days helping in a military hospital.
Several months before, on a long walk in Zasyeka Wood, he'd told
me about his time there.

He was in love with a Cossack girl, "a dark-eyed beauty," he'd
called her. "She was as slender hipped as a boy, with short black
hair—a sign that she was independent. The others wore their hair
long, like gypsies."

He and a young infantry officer, named Ilya, had become close
friends through many months. They spent their days gambling and
riding. They occupied their nights with whoring among the gypsies.
But Leo Nikolayevich was drawn to the Cossack girl, as was Ilya.
They played cards and, jokingly, bet on the girl. The man who lost
would have to sleep alone that night or with another woman.

Each afternoon, the carts would arrive from the battlefield, bringing the corpses. By chance, one day Leo Nikolayevich was nearby when they arrived. "It was the most brilliant day of autumn," he said, with his usual recall of detail. "A cloudless sky. The plane trees tossed in the wind." A senior officer motioned to Leo Nikolayevich. "Here, give a hand!" He rushed to the cart, where several officers lay mutilated among the ordinary infantrymen. One of them, to his amazement, was Ilya.

Ilya's neck was raw where a bullet had got him at the base of the throat, but his face was untouched—"even lovely," as Leo Nikolaye-vich remembered. Scarcely able to control himself, he lifted Ilya from the cart and carried him to the morgue in his arms. The sleeves of his jacket were stained so badly that he threw it in the fire.

Why had this happened to Ilya and not to Leo Nikolayevich? Was life fundamentally irrational? He could not answer these questions.

That night, he went to the house of the Cossack girl. He did not tell her what had happened to Ilya. "I was overcome by a powerful feeling of what was probably lust, but it felt like . . . love." He lay with her till dawn, he said, swearing to himself that this would be their last night together. He was sinning against God, that he knew. But—as Martin Luther put it—he was sinning boldly.

"You know, I still think of her quite often," Leo Nikolayevich told me. There was a strange look in his eyes as he said that, a mingling of nostalgia, regret, and genuine sorrow.

I don't know why, but I was thinking of that Cossack girl as I sat beside Masha, who had come down from St. Petersburg to attend the funeral the next morning. She arrived on the late train at Tula. I met her in a droshky, which I drove myself.

We turned abruptly into the long gravel driveway. Telyatinki was lit up like a skull, with candles burning in the windows. The oak trees, which still retained their leaves, chittered in the cold wind. "Welcome home," I said to Masha, who smiled ruefully.

The household was in mourning, of course, and the place had a ghostly feel to it. Chertkov and Sergeyenko had been with Leo Niko-layevich throughout his ordeal, and reports were just filtering back.

The funeral would attract large crowds. Indeed, the trains from Moscow and elsewhere had been crammed all day, with hundreds of people—most of whom had never met Tolstoy—already camped on the grounds at Yasnaya Polyana.

"I can hardly believe you're here," I said. "I guess I won't have to put today's letter in the mail. You can have it." She grinned as I handed her the envelope and stuffed it into her coat pocket.

I reached for her hand and held it, briefly. She looked at me with an intensity that almost hurt.

We had a glass of tea in the kitchen.

"I think I know you a lot better now," I said to her, softly. "I'm almost afraid that, face to face, we won't speak directly to one another. It's much easier in letters. I'm a more honest person in print."

"You keep too much to yourself—even in your letters."

"I don't want to."

"There's no reason that we can't speak openly," she said.

I saw that she shivered.

"Are you cold?"

"I'm all right."

I took off my coat and put it around Masha's narrow shoulders, inhaling the lovely odor of her hair, which had a slightly waxy sheen that I did not mind. It smelled of water and mud.

"You've been traveling all day. You must be exhausted."

"It's so good to see you, I don't care."

When we had drunk our tea, I carried her leather case to her room, which I had prepared with fresh sheets.

"Thank you," she said timidly.

Closing the door behind us, I reached my hand to her face and let my fingers graze the skin lightly, lightly. She closed her eyes.

"May I kiss you, Masha?"

She said nothing. She just opened her eyes. They were deep and wet, blue-green in the candlelight, large as a calf's.

I could feel the shyness slipping away from me, sloughing off like a snake's skin. Emboldened, I pressed my lips to hers. I put my hands firmly on her hips.

When she reached her arms around my shoulders, I knew that all would be well.

"I love you, Valya," she said.

"I'm so glad."

That night we made love—not the frenzied lovemaking I had expected, but a gentle, almost ceremonious mingling. I knew I would never be the same again.

For several hours we nestled against each other like children. She seemed to sleep hard, but I lay solidly awake, astounded by everything that was happening. I did not even want to sleep. I wanted to feel everything, the swollen sheets, the full length of her body beside mine, her thighs and back and arms and shoulders. I was floating now, permeable, fully human—a creature of skin and hair and bones.

Near dawn, I saw that Masha was awake and kissed her gently on the forehead. "I wish I understood what love is," I said.

"You don't have to understand it," she said. "It's not something that needs analysis."

People were talking at the end of the corridor now, and I realized it was time to get up if we were to meet the train at Zasyeka Station, the train that was bringing the body of Leo Nikolayevich home to rest.

"It's here!" a muzhik shouted.

The train, an hour late, wheezed into the station. It was a briskly cold morning, with a cover of dry snow in the railway yard; milkweed and mullein—the surviving bones of summer—poked through the white crust. In a few places, bare ground showed through, the black Russian dirt I have always loved. I heard eight bells ring in the chapel tower.

The air sparkled, our breath forming a white cloud in front of us. Policemen were everywhere. The tsar, I was told, feared an uprising.

Everywhere in Russia the police and the militia had doubled their ranks, and censorship was in effect for all the papers.

But the feelings of the Russian people could not be stifled. People wept openly in the streets. Theaters in Moscow and St. Petersburg had closed, and university professors refused to lecture. Masha and I stood behind a delegation of students from Moscow.

I knew, intellectually, that Leo Tolstoy meant a great deal to the Russian people. But I had somehow not understood, not fully, the significance of his life. Of his example.

Sofya Andreyevna stepped from the train, looking dignified and at peace. She, like her husband, had been longing for closure. When people saw her, they began to sing "Eternal Memory," an old hymn that Leo Nikolayevich was known to admire. The entire station lifted in song. Even the railway conductors sang from their cars.

The coffin appeared, at last. A plain coffin made of dark yellow pine, long and narrow; Leo Nikolayevich's four strong sons carried it on their shoulders from the railway car to a waiting cart. Muzhiks tossed flowers in their path, singing loudly and weeping. One group of peasants carried a poster that read: "Dear Leo Nikolayevich: We remember your goodness. It will never die." It was signed, "The orphaned muzhiks of Yasnaya Polyana."

We formed a slow procession to the Tolstoy estate, feet scraping along the frozen road, scuffling through snow, a vast train of two or three thousand people who filed through the majestic white pillars at the entrance to Yasnaya Polyana with heads bent low. By ten-thirty, the coffin had made its way to the entrance of the study where Leo Nikolayevich wrote the words that have burned their way into the collective memory of the race.

Sergey, who had taken charge of the day, opened the coffin, revealing what remained of Leo Tolstoy. And the long, sad procession began.

Leo Nikolayevich did not look like himself. He was shockingly thin, his nose bulbous at the tip but shrunken along the sides. His cheeks were hollow. Someone had combed his hair to the wrong side, and his beard was fluffed out like cotton wool. His lips had been sewn shut to prevent his jaw from dropping open. The skin of his face was splintered like an old plate in a million pieces, holding together by force of habit more than physical substance.

When my turn came to stand beside the coffin, I touched his cold fingers. I prayed, "God, accept your son, Leo Nikolayevich, into your eternal arms." And I wept openly for the first time that day.

Masha held my hand.

Leo Nikolayevich had asked to be buried near the edge of a ravine in Zasyeka Wood. It was a place where his brother Nikolenka once said that the secret of eternal love was buried, engraved on a green stick. Sasha pointed out the exact spot, and the funeral was held there in the midafternoon—the time of day when Leo Nikolayevich would usually be riding in these woods on Delire. Had I not, in fact, been riding by that very spot with him less than a month before? It seemed impossible . . .

Wherever one looked, mourners knelt or stood with their heads bent, singing "Eternal Memory." The solid tree trunks rang aloud with the hymn, which gathered now like a great wave and poured through the woods. Photographers snapped pictures from a thousand angles, and cinematographers cranked their strange, modern machines. A sharp wind made everyone huddle as close together as possible.

Sofya Andreyevna insisted that nobody should speak at the grave. No priest would utter the usual words. There would be no ceremony. Even in his death, Leo Nikolayevich was pointing the way to a new world—a world without false praise, empty ceremonies, foolish disguises. He did not require the blessings of authority.

But an old man, a muzhik, took it upon himself to stand on a stump and deliver a brief sermon about the "dear man who had changed their lives." Everyone listened in awe. Though his speech was that of an "uneducated" man, it was eloquent and simple. That a peasant—one of the Russian muzhiks so honored by Leo Tolstoy in his writing—should deliver the final words on his behalf seemed wholly just.

At one point several policemen rode through the crowds on black horses. It was a horrible intrusion, but they were immediately surrounded by muzhiks and forced to get off their animals and kneel. To my relief, they obliged.

Suddenly it was snowing. Just a fluff, at first, but soon it thickened, and the gravediggers became anxious. With a signal from Sergey, they began to pour dirt on the coffin, and the crowds—singing "Eternal Memory" even more loudly—began to leave.

"I feel so empty," I said to Masha.

She put her arm through mine. "Let's go inside, Valya. There will be tea and food. I'm *freezing*!"

"I'm going with you, Masha," I said, holding my ground. "Is that all right?"

"Where?"

"To Petersburg?"

She turned to me with a strange, bright sweetness. "I would like that," she said. "But come along now."

Walking back to Yasnaya Polyana in the midst of the crowd, we said nothing more about where we were going or why or when. We were carried along, buoyed up, by a thousand singing voices, men and women who loved Tolstoy as much as we did, who understood, as he did, that death was simply one of life's many noble transformations, and that nothing mattered in the world but love.

**42**

# J. P.

ELEGY

*Cover him over, clover.*
*Grass, you long-haired, wheezy cover,*
*    hold him down.*

*That dust was man that plucks your roots,*
*that signals from the dark,*
*    again, again.*

*That man was both of us,*
*    my gentle reader.*

*He was fine, they say. No worse*
*    than you are when you leave your bed*
*        unmade, unfilled.*

*No worse than I am when I eat fresh bread*
*    while elsewhere in the world*
*        the bread is stale.*

*No worse, no better,*
*though he tried to heal.*

*Speak, Russian wind.*
*Blow harshly from the steppes*
*and clear the rubble.*

*Rip tall trees to whistling timber,*
*stripped of leaves.*

*The old world's bare in winter as we leave.*

# AFTERWORD

*The Last Station* is fiction, though it bears some of the trappings and affects of literary scholarship. It began half a decade ago when, browsing in a used bookstore in Naples, I stumbled upon Valentin Bulgakov's diary of his last year with Leo Tolstoy. Soon I discovered that similar diaries were kept by numerous other members of Tolstoy's inner circle, which had grown remarkably wide by 1910. I read and reread the memoirs and diaries of Vladimir Chertkov, Sofya Andreyevna Tolstoy, Ilya and Leo, Sergey, Tanya, and Alexandra (Sasha) Tolstoy, Dushan Makovitsky, and others. Reading them in succession was like looking at a constant image through a kaleidoscope. I soon fell in love with the continually changing symmetrical forms of life that came into view.

A novel is a voyage by sea, a setting out into strange waters, but I have sailed as close as I could to the shoreline of literal events that made up the last year of Tolstoy's life. Whenever Tolstoy speaks in this novel, I quote his actual words or, less often, I create dialogue based on conversations reported indirectly. Elsewhere, I have freely imagined what might have, could have, or should have been said.

In addition to the diaries mentioned, I have relied for chronology and circumstantial details on well-known biographies of Leo Tolstoy by Aylmer Maude, Edward A. Steiner, Ernest J. Simmons, Henri Troyat, and A. N. Wilson. Anne Edwards's life of Sofya Andreyevna Tolstoy was also useful. I would refer the interested reader to the book I depended on for bibliographical information: *Leo Tolstoy: An Annotated Bibliography of English-language Sources to 1978* by David R. Egan and Melinda A. Egan (Metuchen, N.J., and London, 1979).

All quotations from Tolstoy's writings—including those from his letters and diaries—have been "Englished" by me, based on previous translations. In this way, I was able to make his voice conform—in cadence and diction—with the Tolstoy of my invention.

I owe a considerable debt to Professor R. F. Christian of the University of St. Andrews in Scotland. He is among the great Tolstoy scholars of this century, and he was kind enough to read my novel in manuscript and provide detailed suggestions and corrections. I am also grateful to Gore Vidal, who offered encouragement, friendship, and practical advice throughout its composition. As always, Devon Jersild, my wife, was my closest reader.